Palgrave Studies of Entrepreneurship in Africa

Series Editors
Kevin Ibeh
Department of Management
Birkbeck, University of London
London, UK

Sonny Nwankwo
Office of the Academy Provost
Nigerian Defence Academy
Kaduna, Nigeria

Tigineh Mersha
Department of Management and International Business
University of Baltimore
Baltimore, MD, USA

Ven Sriram
Department of Marketing and Entrepreneurship
University of Baltimore
Baltimore, MD, USA

The Palgrave Studies of Entrepreneurship in Africa series offers an urgently needed platform to document, promote and showcase entrepreneurship in Africa and create a unique home for top quality, cutting-edge work on a broad range of themes and perspectives.

Focusing on successful African firms, small and medium sized enterprises as well as multinational corporations, this series will cover new and ground-breaking areas including innovation, technology and digital entrepreneurship, green practices, sustainability, and their cultural and social implications for Africa. This series is positioned to eminently capture and energize the monumental changes currently taking place in Africa, well beyond the pervasive informal sector. It will also respond to the great thirst amongst students, researchers, policy and third sector practitioners for relevant knowledge and nuanced insights on how to further promote and institutionalize entrepreneurship, and optimize its benefits across the continent. The series will offer an important platform for interrogating the appropriateness and limits of Western management practices in Africa, examining new approaches to researching the fast-changing continent.

A diverse set of established experts and emerging scholars based in Africa and around the world will contribute to this series. Projects will also originate from entrepreneurship-themed tracks and Special Interest Groups at major Africa-focused conferences, notably the International Academy of African Business and Development, the Academy of Management Africa, and the Academy of International Business African Chapter. The foregoing breadth and diversity of themes, target authors and manuscript sources will produce a richly distinctive series.

All submissions are single blind peer reviewed. For more information on Palgrave Macmillan's peer review policy please see this website: https://www.palgrave.com/gp/book-authors/your-career/early-career-researcher-hub/peer-review-process.

For information on how to submit a book proposal for inclusion in this series please contact Liz Barlow: liz.barlow@palgrave.com. For further information on the general book proposal process please visit this website: https://www.palgrave.com/gp/book-authors/publishing-guidelines/submit-a-proposal.

More information about this series at
http://www.palgrave.com/gp/series/15149

Chi Anyansi-Archibong

The Foundation and Growth of African Women Entrepreneurs

Historical Perspectives and Modern Trends

Chi Anyansi-Archibong
North Carolina Agricultural and Technical State University
Greensboro, NC, USA

ISSN 2662-1169   ISSN 2662-1177 (electronic)
Palgrave Studies of Entrepreneurship in Africa
ISBN 978-3-030-66279-0   ISBN 978-3-030-66280-6 (eBook)
https://doi.org/10.1007/978-3-030-66280-6

© The Editor(s) (if applicable) and The Author(s), under exclusive license to Springer Nature Switzerland AG 2021
This work is subject to copyright. All rights are solely and exclusively licensed by the Publisher, whether the whole or part of the material is concerned, specifically the rights of translation, reprinting, reuse of illustrations, recitation, broadcasting, reproduction on microfilms or in any other physical way, and transmission or information storage and retrieval, electronic adaptation, computer software, or by similar or dissimilar methodology now known or hereafter developed.
The use of general descriptive names, registered names, trademarks, service marks, etc. in this publication does not imply, even in the absence of a specific statement, that such names are exempt from the relevant protective laws and regulations and therefore free for general use.
The publisher, the authors and the editors are safe to assume that the advice and information in this book are believed to be true and accurate at the date of publication. Neither the publisher nor the authors or the editors give a warranty, expressed or implied, with respect to the material contained herein or for any errors or omissions that may have been made. The publisher remains neutral with regard to jurisdictional claims in published maps and institutional affiliations.

Cover credit: Roger Harris/Science Photo Library

This Palgrave Macmillan imprint is published by the registered company Springer Nature Switzerland AG
The registered company address is: Gewerbestrasse 11, 6330 Cham, Switzerland

*To my mother
Mercilina Ama Anyansi, (Nee Nworji)
Who taught me and my siblings the essence of entrepreneurship:*

*Be entrepreneurial in what ever career you choose and maintain integrity
in all your dealings with people*

*Be strategic in your thoughts and actions as you look for options and
alternatives and always perservere*

Preface

Amara loved learning and had always been very curious about the world around her even at the early ages of her life. However, when she reached the middle secondary school age of fourteen, her parents' home was frequented by other parents seeking her hand in marriage to their sons. Amara was not only intelligent and a good student, she was equally very beautiful, well behaved, hard-working, and respectful. These are some of the qualities often sought by men who are looking for the hand of a girl in marriage. She continued to reject many suitors and her parents were very supportive since she continued to do very well in school and even better than some of her brothers.

The pressure to get married continued and got stronger when Amara completed her secondary school education and started to apply for admission to a university. On this one particular occasion, her father's best friend and neighbor approached him to solicit her hand in marriage to his son whom he claimed was about to travel to United Kingdom (UK) for training and is being sponsored by the government Ministry where he worked. He said to Amara's father, "this particular daughter of yours is very intelligent as you often say, and if she marries my son now, she may get the opportunity to join him in UK and who knows, my son may allow her to go for advanced degree?" Amara claimed to be one of the privileged few whose parents do not push into marriage, as her father's response was "it is up to my daughter to decide and not me. I will discuss your request with her and get back to you." With this response her father's friend responded disappointedly, "she is only a girl and you have several male children who should be going for higher education not the girls." Again, Amara's father responded *"all my children, male or female have equal opportunity for any level of education as long as they are doing well in school and I am blessed with the fortune and means to support them."*

Amara was one of the few African young girls who were not pushed into early marriage and denied formal education several decades ago. Traditionally, majority of African girls (women) were not encouraged to engage in formal education. In the past, as shown in Amara's story, culture and tradition encouraged families to give priority for formal education to boys (men) who were expected to "provide for the family through gainful employment and most importantly will carry on the family name and legacy while the girls were expected to marry and take on their husband's family name." Girls on the other hand were encouraged to develop domestic skills such as house-keeping, gardening, farming, cooking, which were often acquired by helping their mothers in house shores and preparing family meals, etc. Informal education and training for girls included apprenticeship in dress making, cooking, and baking at established domestic centers or with an older married woman who has a sewing or baking business.

With these domestic skills, many married women set up roadside restaurants, retail trade consisting mostly of ingredients for meals either in the local bazar and farmers' market or street side stalls.

African women are rarely full-time house wives or "stay-home" mothers. Many set up kiosks in front of their homes, others rent stalls in the open market, while some establish sewing centers to train younger girls as well as design and make dresses for sale. A study by the World Bank Group (2018) reported that Africa is the only region in the world where more women than men choose to become entrepreneurs, and they call it a phenomenon. But to fully explore and understand the foundations of entrepreneurship among African women, it is necessary to examine the historical perspectives and backgrounds of these women. A better understanding of the traditional roles and status of women in Africa will explain and possibly dispel the notion of the African women's tendencies to opt for entrepreneurship as a phenomenon.

This book explores the traditions and cultures in Africa that could be seen as the key driving forces for women entrepreneurial tendencies and business activities. The purpose of this book therefore is to explore and define entrepreneurship in Africa with a focus on women entrepreneurs.

Entrepreneurship in this book refers to all activities relating to women and covers all formal and informal enterprises. It explores the driving forces, the challenges, strategies, the socio-economic environment, organization, supporting institutions, and the interface between Africa ecosystem and entrepreneurial ecosystem, among others.

The book presents its contents in two major sections. However, it should be noted that the sections are not completely discrete but interrelated given the interface of cultural elements and variables in the society. Section one (1930s–1970s) for purposes of this book presents a general perspective on past and contemporary entrepreneurship as a concept, followed by the perspective on entrepreneurial spirit in Africa with a focus on what could be termed the First-generation African women entrepreneurs. This section includes the following topics—An introductory Chapter 1 titled "Global Perspectives on Entrepreneurs and Entrepreneurship," that discusses entrepreneurs and entrepreneurship in general and explores the various definitions and types of entrepreneurial approaches. It covers the literature on the concept or phenomenon as well as its impact on both the micro and macro environment of nations. This introductory chapter also summarizes the literature on the concept with implications for the limited research on African Entrepreneurs. It also presents the types, characteristics, perceived roles on economic development of nations and potential gender differences.

Chapter 2 titled "Africa: Entrepreneurs and Entrepreneurship in the Continent" explores entrepreneurship in Africa covering the literature, scope, and types. This chapter also introduces the roles and status of women, examines the women entrepreneurial activities as driven by culture and traditions. This includes discussions on the concept of entrepreneurship in relation to the types affiliated with women's entrepreneurial activities and entrepreneurial philanthropy.

Chapter 3, "Culture and Traditional Foundations of African Women Entrepreneurs" presents and discusses the cultural and traditional foundations of entrepreneurship among Africa women. It identifies elements of culture and the traditions that could influence the tendencies of African women to become entrepreneurs including summary profile of a typical early African woman entrepreneur.

Chapter 4, "Regional Perspectives of Women Entrepreneurs: Similarities, Differences, and Contributing Forces" assesses the regional perspectives of women entrepreneurs in the continent in addition to examining the traditions, societal expectations, and women's efforts to balance family and career activities outside the family. The chapter also explores the social structures and traditions across the continent and summarizes the key similarities and differences in culture, tradition, and status of women across the continent (North, South, Central, East, and West).

Chapter 5, "Challenges, Opportunities, and Interventions for Women Entrepreneurs" explores and summarizes challenges and trends in entrepreneurship among the first-generation African women entrepreneurs. The profile of an entrepreneur who faced several challenges, survived, and transitioned into the next generation of entrepreneurship was introduced as an example of what the right and adequate interventions could do for the African women. The chapter analyzes and summarizes the potential impact of the Sustainable Development Goals for Women and the continent.

Chapter 6 "Characteristics of the Second-Generation Women Entrepreneurs: Education, Technology, and Globalization Effects," is the first chapter of section two of the book. It explores the identifiable characteristics of this generation's (1980s-present) women entrepreneurs and the potential roles played by access to formal education and training, technological advancement, and globalization processes as they interface with culture and past traditions. The chapter introduces the transition of African women "micro-entrepreneurs" to potentially "classic-entrepreneurs." It also explored the impact of these three factors and other external forces may have on the growth, successes, or failures of this second-generation entrepreneurs. Identification and assessment of the enabling and inhibiting factors as this generations of women entrepreneurs start and scale up their enterprises are the focus of this transition chapter.

Chapters 7 through 11 shifts focus on the future of the continents' economic development potentials and the role of women in the socio-economic development processes. Chapter 7 titled "Africa: Prospects for Entrepreneurial Development" discusses the topics planning which includes but not limited to analysis of Africa ecosystem as it relates to the planning and development of an appropriate entrepreneurial ecosystem and economy for the continent.

Chapter 8 introduces the need, significance, and processes of developing an inclusive entrepreneurial ecosystem that will enable women gain equal opportunities to engage and add value to the socio-economic development of the content; further, the discussions on the potentials and interests of tech companies in the continent will be explored as an inclusive entrepreneurial ecosystem is designed. This analysis will hopefully lead to better understanding of the significance, if any, of integrating all of the national and continent's resources in an appropriate model for entrepreneurship-led economic development in Africa. In addition, information generated about entrepreneurial effect on economic development will lead to better national, regional, and continent's planning for building a sustainable economy.

Chapter 9 titled "Africa's Diaspora: Prospects for her Women entrepreneurs" discusses opportunities for networking and potentials of connecting with the diaspora including the need for women to be courageous and forge ahead for these relationships. Chapters 10 and 11, "Future of Women Entrepreneurs in Africa" and "Conclusions and Trends in the 21st Century", respectively, summarize approaches for growing and sustaining the spirit of entrepreneurship among African women in the future with summaries on roles of Investors, venture capitalist, tech organization, governments, etc. in building Africa's entrepreneurial ecosystem.

The final chapter, Chapter 12 presents profiles and case studies of both tradition-induced, first-generation and contemporary, second-generation women entrepreneurs. The profiles selected are designed to show organization, resource acquisition including funding, and management styles as well as diversity of industry preferences, as the women entrepreneurs learn to compete for resources and market share in a fast-changing global economy.

A common theme in the research topics presented in Encyclopedia of Entrepreneurship (Kent, Sexton, & Vesper, eds., 1982), is "that material improvement in the standard of living and a favorable climate for entrepreneurship are most likely to reinforce one another." This theme could serve as sage way for Africa with several "emerging nations" among the total of 55 nations is more than ripe for strategic restructuring of resources and policies to attract both outward and inward foreign direct investments. Each of the above chapters is introduced or concluded with a theme, an overview, or a personal story of an entrepreneur or both where appropriate.

This book does not claim to explain nor solve all the challenges associated with entrepreneurship in Africa, especially, those relating to women entrepreneurs. Rather it is designed to raise awareness of the impact of culture and traditions on the entrepreneurial spirit of the African woman.

It also presents thought-provoking topics that need further discussion in order to promote a more comprehensive understanding of Africa's ecosystems and its impact on entrepreneurial development with focus on women as well as the implications for socio-economic development.

The book also adds to the research and present information on the continent as it relates to the culture and traditions which created the foundation for African women entrepreneurs. There are so much that needs to be explored. Questions such as the interface between Africa women entrepreneur and social entrepreneurship, entrepreneurial philanthropy among women in Africa, cultural factors and traditions enabling or inhibiting the tendencies of women to opt for entrepreneurship, micro and macro environmental challenges facing Africa women, the impact of external forces such as globalization, advances in technology, and innovation on modern African women entrepreneurs are the focus of the book. The limitations on research and knowledge of both Africa ecosystem and entrepreneurial ecosystems as well as their implications for economic development in the continent are areas of interest as the author atrempts to explore them within the scope of the book. The book adds value to the knowledge about African women entrepreneurs and to the limited literature on entrepreneurship in Africa.

Greensboro, USA   Chi Anyansi-Archibong

Reference

Kent, C. A., Sexton, D. R., & Vesper, K. H. (eds.). (1982). *Encyclopedia of entrepreneurship*. Englewood Cliffs, NJ: Prentice Hall, Inc.

Acknowledgments

I am grateful to several individuals and groups for helping and encouraging me from the start to the conclusion this book. I start with thanking Marcus Ballenger of Palgrave Macmillan for emailing me in Spring 2019 after I postponed the submission of detailed proposal in early 2018. I had told him about my joyful family emergency when I was blessed with three beautiful granddaughters and quickly found that I could not do any research while helping to take care of them. I asked for one-year extension which he accepted and arranged for a go-to-meeting exactly one year later. Thank you, Marcus.

Many thanks to my young colleague, Dr. Stephanie Kelly, professor of Business Information Systems and Analytics, for reviewing and editing the manuscript despite her heavy research schedule and other administrative responsibilities. Thank you so much "spouse"!

A huge thank you to Emeka Anthony Okafor for typing chapters and working on the exhibits and graphics. Most importantly for helping retrieve lost files at the time I thought I was going to re-type several chapters of the book.

Thanks to all the individuals who shared and allowed their stories to be shared, Mrs. Nike Ekundayo for taking time out of her busy schedule at the gallery to tell her stories, Chisolum for her life story, Mrs. Kakhu and her friends; Ms. Martha Catherine Agwang for not only responding to my emails but also compiling her life and entrepreneurial venture stories for this project; Dr. Musheshe, President of Africa Rural University for

Women and Director of Uganda Rural Development and Training as well as the various students of the institution for sharing their stories; Mrs. M. Anyansi (my mother) for all the life lessons and entrepreneurial teaching by examples; Phidora, Amara, etc. and all the other women entrepreneurs identified from the various internet sites.

I acknowledge the impactful contributions your stories made to the understanding of African women entrepreneurs and the motivations for the younger generation of women in Africa.

Thank you to all the individuals who have encouraged and supported the introduction and expansion of Students in Free Enterprise (SIFE/ENACTUS) Education in Africa especially Mr. Tom Moser & Mr. Bernie (Benny) Milano, of KPMG, USA; Dr. Isaac Nnadi, Dr. Ovadje, of Nigeria; Mr. Silvester John, and Engr. Peter Anyansi.

To my professional colleagues whom I have shared not only my mother's entrepreneurial zeal and activities but also the courage and resilience of many African women and their entrepreneurial quests, I give you thanks for listening and encouraging me to share the stories in a book form. Thanks to professor emerita, Marilyn Taylor who has been my greatest advocate, advisor, sister, colleague, etc. since my arrival in the United States as an undergraduate student.

Others including distinguished professor Kenneth D. McKenzie, whose advocacy and belief in me got me through the doctoral program, Drs. Kay keels, Frank Hoy, Vi Narapareddy, Theresa Taylor-Coates, Ogechi Adeola, and Ngozi Ojo, and many others who made it easy and comfortable to discuss entrepreneurship in general and African women entrepreneurs in particular.

This book will not be completed without the push and support of my family especially my three adult children, Emma, Ime, and Tony (Anthony), who called regularly to ask of my progress. I thank them for their respective moral and motivational support. I also thank the Almighty God for keeping me and everyone around me healthy during this COVID-19 pandemic and for giving me the strength to focus on the project.

My sincere apology to anyone or program I may have failed to acknowledge.

Contents

Part I   Introduction and First-generation Micro Entrepreneurs

1   Global Perspectives on Entrepreneurs
    and Entrepreneurship   3
    Entrepreneurs, Entrepreneurship, and Economic Impact   4
    Gender and Entrepreneurship   8
    Entrepreneurship as an Academic Discipline   10
    Overview of the Book Structure and Chapters   13
    References   15

2   Africa: Entrepreneurs and Entrepreneurship
    in the Continent   19
    Introduction   19
    Changing Perspectives of the Continents   21
    Literature and Profile Review   22
    Select African Entrepreneurs   29
    Summary   35
    References   37

3   Culture and Traditional Foundations of African
    Women Entrepreneurs   41
    Introduction   41

Traditional Wedding Gifts and Dowry	42
Culture, Traditions, and Multiple Roles of the African Woman	44
Entrepreneurs by Default	47
Characteristics of a Traditional and Culture-Driven African Woman Entrepreneur	49
Summary	52
References	54

4 Regional Perspectives of Women Entrepreneurs: Similarities, Differences, and Contributing Forces — 55
Introduction — 55
Regional Markets and Culture — 56
Regions and Countries of Africa — 57
Cultural Elements: Similarities and Differences — 58
Summary of Regional Cuisines — 62
Colonization, Colonial Cultures, and African Women — 65
Summary — 73
References — 74

5 Challenges, Opportunities, and Interventions for Women Entrepreneurs — 75
Introduction — 75
Key Challenges — 77
Potential Benefits of Women Education — 82
Summary — 85
References — 86

Part II 21st Century Second-generation Entrepreneurs and Entrepreneurial Development

6 Characteristics of Second-Generation African Women Entrepreneurs: Education, Technology, and Globalization Effect — 89
Introduction — 89
Interventions and Charateristics — 93
Women Organizations and Networking Interventions — 98

	Summary	106
	References	109
7	**Africa: Prospects for Entrepreneurial Development**	111
	Introduction	111
	National Development Planning in Africa	112
	Entrepreneurship and National Development	113
	Women and Socio-Economic Development	117
	Summary	121
	References	122
8	**An Inclusive and Diverse Entrepreneurial Ecosystem for Africa**	123
	Introduction	123
	Decision-Making and Planning Process	124
	The Need for Entrepreneurial Ecosystems for Africa and Its 54 Nations	126
	Ecosystem Frameworks/Models	127
	The Generic Incremental Value-Added (GIV) Model	131
	References	138
9	**Africa's Diaspora: Prospects for Women Entrepreneurs**	139
	Introduction	139
	African Population in the Diaspora	142
	Diaspora Women Organizations	146
	References	153
10	**Future of Women Entrepreneurs in Africa**	155
	Introduction	155
	Summary	163
	References	168
11	**Conclusions and Trends**	169
	Introduction	169
	Trends and Challenges	170
	Conceptualized Trends for the Twenty-First-Century Women Entrepreneurs	172
	Conclusions	180

Reference 183

12 **Profiles of Select African Women Entrepreneurs: Their Stories, Successes, Inspirations, and Challenges** 185
Introduction 185

References 219

Index 233

PART I

Introduction and First-generation Micro Entrepreneurs

CHAPTER 1

Global Perspectives on Entrepreneurs and Entrepreneurship

The title of this book indicates its focus but does not provide the purpose and approach used in examining this phenomenon in the continent of Africa. The book proposes to examine the ecological factors that drive or motivate women in Africa to opt for entrepreneurship. It also proposes to assess the entrepreneurial ecosystems as it interfaces with Africa's ecosystem and thus analyze and propose frameworks and models for enhancing entrepreneurial spirits among twenty-first century Africans, especially women. To achieve these goals, the book is designed to define and explore the business activities that were performed by women prior to the current era of modern business operations. The book focuses on the culture and traditions that drove African women, often referred to as "Market Women" to start and grow or not grow their business operations.

This introductory chapter which explores the global perspectives of entrepreneurs and entrepreneurship is thus organized and presented in the following order: general perspectives on select definitions of entrepreneurs and the process of entrepreneurship including economic impact, types and characteristics, gender and entrepreneurship, and the concept as an academic discipline. Following the above sections of the chapter, is a summary discussion of how these studies and perspectives play out in the continent of Africa.

Entrepreneurs, Entrepreneurship, and Economic Impact

Early discussions on the concept, mostly by economists (Schumpeter 1939; Smith 1937; Chandler 1977) described entrepreneurs as the engine that starts and moves the economy of nations. Many argue on the positive impact entrepreneurs and entrepreneurship have on economic development of nations and although these studies were conducted in developed nations, evidence exists to show that same effect is happening in the emerging and developing economies. All the same, many researchers found limitations and issues that inhibit successful entrepreneurial programs. Differences in infrastructure, government policies, and existing levels of natural resources are a few of the issues noted.

Adam Smith's theory of the "Invisible hand" may be credited with the early attempts to define the intentions and activities of an entrepreneur and the impact in the society. In his publication, the "Wealth of Nations" (1937), he wrote, that as each businessman starts with "intent to create and develop his personal gains, he is led by an invisible hand to promote an end which is not his intention." He continued that "by pursuing his own interest he frequently promotes that of the society more effectively than what he really intended to promote." Later in another book, "The Visible Hand," Chandler, Jr. (1977), described a modern business enterprise as the "entrepreneurial or family firm, and thus an economy or sectors of an economy dominated by such firms may be considered a system of entrepreneurial capitalism."

Chandler proposed that in the "very beginning, however, modern business enterprise required more managers than a family and its associates could provide." He argued that in some firms, the entrepreneur and his close associates (and the families) who built the enterprise will continue to hold majority ownership as well as the control of finances and distribution of key resources even when they had to hire professional managers. He maintains that the entrepreneur often continued to dominate in an entrepreneurial capitalist economy.

Other early writers on entrepreneurs and entrepreneurship include Schumpeter (1937) who described the entrepreneur as "a special kind of creative person, one who brings about growth through changes in production functions."

The scope of studies on the concept has expanded beyond the question of "what it is?" and "what it does" to new areas of research including entrepreneurial ecosystems, innovation and entrepreneurship, entrepreneurship education, gender and entrepreneurs, entrepreneurship across cultures, types of entrepreneurial activities, challenges, frameworks and models of entrepreneurship, etc. The study of the concept has equally become complex, more diverse, and global.

Research on several of the above areas were presented in the "Encyclopedia of Entrepreneurship" (Kent et al. 1982). The editors defined the field of entrepreneurship as "the creation of new business enterprises by individuals or groups." The book summarized various early research on the concept of entrepreneurship including topics on innovation and entrepreneurship, the environment of entrepreneurship, psychology and sociology of entrepreneurship. The impact of the concept on economic development of nations was extensively explored. For example, Broel (1978) discussed the issues facing entrepreneurs in less developed countries. This limited study examined both the sociological characteristics of the select countries and the economic effects of entrepreneurship on them. This author's (Broehl) economic impact discussions centered around Schumpeter's ideas and the role of the entrepreneur as an innovator. He indicated that there are differences between developed and developing nations and that there is a need for more explicit research on entrepreneurs and entrepreneurship at various levels of economic development. He also noted that only eight out of the fifty-one references he cited included either term (entrepreneur and entrepreneurship) in the title.

In another study, Kirzner (1973) argued that it is **lack of economic equilibrium** in societies that creates the opportunity for entrepreneurship. In addition, he theorized that although the entrepreneur's activities will move the economy toward equilibrium, changing circumstances will always create new profit opportunities if the government does not impose rigid and constraining policies. This argument could apply in the African women's situation where culture and tradition created **economic inequality and disequilibrium among women and men.**

On the impact of the environment (micro and macro) on entrepreneurship, Bruno and Tyebjee (1982) examined several factors that influence entrepreneurial start-up. The researchers identified twelve variables including the lack of systemic data concerning dependent and independent variables relating to "regions of the Country" selected for the research study. This identification and finding could be termed the ecosystems and thus call for the need to relate and design entrepreneurship programs that fit the national or regional environment.

Other definitions or explanations of entrepreneurs and entrepreneurship processes include studies by Hirsch and Bush (1985), assessment of the concept as "the process of creating something with value by devoting the necessary time and effort, assuming the accompanying financial, psychic, and social risks, and receiving the resulting rewards of monetary and satisfaction." In their book entitled, The Woman entrepreneur: Starting, Financing, and Managing a Successful New Business, the authors explored challenges and strategies employed by women entrepreneurs in building a successful business operation. All the same this rare study of women entrepreneurs' challenges and strategies involved mostly women in developed societies who were operating in a different environment than the women in Africa. Their definition of the concept is equally debatable as it relates to the term psychic, risks and rewards of monetary and satisfaction. The question could be whether all items of value bring satisfaction? What is the goal of the value creator and what type of satisfaction is sought—intrinsic or extrinsic?

As the study of entrepreneurs and entrepreneurship evolved into diverse field of studies including innovation technology, institutions, psychology, sociology, and economics, the definitions became equally diverse depending on the background and focus of the researcher. **To an economist, "an entrepreneur is one who brings natural resources, labor, other materials and assets into combinations that make their values greater than before, and also one who introduces changes, innovations and new order**." To a psychologist, this is an individual or group typically driven by certain forces—"the need to achieve or accomplish something, to experiment, or escape the authority of others, ………." In another field, such as management, one businessman may see the entrepreneur as a threat and an aggressive competitor while another sees the same entrepreneur as an ally, a source of supply, a customer, or someone to invest in. This same individual (entrepreneur) is seen by a capitalist philosopher as one who creates wealth for him or herself as well as others, someone who finds better ways to utilize resources, reduce waste, and produce jobs (Vesper 1980).

> *With diversification in the fields of Entrepreneurship, terms have also grown from classical, serial, micro............. to such terms as edu-preneur (entrepreneurial educator), med-preneur (medical entrepreneur), tech-preneur (entrepreneur in technology), entrepreneurial government, entrepreneurial leadership, etc. indicating that the process is applicable to diverse areas of activities and not just in business.*

Again, it should be noted that the above descriptions of the entrepreneur and entrepreneurial man are taken from studies conducted in developed economies. Few studies, if any, at this point were focusing on entrepreneurs in developing economies, and fewer still on entrepreneurial women.

However, many twenty-first century researchers (Nickels et al. 2019) are making additional efforts to study entrepreneurial activities in emerging and developing economies. In addition to perspectives and definitions, researchers identified what they believed to be key characteristics or traits of a successful or potential successful entrepreneur. These notable characteristics include but not limited to creativity and innovative, internal locus of control, tolerance for uncertainty, highly energetic, action-oriented, self-nurturing, etc.

These characterizations were followed by general classification of the individual or group based on their motivations, entrepreneurial practice, or goals for engaging in entrepreneurial activity. Major classifications included but not limited to:

- the Micro-preneurs (Home-based business, starts and manages the business that stays small, thus allowing the entrepreneur to balance family and lifestyle);
- Serial entrepreneur (one who takes the risk of starting one business, grows it to a certain stage, then sells it, and starts a new one);
- Social entrepreneur (an individual or group who uses for profit entrepreneurial business approach to solve a social problem);
- Intrapreneurs (creative or innovative person or group who works as entrepreneur in large corporations);
- Web-based Entrepreneurs (individual or group who develop and sell products or services online, these are mostly seen in service industry); and

- Entrepreneurial Team (group of experienced people with diverse skills who come together to create a new product/business, grow, and manage it).

These characterizations and classifications indirectly created a distinction between the entrepreneur as the person or persons and the entrepreneurship as a process. The motivations and goals had limited references as to intention to explore and exploit opportunities or pushed by necessity to go into entrepreneurial activities. These two factors are significant in exploring and understanding entrepreneurship in Africa and especially among African women. The same goes for the measurement of success as presented by Hisrich & Bush especially for the African woman entrepreneur. These situations will be examined further in the later chapters of the book.

Gender and Entrepreneurship

The Global Entrepreneurship Monitor (GEM) and other related organizations and conferences have done some notable job of encouraging and supporting research studies with focus on emerging economies including African economies. GEM credits Josef Schumpeter's "ground breaking" work on invention, innovation, and entrepreneurship, presented in his book titled The Theory of Economic Development (1911), as the foundation or platform on which GEM's entrepreneurial research activities were built. GEM has been collecting and reporting data from an array of circumstances found in 51 countries and territories from around the world since 1999. In addition, the organization claims to be the corner stone in the rapidly expanding field of entrepreneurship.

The 2006 International Entrepreneurship Exchange held in Auckland, New Zealand, presented diverse issues on international agenda of entrepreneurial related activities. The diversity of participants' presentation was encouraging but was focused mostly on developing nations of Eastern Europe and South America. South Africa was the only African country with a study center. All the same credit should be given to the 2006 conference organizers for the diversity of topics presented. Of the one hundred and twenty-one papers, five mentioned or included the term culture in its title, six included education, and eight included issues of women entrepreneurs. These topics, especially the education papers, seem to indicate the trend that is becoming the corner stone of many business schools. Many business schools today, including accredited and non-accredited are developing and offering entrepreneurship curricula and degree programs.

Topics such as "Search for Equity Capital: Implications for Women Entrepreneurs" (Bruin and Flint-Haitie 2006) and "Rural Women Entrepreneurs and Access to Socio-economic development in Northern Ghana: A Case Study of the Shereponi Sub- district" (Lambini 2006) resonate with the focus of this book. The later argued that women entrepreneurs play important role in the socio-economic development of Chereponi sub-district as their major roles include principal caretakers of the household, educating (raising) the children, health delivery, and other family livelihoods. These roles are common among African women and it should also be noted that one of the communities of Ghana, in West African region is a matrilineal society. Also, in another article, entitled "Inspirational parables: Ethnic minority Indian Women Entrepreneurs in New Zealand," Pio (2006) identified the issues of culture and ethnicity in the study designed to assess the impact of ethnicity on entrepreneurial choice, the nature of the enterprise, and the entrepreneurial trajectory as minority women entrepreneurs. The author found that family traditions, the significance of the male figure in the woman's life (Indian culture is primarily patriarchal), and the role of mother figure with restricted mobility in the labor market, have positive influence on the woman's entrepreneurial aspirations. These findings among Indian women may have significant similarities with some African cultures and traditions in relations to male dominance and roles of the women in the societies.

Another seemingly relevant study and findings by the GEM organization (2005 Report) was the analysis of entrepreneurial startups between men and women in its thirty-six participating countries. Hungary topped other countries with the highest percentage of overall female participation in entrepreneurial activities. Brazil came in second followed by Venezuela, with Jamaica ranked fifth while South Africa was ranked number eight. It should be noted that the percentages with which women out numbered men in startups were minimal ranging from .02–.5%. However, it is interesting to note that the top three countries are developing or emerging economies. In a related study focusing on the growth of early stage entrepreneurship between men and women, Hungary, again, topped the list with 2.4% of women startups versus 1.4% of men. Another study also measured the tendencies toward opportunity and necessity entrepreneurship between men and women in each of the participating countries. Analysis indicated that Hungary, once more, is the only country where women edged men (1.2–.5%) in opportunity entrepreneurship. However, when it comes to necessity entrepreneurship, ten countries (Brazil, Denmark, Greece, Hungary, Mexico, New Zealand, Slovania, Venezuela, with a tie between Austria and Japan) show more women startups as a result of necessity. Reasons for these findings are potential research questions for the future.

Entrepreneurship as an Academic Discipline

The trend toward entrepreneurship as an academic discipline has continuously expanded in the past two decades. Most accredited, and even unaccredited institutions of higher education have either established a course or a full program of studies with a focus on the teaching of this concept or phenomenon. Many larger educational institutions and philanthropic organizations have established centers of entrepreneurship with the goals of motivating innovations and commercialization of ideas and products for cities and regions. Notable among these in the USA are Babson College Entrepreneurship Center, Stanford Center for Entrepreneurship, The Ewing Marion Kauffman Foundation, regarded as the world's largest foundation devoted to entrepreneurship. This organization is currently exploring the African entrepreneurial landscape to further study the opportunities and challenges in fostering high-growth entrepreneurship in developing countries (www.Kauffman.org).

The Global Entrepreneurship (GEM) Report has also been a significant influence in the gathering and dissemination of data plus an array of entrepreneurial circumstances in over fifty countries and territories around the world since 1991. GEM presents itself as the cornerstone in the rapidly expanding field of entrepreneurship education and research. GEM works with universities and private organizations to organize and host several entrepreneurship conferences and workshops across the globe (GEM 2005 Executive Report: www.lulu.com/hfrederick).

Other notable centers and institutions across the world include but not limited to ESBRI Entrepreneurship and Small Business Research Institute (Sweden); Hunter Center for Entrepreneurship, University of Strathclyde, (Scotland); IESA Centro de Emprendedores, (Venezuela); UCT Center for Innovation and Entrepreneurship, The Graduate School of Business, Cape Town, (South Africa); National University of Singapore; Tec de mon terrey, Business Development Center, EGAP

Strategic Studies Center, (Mexico); National Entrepreneurship Center, Tsinghua University, (China); Center for Entrepreneurship, IEA Management and Business School, Universidad de Austral, (Argentina); HEC Montreal, The Sauder School of Business at UBC, (Canada); Centro de Entrepreneurship, Grupo Santand, Universidad Adolfo Ibanez, Centro para el Emprendimiento y la Innovacion, Universidad del Desarrollo, (Chile); Stockholm School of Economics in Riga, (Latvia); Young Entrepreneurs Association, ministry of Planning and International Cooperation, (Jordan); University of Technology, (Jamaica); Foundation for Economics and Industrial Research (IOBE), (Greece); and many others.

It is evident from the above select centers and programs that many of **the programs in emerging and developing countries are rooted in the national universities with a tie to economic development studies.** This is contrary to the situations in the developed economies where independent organizations such as Kauffman Foundation (USA), GEM (New Zealand), and Fundacion Xavier de Salas (Spain), organize, fund, and encourage entrepreneurial education, and development.

Also, in the past three decades, many of the entrepreneurship centers and academic programs are located in business schools and tied to the business discipline, especially management (Schreier 1975). However, in recent years, the study of entrepreneurship as a discipline has expanded from a business-centered study to that of interdisciplinary programs (Schoch 1979; Vesper 1976 [1979], 1980). Current academic conferences and symposia have tracks and special calls for submissions with titles such as "Interdisciplinary and Experiential Entrepreneurship Education under Emerging Research: Research papers in engineering, humanities, music, arts, computer science, education, business, etc. are welcomed" (www.usasbe.org/page/2020conference).

This expansion of interest in entrepreneurship among several academic programs calls for the need to be more inclusive in the study of the concept and also draws attention to the need to revisit earlier definitions of both the entrepreneur and entrepreneurship, an idea that is also echoed in the article "Rethinking Entrepreneurship Methodology and definitions of the Entrepreneur" (Howorth et al. 2005). This expansion into other disciplines further raises other questions such as—whether entrepreneurship can be taught? (Kierulf 1973, 1974; Roscoe 1971) also raised the question of whether entrepreneurs are born or developed? If yes is the answer to the teachability of the concept, what would an effective entrepreneurship curriculum look like and how would the results and impact be measured (Kramer 1971; Schrein 1975)?

Researchers are at cross roads on the impact of educational programs and training for entrepreneurship. In their studies and development of an educational approach for enhancing self-efficacy, Lucas and Cooper (2006) argue that self-efficacy is a strong predictor of successful entrepreneurship and that it can be enhanced by properly designed educational programs. The study termed Enterpriser Approach, designed a curriculum to enhance self-confidence of students with a goal of enhancing their entrepreneurial skills. The authors found an enduring impact of the program on the participants for about six months. There was no evidence of the influence of the program for a longer period. In a similar program, Start and Improve Your Business (SIYB), a global entrepreneurship education program, sponsored by United Nations International Labor Organization (ILO), researchers Moremong-Nganunu et al. (2006) found that an attempt to measure impact of the training on participants in Botswana and Southern Africa was unsuccessful.

The above authors believed that both the evaluation instrument and the periods of application were "unsystematic, non-quantitative, and unsatisfactory." The concluded that after over ten years of this training program in Botswana, it continues to run in the absence of any knowledge concerning its efficacy. In addition, the SIYB programs operating in other developing African countries including Uganda and Zimbabwe continue to suffer from inadequate evaluation instrument and application. Also, in other studies of entrepreneurship education and training (Saee 2006; Tanas and Yamin 2006; Braukman 2006), the authors present and argue for appropriate government programs designed to integrate entrepreneurship programs in both secondary and university curricula. However, same authors and other researchers were equally concerned about curriculum development and teaching methodologies. The challenges of creating and developing entrepreneurial spirit among the citizens abound even as various governments and international organizations (Germany: EXIST; European Commission on Education: The European Agenda for Entrepreneurship Education [2004]; ILO: SIYB; etc.) continue to recognize and fund entrepreneurship as a process that creates new businesses and as well as the underpinning engine for socio-economic development.

If it is determined that entrepreneurs can be developed and that entrepreneurship process engineers and energizes economic growth, several key issues that must be considered and addressed include but not limited to:

- The level of school years when entrepreneurial learning be introduced?
- Type of educational policies are needed to initiate relevant pedagogical changes?
- How researchers and educators determine and manage the contextual and process issues of entrepreneurship?
- How will the impact of entrepreneurs and entrepreneurship activities on the economy of a society be adequately measured?

Adequate considerations and discussions, not only of education policies and curricula, but also of leadership (entrepreneurial leadership, entrepreneurial ecosystems, entrepreneurial philanthropy, etc.) and other institutional issues (micro and macro), are necessary for effective transition to entrepreneurial socio-economic system of development. This effort is paramount, especially in the new millennium and especially for potential Africa's entrepreneurial economic development.

Overview of the Book Structure and Chapters

The book is about African women entrepreneurs in the pre- and post-colonial (1930s–1970s) and their transition into the modern globally and technology-driven entrepreneurs (1980s–present). In addition, and prior to the above focus, the book starts with an introductory chapter on the historical background and literature on the concept of entrepreneurship and the phenomenon of the "entrepreneurial man or woman." The chapter covers other perspectives including academic and entrepreneurial training approaches across the globe.

Chapter 2 presents discussions on Africa's entrepreneurs and the concept of entrepreneurship within the continent. It also presents the examined Africa's potential for sustainable entrepreneurial economy. The chapter covers an overview of entrepreneurship and entrepreneurs in Africa while focusing on the status, and research on women. With its focus on women entrepreneurs, it considers every activity in which the African woman engages in for purposes of improving the economic well-being of her family and the community at large as an entrepreneurial venture. These activities include both formal and informal businesses

Chapter 3 discusses the cultures and traditions as they influenced and directed the African's women entrepreneurial tendencies.

Chapter 4 explores the regional perspectives of women entrepreneurs across the continent with a focus on cultural similarities and differences.

Chapter 5 identifies and discusses challenges, opportunities, and interventions for women entrepreneurs. Starting with a mini profile of an entrepreneur, the chapter expands on the need and potential impact of women's education for the society.

Chapter 6 introduces the second-generation women entrepreneurs. The chapter summarizes key characteristics as well the effect of education, technology, and globalization on the entrepreneurial activities this women. The need for appropriate educational programs and training were explored.

Following this discussion, Chapter 7 explores the prospect for Africa's economic development. It challenges the continent to engage a pragmatic development plan that takes its abundant resources into consideration.

Chapter 8 presents and discusses a potential inclusive and diverse entrepreneurial ecosystem development for Africa. Given the issues raised in Chapter 7, it proposes a model of economic development that considers Africa's resources, especially the human recourses in developing a dynamic plan.

Chapter 9 explores and discusses the potential contributions of Africa's diaspora in the continent's development. Diaspora is considered a major prerequisite for national strategic development efforts and the areas of diaspora contributions are the focus of the chapter.

Chapters 10 and 11 present summaries and conclusions on the future of African women entrepreneurs and the identified key conceptualization of the future status, respectively. Recommendations were made for creating an enabling environment for growing women entrepreneurial efforts and growing the continent's entrepreneurial development.

The final chapter, Chapter 12 presents profiles of select women entrepreneurs with a focus on their characteristics, inspirations, aspirations, challenges, and most importantly their operating strategies and successes.

Overall, the book continues with discussions of the impact or potential impact of entrepreneurship as a factor of production and its contributions to the economic development of the continent, and the role or impact that African women entrepreneurs play or have on the socio-economic development. In final analysis the question of what entrepreneurship is and who entrepreneurs are, continue to be topics of discussion for researchers and educators and the following are some specifics for African continent:

- Whether we can teach entrepreneurship, and if yes, how and at what levels of human development can we introduce training programs,
- What contextual and process approaches are appropriate for the African environment and ecosystem, does one size fit all?
- Are there differences in entrepreneurship education and training in developed versus developing economies?
- Are the motivations for women entrepreneurs in Africa similar to men's?
- Are the strategic and organizational approaches the same for men and women entrepreneurs?
- What is the predominant type of entrepreneurship style among African women and why?
- What policies (educational, government, ecosystems, etc.) should be put in place for an inclusive and effective development of entrepreneurship in Africa?

These and many other questions relating to entrepreneurship in Africa, especially women entrepreneurs will be touched upon throughout the book.

References

Braukman, U. (2006, February 8–10). *Entrepreneurship career development: An innovative impulse from Wuppertal entrepreneurship education*. Presented at the Third AGSE International Entrepreneurship Research Exchange, Auckland, NZ.

Broel, W. G., Jr. (1978). *The village entrepreneur*. Cambridge, MA: Harvard University Press.

Bruin, A., & Flint-Haitie, S. (2006, February 8–10). *The search for equity capital: Implications for women entrepreneurs*. Presented at Third AGSE International Entrepreneurship Research Exchange, Auckland, NZ.

Bruno, A. V., & Tyebjee, T. T. (1982). The environment for entrepreneurship. In C. A. Kent, D. L. Sexton, & K. H. Vesper (Eds.), *Encyclopedia of entrepreneurship*. Englewood Cliffs, NJ: Prentice-Hall, Inc.

Chandler, A. D. (1977). *The visible hand: The managerial revolution in American business*. Cambridge: Harvard University.

Hirsch, R. D., & Bush, C. (1985). *The woman entrepreneur: Starting, financing, and managing a successful new business*. Lexington, MA: Lexington Books.

Howorth, et al. (2005). Rethinking entrepreneurship methodology and definitions of the entrewpreneur. *Journal of Small Business and Enterprise Development, 12*(1), 24–40.

Kent, C. A., Sexton, D. R., & Vesper, K. H. (Eds.). (1982). *Encyclopedia of entrepreneurship*. Englewood Cliffs, NJ: Prentice Hall, Inc.

Kierulf, H. E. (1973, June–July). Can entrepreneurship be taught. *MBA Magazine*.

Kieruff, H. E. (1974, October–December). Developing a curriculum for effective teaching of entrepreneurship. *MBA Magazine*.

Kirzner, I. M. (1973). *Competition and entrepreneurship*. Chicago: University of Chicago.

Kramer, H. E. (1971). New entrepreneurial dimensions of business education. *Collegiate News and Views, XXV*(1, Fall).

Lambini, C. (2006, February 8–10). *Rural women entrepreneurs and access to socio-economic development in Northern Ghana: A case study of Chereponi sub-district*. Presented at the Third AGSE International Entrepreneurship Research Exchange, Auckland, NZ.

Lucas, W. A., & Cooper, S. (2006, February 8–10). *Enhancing self-efficacy for entrepreneurship and innovation: An educational approach*. Presented at the Third AGSE International Entrepreneurship Research Exchange, Auckland, NZ.

Moremong-Nganunu, T., Hindle, K., & Cunningham, E. (2006, February 8–10). *A preliminary evaluation of the world's largest skills enhancement program for entrepreneurs*. Presented at the Third AGSE International Entrepreneurship Research Exchange, Auckland, NZ.

Nickels, G. M., Mchugh, J. M., & McHugh, S. M. (2019). *Understanding business* (10th ed.). New York: McGraw-Hill Education Publishers. ISBN 978-1-259-92943-4.

Pio, E. (2006, February 8–10). *Inspirational parables: Ethnic minority Indian women entrepreneurs in New Zealand*. Presented at the Third International Entrepreneurship Research Exchange, Auckland, NZ.

Roscoe, J. (1971, June–July). Can entrepreneurship be taught? *MBA Magazine*.

Saee, J. (2006, February 8–10). *Entrepreneurship education and training: A Panacea for the European Economic Malaise in the third millennium*. Presented at the Third AGSE Entrepreneurship Research Exchange, Auckland, NZ.

Schoch, S. (1979, September). How business schools handle entrepreneurship. *Venture Magazine, 1*(8).

Schrein, J. W. (Ed.). (1975). *Training and education for entrepreneurship.* Proceedings of Project ISEED. Milwaukee Center for Venture Management.

Schumpeter, J. A. (1939). *Business cycles: A theoretical, historical, and statistical analysis of the capitalist process.* New York: McGraw-Hill Inc.

Smith, A. (1937). *The wealth of nations, editor, Edwin Cannon.* New York: Modern Library.

Tanas, J. K., & Yamin, S. (2006). *Entrepreneurial education for the new millennium.* Presented at the Third AGSE International Entrepreneurship Research Exchange, Auckland, NZ.

Vesper, K. H. (1976 [1979]). *Entrepreneurship education: A bicentennial compendium.* Milwaukee Center for Venture Management.

Vesper, K. H. (1980). *Research on entrepreneurship education.* Presented at the Conference on Research and Education on Entrepreneurship, Baylor University, Texas.

CHAPTER 2

Africa: Entrepreneurs and Entrepreneurship in the Continent

INTRODUCTION

The continent of Africa is fast evolving economically, socially, technologically, and globally. As the continent moves toward an entrepreneurial-based economy, earlier perspectives and opinions are slowly but surely changing.

Reflecting on an event in the year 1988—an eight-year-old girl stepped outside an international airport in the most populous country in West Africa (Nigeria), and looking confused asked the parents, "Mom, Dad, where are the animals?" What do you mean? The parents responded. The third grader explained that her teacher (when she told her she was traveling to Nigeria with her parents for Christmas holidays), asked her where they will be staying because Africa is populated mostly by large animals and could be seen roaming all over the towns. Before the parents could respond, the two younger brothers simultaneously intercepted with "hey, we are not yet in Africa, this might be another flight connection in the United States!"

Fast forward to 2019 when I had the pleasure of traveling to another African country with some professionals. I spent several times in pre and during the three weeks stay in this popular east African country reminding my US traveling companions and friends to stop referring to our trip as a "visit to Africa" but to use the name of the country which is in Africa. One

© The Editor(s) (if applicable) and The Author(s), under exclusive license to Springer Nature Switzerland AG 2021
C. Anyansi-Archibong, *The Foundation and Growth of African Women Entrepreneurs*, Palgrave Studies of Entrepreneurship in Africa, https://doi.org/10.1007/978-3-030-66280-6_2

colleague was proud to let me know that this trip was the second visit to "Africa" and I politely asked which country she visited and she had think twice before remembering the name of the country. To many, Africa is just another country alongside China, United Kingdom, Germany, etc. Several incidences in my teaching career in the US also attest to this apparent lack of interest in the continent. I usually introduced myself to my class on the first day of each semester. By the end of the day, I usually get one or two students approaching me to talk about the friend from Africa. When I asked the students which country their friends came from, I got a look like "what do you mean? I just told you he/she is from "Africa."

A disturbing incidence which offered a teaching moment was when I had a graduating senior student in my class walked up to me in the hall way, very excited to tell me that his friend from Africa was traveling home for the Christmas break and had invited him to come along. He had talked to his parents and they have agreed to help him buy the plane ticket which was all that his friend had requested. "I will be staying with him and his family once we get to Africa and every other expenditure will be on them." Happy for him, I asked which country he will be traveling to? He hesitated and then responded, "The name escaped me now but if I see map, I will show you." I responded with an invitation to join me in my office after class because I have a map of the world with countries and flags in my office.

Upon arrival, I pointed to the large map on the wall and asked him to find the country in Africa. Several minutes later he put his finger on Beijing, China, and exclaimed, "Here Dr. Archibong, I found it but I have forgotten how to pronounces it." Shocked and disappointed, I gave him a new assignment for the class, which was to not only identify the map of Africa, list the then 53 countries and select the very country he was supposed to visit with his friend for a detailed analysis of the country's socio-economic status.

If this happens with students, what can you say to a colleague and fellow professor who for over 20 years introduced you as "my friend from Africa" and when asked by someone who is more knowledgeable—which country? She turned to me for the answer.

The above incidences are not unusual, even as Africa and Africans move toward economic independence. Many in the western world are ignorant of the continent of Africa and its diverse ecosystems and often refer to Africa as a country. Opinions of the continent are often based on movies such as "Tarzan," "Roots," "African Queen" or "The Gods Must be Crazy." Others gather information from publications such as "Heart of Darkness," "Gorillas in the Mist" or the popular Achebe's "Things Fall Apart" to name a few. Perceptions, even among the educated, are more of a place for wild life expeditions, populated by highly illiterate people, who are economically deprived and surrounded by regional conflict, corrupt leaders, and marginalized women.

Changing Perspectives of the Continents

In the past two decades opinions are gradually changing as globalization and advancements in technology, especially telecommunications provide avenues and often report current events from the continent. There is a growing interest in the continent as it is being positioned as the next emerging global market with potentials for profitable investments. The media reports of its abundant resources with opportunities for entrepreneurial development. However, constructive and empirical research on the continent's potentials for growth remain elusive. Analysts who study historical and economic trends are predicting that this will be Africa's century.

According to an African industrialist, entrepreneur and philanthropist, Ivor Ichikowitz, "Africa can stand toe-to-toe with the big guys." He touts the huge "market power" within Africa's potential for greater intercontinental collaboration, its commitment to market liberalization, internal trade, and its embrace of "Fourth Industrial Revolution-inspired technological innovation." He believes that considering some fundamentals including the fact that the continent comprises 20% of the planet's landmass, with an immense wealth of natural resources, including critically strategic minerals used in today's cutting-edge technologies, contributes to the continent's extraordinary market power. However, he cautions that there are still massive risks and challenges which Africa needs to overcome in order to succeed. These challenges include but not limited to: lack of basic capacity for proper security and economic development, economically fracture trade zones, and migration.

Encouraging trends provided by the Boston Consulting Group (BCG 2019) are summarized as follows:

1. The amount of capital African firms invested in Africa itself increased from 3.7bn to 10bn between 2006–2007 and 2015–2016

2. Within the same period intra-regional mergers and acquisitions jumped from 238 to 418
3. Average annual intra-African exports increased from $41bn to $65bn and
4. Average number of African tourists traveling within Africa rose from 19 m to 30 m, accounting for almost half of all tourists on the continent.

The above statistics underscores the potential for further growth if the continent is able to implement the recently created African Continental Free Trade Agreement (ACFTA). Africa's huge market potential is attracting lots of Foreign Direct Investment (FDI) which many African tend to see this new Scramble for Africa' as a form of "economic colonization." Prominent among these foreign investors are China (China Safari, with multilateral projects in resource extraction and infrastructure), Germany's "Marshal Plan for Africa," an agenda with development of controlled production chains, Russia with Putin hosting the Russia-Africa Forum October 2019), and USA lunch of "Prosper Africa Initiative." The onus is on African leaders to take note and plan strategically by addressing its critical challenge of investing in financial inclusion, renewable energy, appropriate infrastructure, and intercontinental security to name a few.

Literature and Profile Review

There is limited literature on Africa's journey toward entrepreneurial economy and even less on Africa's entrepreneurs and the nuances of the phenomena within the continent. Nonetheless, a more significant and compelling issue than the limitation of research on Africa's entrepreneurs, their activities, and the potential impact on socio-economic development is the tendency to apply foreign or developed economies research models, techniques, concepts, perspectives, etc. that often ignore the Africa ecosystems or ecological factors. The questions that needs to be answered include whether one size fits all when it comes to economic development models? Also, if entrepreneurs are people who put productive resources together and thus become engines for economic development, what factor is missing in the continent given her abundant mineral resources which include large reserves of fossil fuel, metallic ores, gems, and precious metals. In addition to these minerals are the diversity of biological resources such as equatorial rainforest of central and wildlife of eastern and southern parts of the continent.

This chapter reviews identifiable and select literature on entrepreneurs and entrepreneurship in Africa, discusses potentials for developing an entrepreneurial economy, and examines the key factors of production as it relates to Africa's society and economic environment. Special focus is paid on the existing and selected literature on African women entrepreneurs, their prescribed roles in the society, their challenges, and impact of their respective roles and activities in the communities and society.

Exhibit 2.1, titled Profile of Africa, presents some facts in numbers and percentages. The information (www.Britannica.com/place/africa 2020) included the richest and poorest countries in the continent, literacy rate, life expectancy, infant mortality rate, percentage of population under age 25 years, annual rate of growth in urban population, as well as religious diversity and the respective populations.

To envision an effective prospect for Africa's entrepreneurial and economic development, it is necessary to review and understand some facts about the world's youngest, second-largest, and second-most populous continent after Asia. It is the continent with the world's oldest university, "University of Karueein" founded in 859 AD by Fatima Al-Fihri, in Fez, Morocco, and referred to as "Athens of Africa" (Guinness World Record). The University was founded by the daughter of a wealthy merchant, Mohamed Al-Fihr, as multi-functional institution which serves as a mosque and an education center. By the twelfth century, curriculum included religious subjects such as the Qur'an and Fiqh (Islamic Jurisprudence). Other subjects include grammar, rhetoric, logic, Medicine, mathematics, astronomy, and geography. In 1947 the university (Madrasa) was integrated into the state education institution system by royal decree.

> *It is interesting to note that this world's earliest university which was started by a women did not admit women until 1963. This situation underscores the marginalization of women and limitation of women's access to formal education.* (www.en.m.wikipedia.org)

Research studies by both individual and groups present comparable highlights of the past and current status as well as potentials for the continent's development. Economically, the profile indicated that thirty-two (32) of the thirty-eight (38) nations of the world's most heavily indebted

Exhibit 2.1 Africa: profile in numbers and percentages −1

Profile Item	Numbers and percentages (%)—2005	Numbers and percentages (%)—2019
1. % of Earth's total landmass	20+ % [11,724,000 sq. miles/30,365,000 sq. kilometer]	Same
2. Population	900 million; [14% of world]	1.335 billion; [16.72% of world]
3. % of Population under age 25	71%	60% [median-19.8 in 2020]
4. Annual rate of Growth in Urban population	3.5%	4.1% [global rate of 2%]
5. Most populous city	Lagos, Nigeria	Lagos, Nigeria
6. Most populous nation	Nigeria [131 million]	Lagos, [196 million]
7. Percentage of population dependent on agriculture	66%	60% [32% of GDP]
8. Average Income	50% live on less than a $1 a day	$315 average per year/no change
9. Richest nation in GDP (PPP)	Mauritius [GDP $12,800]	Nigeria by GDP and Seychelles by GDP per capita
10. Poorest Nation per capita	Burundi and Malawi [capita income less than $600]	South Sudan and Central Africa Republic [per capita income of less than $700]
11. Number of heavily indebted nations	32 of 38 listed by IMF	31 of 37 [IMF listing]
12. Infant mortality rate	102/1000 in Sub-Saharan & 33/1000 in the North	78/1000 in Sub-Saharan & 30/1000 in the North
13. Average life expectancy	46 in Sub-Saharan & 67 in North;	56.2 in Sub-Saharan; 61 for males and 65 for females
14. Average literacy rate	60%	65%
15. Number of Christians	410 million	570 million
16. Number of Muslims	358 million	393 million
17. Percentage population of Women	Not shown	672,174,623[50.5%]/men: 672,167,420. [49.5%][countrymeters.info/13/2020
18. Female population within ages 25–29	Not shown	7.7% of population [51,757,446]

countries are in African according to the International Monetary Funds (IMF) and National Geographic, Africa Special Edition (Cobb 2005). This data is almost fifteen years but serves as a yard stick for measuring or determining how far African countries have gone in improving its social and economic conditions. For start, it should also be noted that the population under age 25 years which was 71% in 2015 is now 60% in 2019? These young citizens have potentials for contributing to the entrepreneurial economy if given the right tools such as education, training, and implementation of policies that create enabling environment. But with the percentage drop in population of this age group, it is not known whether birth rate has dropped, which is possible with women access to education, tendency for birth control, and aspirations for careers, or whether there has been an increase in the death rate or lower life expectancy of the youth? Data also show improved showed improvement in literacy rate which could be related to the decline in infant mortality rate.

Mo Ibrahim (2019) in his discussion at the World Economic Forum stated that Africa's first challenge is "youth bulge that stuck in the waithood." The United Nation (UN) demographic projection is that the median age in Africa is going to be 19.8 in 2020 and with this, Ibrahim believes that the youth offer great potential and are Africa's biggest resource for economic development. He called for improvement in health and education that will put the growing youth population in a more productive position. He also called for creation (by both government and private sector) of better condition and enabling environment for advancing human capital. He blamed poor government policies for youth migration to cities and out of the country and believed that there is an urgent need for the continent to address issues of poor education system, health, unemployment, and inadequate access to programs or trainings that prepares youth from school to work positions.

This call for changes in education and health systems is underscored by the statistics that still keep 31 of African countries among 37 nations listed in International Monetary Fund (IMF) group study of the most indebted and poorest nations. This indicates no change in past 15 years. Average income and population of people dependent on agriculture did not change much within the same period yet the continents population has grown from 14 to 16.72% of the world's in the same period. Policy changes (in) in education system is a must as the states reassess the measurement of literacy within the nations. Current education approaches that focus on oral learning with a focus on listening and speaking will not advance Africa's economy. Twenty-first century society economic development requires literacy education that focuses on reading, writing with ability to analyze and synthesize information or data. Further, the twenty-first century global and technology-driven economy demands not only education literacy but also competencies in computer, media, and information literacy. Africa has an urgent need to develop her human capital for effective entrepreneurial economic development in a knowledge global economy.

Examination of Exhibit 2.2 underscores the perception of poverty in many African countries as the study by the World Bank (2016) listed twenty-five (25) poorest countries in the world based on the Gross National Income (GNI). Again, the continent of Africa claimed 22 of these 25 poorest nations. However, the 2017 and 2018 updates of the 22 countries show improved GNI in almost all of the countries. Additionally, two African countries, Seychelles and Mauritius, made the top 50 rich countries of the world. The table also shows that forty-four African countries made the World Bank's one hundred and sixty-seven nations' list, with the last twenty-three lowest GNI (144–167) nations recorded as African's. Another significant information in table is that nineteen (19) of these less-rich countries were also listed among the top twenty-five poorest countries in the world with Central Africa Republic listed as the poorest (World bank 2018). These findings raise a lot of questions regarding economic development in Africa. Where did the increases in the GNI of the nations come from? Why are the African economies still lagging behind others given the national resources the establishment of higher education institution in the continent ahead of the western world? This data reaffirms the need for the governments to revisit policies and develop programs that create enabling environment for effective entrepreneurial economy.

Another area of concern is knowing that comparatively Africa's fifty-four nations are poor economically but very rich in natural resources. An examination of key factors of production (Labor, land, Capital, Entrepreneurship, knowledge) indicate abundance of labor (skilled and unskilled), natural resources (what is under and above land), and Africa also claims twenty percent of world land mass with various minerals and diverse ecology/ecosystem. These include but not limited to coastal, deserts and semi-deserts, mountain, savannah, tropical grasslands, rain forests, etc. Capital which may not necessarily be money is limited and

Exhibit 2.2 Africa economic development as per World Bank Ranking and measured by PPP (GNI)

Country	World ranking out of 167 countries	2018 Gross National Income (GNI)	2017 GNI	2016 GNI	Listed among top 25 poorest nations in the world—2016 (Ranking #)
1. Seychelles	42*	29070			
2. Mauritius	45*	26030			
3. Libya	51	20990			
4. Equatorial Guinea	58	18170			
5. Botswana	61	17970			
6. Gabon	66	16580			
7. South Africa	74	13230			
8. Egypt	82	12080			
9. Tunisia	83	12060			
10. Morocco	98	8410			
11. Angola	113	6150			
12. Nigeria	117	5700			
13. Republic of Congo	120	5050			
14. Ghana	122	4650			
15. Sudan	124	4420			
16. Zambia	128	4100			
17. Ivory Coast	131	4030			
18. Cameroon	133	3700			
19. Senegal	134	3670	2678	2299	(22)
20. Lesotho	135	3610			
21. Kenya	136	3430	3496	2897	(25)
22. Tanzania	138	3160	3283	2542	(24)
23. Zimbabwe	141	3010	2277	1677	(16)
24. Guinea	144	2480			
25. Benin	145	2400	2160	2011	(21)
26. Mali	147	2230	2169	1909	(20)
27. Rwanda	148	2210	2081	1727	(17)
28. Ethiopia	149	2010	2113	1602	(13)
29. Uganda	150	1970	2352	1657	(14)
30. Chad	152	1920*	2433	1817	(18)
31. Burkina-Faso	152	1920*			

(continued)

Exhibit 2.2 (continued)

Country	World ranking out of 167 countries	2018 Gross National Income (GNI)	2017 GNI	2016 GNI	Listed among top 25 poorest nations in the world—2016 (Ranking #)
32. Guinea-Bissau	155	1790	1806	1431	(11)
33. Togo	156	1760	1612	1220	(8)
34. Gambia	157	1680	1686	1570	(12)
35. Madagascar	158	1580	1554	1339	(10)
36. Sierra Leone	159	1520	1791	1221	(9)
37. Malawi	160	1310	1172	1048	(6)
38. Mozambique	161	1300	1266	1100	(7)
39. Liberia	162	1130	none	667	(2)
40. Niger	163	1030	1153	897	(5)
41. D R Congo	164	900	787	723	(4)
42. Central Africa Republic	165	870	none	649	(1)
43. Burundi	166	740	808	716	(3)
44. Mauritania	167	420			

so are knowledge and entrepreneurship. Thus, there is a need to figure out the missing factors for sustainable economic development of African nations and assess the potentials for effective and inclusive development of the continent.

The past two decades have seen some growing interest among scholars, researchers, and investors in Africa and its economic development potentials. The continent's projection as the fourth and next economic renaissance is also attracting foreign investors and researchers. In addition, the continent is seeing an increasing number of indigenous researchers on the entrepreneurial phenomenon as well as a growing number of indigenous entrepreneurs. A review of one hundred and sixty Google Scholar articles revealed several studies with some focus on Africa's entrepreneurial ambitions and economic development issues and successes.

A West African indigenous entrepreneur and entrepreneurial philanthropist, Tony (Anthony) Elumelu is noted to be a driving force behind the concept of "Africapitalism" and committed to the economic transformation of Africa (Babooza 2013). Elumelu's goal and desire is to see "Africans taking charge of the value creation sector of the economy and ensuring that those value-added processes happen in Africa." He shuns government policies and programs that do not create the environment that will support private sector potential entrepreneurs with the vision, tools, and opportunities to shape the destiny of the continent. His foundation (Tony Elumelu's Foundation) is credited with the dedication and promotion of excellence in business leadership with a strong support for start-up enterprises across the continent. He refers to the young start-ups he funds and mentors as "Africapitalists" who will move Africa forward (www.tonyelumelufoundation.org). It is obvious that Elumelu is a proponent of real entrepreneurial activities in Africa and promotes the need for the private sector that will take the necessary risks to organize the resources in Africa for value-added production that will enhance socio-economic development. It is equally, evident that he sees entrepreneurship as the missing factor in the development of Africa.

Select African Entrepreneurs

In a chapter contribution to Handbook of Research on Entrepreneurs' Engagement in Philanthropy (Taylor et al. 2014), the author identified ten distinguished entrepreneurs who were also philanthropists as listed in Forbes top 40 African millionaires and billionaires. Among these are the globally known Aliko Dangote of Nigeria, Anthony Elumelu mentioned in above paragraph, Foloronsho Alakija (Nigerian female), Alan Gray (South Africa), Francois Van Niekerk (South Africa), James Mwangi (Kenya), Mo Ibrahim (Sudan), Ashish Thakkar (Uganda), Mark Shuttleworth (South Africa) and Theophilus Y. Danjuma (Nigeria). A case study of these select entrepreneurs indicated involvement of African entrepreneurs in various activities and could also be classified as classic, serial, social, lifestyle, intrapreneurs, and venture-preneurs. There are a growing number of young entrepreneurs such as Tony Elumelu of Nigeria, Mark Shuttleworth of South Africa, and Ashish Thakkar of Uganda. These entrepreneurs are visionaries, opportunity seekers, and risk-takers who are equally concerned about bottom line as is among Western developed countries entrepreneurs.

Most of the above entrepreneurs (70%) have college degree and about 80% are self-made entrepreneurs who started business at the young age of 13–15 years. For example, Alahaji Aliko Dangote who is the founder, president, and Chief Executive Officer (CEO) of Dangote Group of Companies, started his entrepreneurial ventures when he was in primary school where he purchased and sold candy to fellow scholars and in the community. Today, the conglomerate headquartered in Lagos, Nigeria has subsidiaries all over Africa including Benin, Cameroon, Zambia, and South Africa. He is very supportive of developing Africa by Africans. He is quoted as encouraging people to invest in Nigeria and Africa because, as he argued, it is the only way to develop the continent's economy (www.dangotefoundations.org).

Like Dangote and Elumelu, other African entrepreneur philanthropists are equally focused (and) on building and supporting young emerging entrepreneurs. Thakkar of Uganda, East Africa, works to create sustainable economic and business development opportunities for young business owners through his Mara Launchpad incubation centers and the Launchpad Fund. In launching the Fund, Thakkar said, "Funding has been the missing link, but with Mara Launch Uganda Fund now in place, we complete the ecosystem for supporting young entrepreneurs- after all, young people are our future" (Imaralu 2012).

With Folorunshe Alakija, the multi-millionaire business woman, it is not surprising that this female entrepreneur philanthropist focuses her attention to women issues. She explained her focus on widows as follows: "We found out that being a widow is a stigma in the Nigerian society...Once they lose their husbands, the society turns its back on them, their in-laws begin to mistreat them, they become depressed, they don't know where the next meal is coming from ... We try our best to bring hope back into their lives, We have helped over 2700 widows with workshops and pro vision of monetary support for scholarships for their children and interest-free loans to start small business operations" (Soetan 2012). This widows' situation is worse among the Igbos of Southeast Nigeria where women do not inherit neither husband's nor father's property. A recent Supreme court ruling (Chocomilo 2020) in favor of a daughter to get a share of the deceased father's wealth indicate that this old tradition is not going away even when there is a government law that says otherwise. In addition, a Nollywood movie "Castle Vs. Castle" (Netflix) also depicts the plight of a widow who was about to lose everything following the death of her husband.

It is apparent that Africans need to grow entrepreneurs for sustainable economic development. Thus, Anyansi-Archibong (2006), in an article presented at global entrepreneurship forum proposed that entrepreneurship is the critical and necessary factor that is missing in the development of poor nations. It is a necessary factor for effective and sustainable development of African nations. In the paper which examined the factors of production and their respective impact on socio-economic development, the author cites Nickels et al. (2019) which in its analysis of the rich and poor countries concluded that the major differences in the levels of wealth resulted from the production factors of entrepreneurship and knowledge. The fact that most of the poor countries, especially in Africa, are endowed with abundant natural resources and labor, but lack entrepreneurs and knowledge workers who are the driving forces in the risk-taking processes that ultimately put the resources together for value-added production.

Anyansi-Archibong also argued that capital as another factor of production could not be the missing ingredient since capital (tools, machinery, etc.) could be and has often been funded by foreign aids and global organizations such as the International Monetary Fund (IMF), World Bank, and the respective national governments. It could also be argued that the available capital, mostly financial in nature has been ineffective because there are no entrepreneurs with knowledge to effectively apply this resource for productive activities. This statement underscores what Elumelu alluded to in the need to inspire and support growth of entrepreneurs and create an environment (government policies) that facilitates private sector development.

In a series of publications on Africa, such as Fick (2002, 2006, 2014, 2016) explored and documented the success stories among African entrepreneurs, discussed the economic opportunities in the continent, as well as the continent's entrepreneurship potentials in the twenty-first century. In his first publication, Entrepreneurship in Africa: A Study of Successes (2002), Fick like most nonacademic researchers presented select successful entrepreneurs in terms of what business they are in, how the business was started, their strategies, challenges, solutions found and social impact on their respective communities. Following these documented profiles, Fick stated that "there is no shortage of entrepreneurs in Africa; in fact, over the centuries, there has always been entrepreneurs in Africa and that given the opportunity, entrepreneurs in Africa and from around the world will drive Africa's economic trains forward." This study concluded with prospects for improving Africa's economic and social environment by creating opportunities for innovative, skilled, and passionate entrepreneurs in Africa. Fick cites another indigenous African scholar, Ayitte (1998) and author of Africa in Chaos, who argued that the environment maybe such that it retards or inhibits entrepreneurship in the continent. Ayitte re-iterated by indicating that the prevailing environment in Africa in the 1990s were characterized by government hostility to private enterprise, stifling bureaucracy, insecurity, absence of property rights, crumbling infrastructure, corruption, lack of economic freedom, etc. and believed that if the above situations are improved, there will be many more African entrepreneurs and better prospects for African development.

> *There is no shortage of entrepreneurs in Africa; in fact, over the centuries, there has always been entrepreneurs in Africa and that given the opportunity, entrepreneurs in Africa and from around the world will drive Africa's economic trains forward.* (Fick 2002)

In his second book, Africa: The Continent of Economic Opportunity, 2006, he summarized both opportunities and challenges for entrepreneurship from external and internal sources. He assessed the opportunities in regional ecosystems and trade blocs including the biodiversity of the continent. In conclusions, Fick argued that Africa is not only rich in resources but in creative citizens as shown in the profile of successes including women. He believes that the most significant issue is "how to best create economic environment and opportunities for skilled, innovative, and passionate entrepreneurs in Africa to successfully implement their ideas, achieve their dreams, and bring benefits to their communities." He believed that by relying on this tremendous richness Africans will build a "new" Africa—independent, self-reliant, and prosperous.

This line of argument supports Elumelu's concept of "Africapitalism" but with a push for integration of trade from regional economic blocs. Although Fick's publications continued to identify various industries where opportunity for entrepreneurial activities exist for both indigenes and foreigners, the featured five hundred and seventy-five enterprises from fifty-six countries failed to separate nor distinguish the entrepreneurs by gender. Some women operated enterprises made the list; however, their contributions or differentiations from the male-dominated operations were not identified.

When you think of the limited entrepreneurship research or study on emerging economies granting the importance and steady economic growth of these nations, it will not be surprising to see even a smaller number of studies on African nations and their entrepreneurial activity. In their 2008 literature review, Bruton, Ahlstrom, and Obloj found that only 34 articles relating to entrepreneurship in emerging economies were published in a period of seventeen years (1990–2007). All the same, entrepreneurship continues to be presented as the engine that sparks and pushes economic development.

> *Africa is not only rich in resources but in creative citizens..................in-cluding women, the most significant issue is how to best create economic environment and opportunities for skilled, innovative, and passionate entrepreneurs in Africa to successfully implement their ideas, achieve their dreams, and bring benefits to their communities.* (Fick 2006)

In another study designed to challenge research methodologies and perspectives on African entrepreneurs and entrepreneurship, the authors Hayes and Robinson (2012) argued against and challenged the application of standardized methodologies, tools, and perspectives of entrepreneurship used without consideration to the culture and the nuances of the society. They argued for an economic sociological perspective that considers cultural measures such as religion, ethnicity, colonial heritage, and role of traditional rulers in determining the level of entrepreneurial activities in Africa. For this study, entrepreneurial activity was broadly defined to include formal and informal activities—"traditional entrepreneurship as formally registered operation and informal as other self-employment activities".

The authors concluded with several propositions including but not limited to: 1. "That higher degree of religiosity will be correlated with higher rates of entrepreneurial activities (formal and informal) in consistence with the Weberian perspectives; 2. That nations with strong national identities will have higher level of entrepreneurial activities than nations with weaker national identity; 3. Highly fractionalized countries will have a high level of entrepreneurial activities for the minority ethnic groups; 4. That African nations with French colonial legacies (Francophone) will have lower entrepreneurial activity than Anglophone nations (nations with British colonial legacies); 5. Stable political systems will have higher level of formal entrepreneurial activity while unstable political systems will have high level of informal entrepreneurial activities; and 6. Authors predict that government bureaucracy will stifle formal entrepreneurial activity and increase informal activity."

The above propositions appear to be highly relevant and depicts characteristics of African nations—multiple ethnicity, religious diversity, unstable political systems, and complex traditional issues that when taken into consideration will impact the development of entrepreneurial activities. The inclusion of cultural elements in the measurement and determination of African nations' entrepreneurial aspiration and development is a noteworthy concept; however, the sociological approach failed to identify and discuss the potential impact of these cultural-induced tendencies on women. The impact of culture and traditions (norms) on social structure and roles of women in Africa is critical to the study of women entrepreneurship and their contribution to socio-economic development is the focus of this book.

Other related literature with a focus on Africa's entrepreneurial activities especially women include a 1998 study by Spring and McDade who argued for the importance and inclusion of women entrepreneurs as inspirational in small-scale traders who dominate the informal sector. In the same context, Maswana (1998) asserts that a great deal of developing nations of Africa's economic activities take place in the informal sector and as such this sector should be included in policy planning since it represents the real image of Africa's economic dynamics. This significance of women's contributions to the African economy was recognized in the actions of the colonial masters when in the mid 1920s, local Warrant Chiefs in Nigeria, West Africa were authorized to collect taxes from local market women. The market women rebellion or the Aba women riot of 1929 was a protest against taxation of their revenue from informal entrepreneurial earnings. The Aba, Owerri, and Onitsha (all major cities in the Southern Nigeria) were organized and carried out by women to protest against the taxation scheme. This was followed by other series of women's protests including another Aba women riot of 1938–1940, oil mill protests in Owerri and Calabar provinces resulting in women being appointed to serve on the "Local Native Courts." There were women riots in other regions of the country including the Abeokuta (western region) women's revolt (1947–1949) and Kano riot in 1953. All of these riots or protests were caused by women dissatisfaction with increase in school fees (which mothers were often responsible for), forced female labor, and corruption by local officers who were appointed by the colonial governor with full power to seize properties, imprison non-compliers, and make changes in taxes (Native revenue ordinance of 1927). The officers changed existing tax role to include separate taxation of wives, children, and livestocks mostly reared and owned by women.

Summary

It is noteworthy that even at the early stage of colonial rule, women were able to organize themselves and achieve results that affected their families and the respective communities. The Abeokuta women's revolt is equally noteworthy as it was a nonviolent movement organized and led by Mrs. Ransom-Kuti, one of the early educated and respected women in Nigeria and Africa. Mrs. Ransom-Kuti initially formed a union of elite and equally educated women but with inspirations from the events in the 30s and 40s, she opened up the "Abeokuta Ladies Club" to market women and artisans. Over 200,000 women joined the new "Abeokuta Women Union" with the objectives of fighting to replace flat tax on women with taxation on expatriate companies and investments on local enhancement, end the Sole Native Authorities price control on food items which have negative impact on women operations, and inclusion of women on Sole Authority since women pay taxes.

The Abeokuta Women's Union later became Nigerian Women Union with branches all over the country (Olusoluon 2012). The women achieved all of the objectives including abolition of tax on women and an increase on men's taxation. Other women protest in various regions of the continent will be presented later in the book.

It is important to note the growing research interest among African scholars who are now devoting their research activities to study the entrepreneurial activities of African women. Although significant and systematic study of the place and role of women in Africa is a recent concept, only dating from the 1980s, there are gender-related studies including comparative analysis of roles and implications for socio-economic development. This author also indicated the need to understand that most research were by European authors who have limited or second-hand knowledge of culture and traditional nuances in African society. Many also ignored dynamic changes and historical perspectives in the continent. In their 2012 article, "Diverging Pathways: young female Employment and Entrepreneurship in Sub-Saharan Africa" Langevin and Gough examined the reasons for growing women entrepreneurs especially in retail, seamstress, and hairdressing with a focus in Ghana, West Africa. They found that limited opportunity for formal wage in the private sector and the shrinking public sector are some of the reasons why many women entrepreneurship is on the rise even when it is challenging to succeed.

Following the above argument, Baharul-Islam (2012), found that Africa's rural entrepreneurship by women, even in the midst of global financial and economic crisis, helped in poverty alleviation, and social uplifting in the rural communities. Islam also highlighted some challenges and opportunities with such examples as the successful Women Business Solutions in Zambia and Busy Incubator in Ghana. Islam further defined a woman entrepreneur as "a person who accepts challenging role to meet her personal needs and become economically self-sufficient. They are moved by a strong desire to do something economically gainful and that which will bring 'value-addition' to both their family and society."

In 2008, another study titled "Entrepreneurship and SMEs in Ethiopia: Evaluating the role, prospects and problems faced by women in this emergent sector" Singh and Belwal found that lack of financing, competence, exposure, distribution network and finding new market opportunities limit female entrepreneurs' success. In addition, the authors found that limited government and institutional support, absence of technical know-how, integration mechanism, and rampant corruption also contributed to the difficulties faced by women entrepreneurs in Ethiopia, East Africa.

Across the globe, a study of women entrepreneurs in Western and Eastern European countries underscores the above findings when it reported that the inhibiting factors to women entrepreneurs' progress include the fact that society do not take women business owners seriously, they are conflicted by child and dependent on care responsibilities, lack of capital, lack of entrepreneurial education, and training in technical knowhows. Other non-African country studies indicate similar issues, as shown in the study conducted in Turkey, where married female entrepreneurs reported role conflicts in personal and professional lives. Becoming an entrepreneur had a negative impact on their family life but positive effect on social, economic, and individual lives (Ufuk and Ozgen 2001).

The select literature cited above indicate some similarities in the challenges facing women entrepreneurs across the globe; however, none of these studies including the statement that foreign researchers do not take into consideration the traditions and changing cultures in Africa, have attempted to examine the potential relations among cultural elements, traditions, and women entrepreneurial activities. Entrepreneurship and its nuances among African women are still understudied and there is a need for an integrated studies or examination of the phenomenon and the contributions women entrepreneurs make to the society.

The traditional roles of women as mothers, spouses, caregivers, nurturers, etc. in the early 30s have been talked about and so have the challenges they faced with limited formal education as they venture into professional career. It should not be surprising that most African women often opt for entrepreneurial activity and that these women (referred to as market women) prefer or focus on retail operations. They are also mostly in the fashion industry, restaurant or food related operation. There has to be some interface among African cultures, traditions, and the entrepreneurial tendencies of women. African leaders need to build on the growing research and investment interests in the continent especially the issues relating to the youth and women. National and continental leaders should follow up on the activities of young and inspiring African entrepreneurs such as Toney Elumelu, Ashish Thakkar, Mo Ibrahim, and Folaronsho Alakija, to name a few, who have shown interest in motivating the youth and women to engage in entrepreneurship. The need for development of adequate programs and training centers of entrepreneurship can never be overstated. Purposeful and targeted programs that inspire entrepreneurial spirit are needed across the nations. Adequate infrastructure, especially in the telecommunication technology and enabling environment are a must for the achievement of the goals of an entrepreneurial economy.

Research studies leave many questions unanswered and the exploration of the above propositions on women entrepreneurs is the focus of next chapter. It is not known why African women engage in the type of entrepreneurial activities identified by researchers; however, the role culture and traditions play on the tendency of the African women to engage in such activities will be explored. The chapter will attempt to present available facts and examine relationships among the variables.

It is believed that there is a strong interface and relationship among Africa's culture, traditions, and Entrepreneurial tendencies of the African woman.

References

Africa Continent. (2020). www.Britannica.com/Place/Africa.
Anyansi-Archibong, C. B. (2006). Entrepreneurship as the missing factor in the economic development of developing nations. *Global Entrepreneurship Monitor*.

Ayitte, G. B. N. (1998). *Africa in chaos*. New York: St Martins Press.
Babooza, S. (2013). *Why African philanthropists seek "Africapitalism"*. Retrieved at http://www.thisdaylive.com.
Baharul-Islam, K. (2012). Rural entrepreneurship for women: A case of wealth creation by African rural poor amidst global financial crisis.
Boston Consulting Group Study, in I. Ichikowitz. (2019). Africa can stand toe-to-toe with the big guys. *New African Magazine* (An IC Publication), December 2019/January 2020, No. 599.
Chocomilo, A. S. (2020). *Igbo laws: Igbos disagree as supreme court upholds the right of a female child to inherit her father's property*. https://www.lifeandtimesnews.com/08/27/2020.
Cobb, C. E. Jr. (2005, September). Africa in fact: A continent's numbers tell its story. In *National Geographic*, Africa special issue. http://www.nationalgeogrphic.com/magazine.
Fick, D. (2002). *Entrepreneurship in Africa: A study of success*. www.amazon.com/books/dp/1567205364.
Fick, D. (2006). *Africa: A continent of economic opportunity*. www.realafricanpublishers.com/most-popular/business/africa-continent-of-economic-opportunity-detail.html; www.amazon.com/books/dp/1919855599.
Fick, D. (2014). *African entrepreneurs in the 21st century and their stories of success*. Ghana: Excellent Publishing and Printing. ISBN 978-9988-0-7807-2.
Fick, D. (2016). *Africa entrepreneurs: Success studies*. www.eppbookservices.com.
Hayes, R. N., & Robinson, J. A. (2012). An economic sociology of African entrepreneurial activity. *International Journal of Entrepreneurship, 16*(Special Issue), 51–67.
Ibrahim, M. (2019). African youths: Jobs or migration, governance weekend. Mo Ibrahim Forum, Abijan, Cote d'Voire.
Imaralu, D. (2012). *Ugandan billionaire Ashish Thakkar launches venture capital fund for young entrepreneurs*. Available at www.maragroup.com/2010; http://www.ventures-africa.com/2012/07/ugandanbillionnaire.
Maswana, J.-C. (1998). Africa's future needs to include the informal sector. In Spring & McDade (Eds.), *Entrepreneurship in Africa: Theory and reality*. Gainesville: University press of Florida.
Nickels, G. M., Mchugh, J. M., & McHugh, S. M. (2019). *Understanding business* (10th ed.). New York: McGraw-Hill Education Publishers. ISBN 978-1-259-92943-4.
Olusoluon, S. (2012). *Aba women riot: Women's war*. http://www.en.m.wikipedia.org%3Ewomen%5Fwar; www.blackpast.org%3Eaba-women-riot.
Soetan, F. (2012, August 2). *Finance, Fashion, Philanthropy: Folorunsho Alakija, FAMFA Oil*. http://www.ventures-africa.com/2012/08/finance-fashion-philanthropy-folorunsho-alakija.

Taylor, M. L., Strom, R. J., & Renz, D. O. (2014). *Handbook of research on entrepreneurs' engagement in philanthropy: Perspectives.* Northampton, MA: Edward Elger Publishing Limited. ISBN 978-1-78347-100-3.

Ufuk, G., & Ozgen, A. (2001). Role conflict for married women entrepreneurs in Turkey.

World Bank Economic Report. (2016). https://www.worldbank.org/Africa.

World Bank Economic Report. (2018). https://www.worldbank.org/Africa.

CHAPTER 3

Culture and Traditional Foundations of African Women Entrepreneurs

INTRODUCTION

The traditional marriage ceremonies and celebrations have just ended and guests are leaving the bride's family premises. Nneka, the bride, is with her close friends and family members taking stock of the wedding gifts from both her parents and other immediate community mothers. It is usually the norm or custom in most African countries, following the discussions, agreement, and payment of dowry from the bridegroom and his family, for the bride's family to spend some of the dowry on gifts for their daughter, the bride. These gifts were intended to help the bride settle down in her new home. She is expected by tradition to support the husband and help maintain a self-sufficient family.

Nneka's bridal gifts, consistent with tradition included a wooden mortar and pestle set (large, medium, and small), assorted sizes of cooking pots and pans (aluminum, wrought iron, clay), dishes and spoons, local brooms, metal tripod stand, grinding stone, medium size hoe, sewing machine, select number of materials (wrapper and other pieces of materials), luggage, etc. The quality, quantity, and diversity of gifts are very much dependent on the wealth of the family and the dowry presented. These gifts were not only symbolic but practical as it immediately identified the various roles and cultural, as well as the traditional expectations from the newly married girl.

© The Editor(s) (if applicable) and The Author(s), under exclusive license to Springer Nature Switzerland AG 2021
C. Anyansi-Archibong, *The Foundation and Growth of African Women Entrepreneurs*, Palgrave Studies of Entrepreneurship in Africa,
https://doi.org/10.1007/978-3-030-66280-6_3

Traditional Wedding Gifts and Dowry

Exhibit 3.1 presents some wedding gift items and their respective significance for the woman as she transitioned to her husband's home. The newly weds, especially the woman was expected to be responsible for building a new family with the support of the husband. She was to understand the familiar voices and statements, even from her own family that "a woman's pride is defined by her marriage status" or that "a woman is mostly defined by her husband's status." These statements made marriage an important stage in an African woman's life and thus the attempt through which entrepreneurial activities designed to support her husband in building and sustaining the family in her first exit according the Moroccan saying that girls have two exits in their lives—"one to the husband's home and the other to the grave" (Kadri 2020).

Exhibit 3.1 Traditional marriage gifts, symbolism, and influence on entrepreneurial tendencies

Select items	Symbolism/role intent
Set of Mortars and Pestles	The largest is for pounding heavy items like corn, cassava, millet, yam, rice, etc. for meals; the medium size mortar is for soft items such as grinding tomatoes, egusi (melon seed), ogbono, coco yam, etc.; and the small mortar is used for grinding pepper, crayfish, and other condiments and spices used in preparing various meals
Pots and pans	The tools—pots and pans of different sizes symbolize feeding responsibilities and remind the newly married woman of her duty to cook and feed her new family and sometimes the extended members
Dishes and spoons	Tools for serving food to the family
Metal/Iron Tripod	An important tool used in the outdoor kitchen for holding the cooking pots— more like the stove top but with fire wood supplying the flames
Wrappers and Dress materials	Wrappers and materials for personal use
Sewing Machine	Potential tool for sewing and fashion business
Brooms	Home keeper role—sweeping and cleaning the house and surroundings
Bicycle	Luxury item for few used for carrying tools to farm and crops to market
Other related items	Depends on the wealth or poverty status of the family or the wealth of the husband

With very limited education and the tools/gifts received from wedding, many women rely on the domestic skills acquired from home for diverse business startups. Most of the Sub-Saharan African women established businesses in food-related industry. Popular among them was the roadside restaurants, retail trade of food items at home or in the open bazar markets, and those lucky or wealthy enough to receive a sewing machine and learned needle work in the primary school open up small sewing business and craft centers.

Compare the above to Phidora's situation in Uganda, East Africa, or Njiri in Kenya, where dowry is negotiated in terms of livestock. Phidora's parents received seven cows, a dozen goats, and five thousand shillings (80shillings/$) for her dowry. Phidora received three cows and six goats to take to her new marital home. Upon arrival, her husband allotted her a small portion of his farm land to grow vegetables and other crops. This tradition was common to most of the East African cultures.

Literature on societal roles, the impact, definitions of traditions and culture on African women is limited and often not comprehensive. Boserup (a historical economic scholar) made waves among historians in her 1970 book titled, "Women's Role in Economic Development." She presented women as economic producers but argued that those economic systems were disrupted by colonialism which moved or shifted women's status to become marginalized and unappreciated.

Several scholars have picked up from Boserup including the study of women traders in Senegal, West Africa (Brooks 1976); a study of how economic changes in Kenya, East Africa, affected Luo women (Jean Hayes 1976); and Mann's 1985 study of Marriage in Nigeria. These studies and a few others focused on roles and status of women in pre- and during colonial era. They explored the processes employed by women in dealing with changing forms of oppressions and examined how "phenomena" such as "domesticity" became gendered. Many unearthed women's role in national struggles for independence (Shilcola and Presley 1998 [1992]) and argued that these categories of women cases can now be applied in pre-colonial context (Oyewunmi 1997).

Generally, but more traditionally, most African women receive less formal education, they are marginalized, engaged, or forced into early marriage, do not inherit or own property. They are, at least in the past fifty years and to some extent at the present time, small vegetable farmers, and retail traders, who are mostly referred as "market women." Their roles include but not limited to child bearing, nurse and raise children, manage homes with very limited resources, and responsible for household healthcare.

Many individuals and groups in today's society may regard the above characterization of women as archaic old customs but take a good look at the current status of women and it could be seen that the only change happening is the increase in the percentage of women who engage in formal education. Many African women have university degrees and professional careers but roles and expectations have not changed and so are many tradition and culturally driven status.

Many still believe that a woman is defined by her husband's status and that an unmarried woman has little or no respectful status in the society. Men still maintain the attitude of having the ultimate authority in the household irrespective of the education and career position of their spouses. Recent example is a 2019 situation, where a couple (both with Ph.D. degrees) had the usual husband and wife disagreement. In the middle of their discussions the husband busted out—"listen, I married you, you did not marry me, I am the head of this family, and no matter what, what I say is final!"

This outburst from a highly educated African man underscores the fact that the cultural or social structure that placed African woman in subordinate position to the man have not changed even with open and more liberal access to formal higher education for women.

There are other similar situations where the woman was marginalized such as the requirements to surrender a woman's earnings to the husband (Okundayo 2020).

Culture, Traditions, and Multiple Roles of the African Woman

Social structures as well as several elements of culture (religion, life style, values, norms, attitude, cuisine, language, fashion, etc.) and cultural characteristics (transgenerational, dynamic, learned, etc.) play a major part in determining the African woman's roles and status. For example, traditional division of labor gives Senegalese women the responsibility of household tasks of cooking, cleaning, and child care. These women are expected to and do share a large responsibility in agriculture such as weeding and harvesting of produce such as rice and millet. Recent changes in economic planning has added management of village forestry resources and operating millet and rice mills as the men migrated to the cities (Wikipedia 2018) to seek opportunities for better life.

In Uganda women are required to concede to the authority of all males (father, brother, uncle, husbands, etc.) in the immediate and extended family. In early 1980s, evidence show that women in the Buganda area of Uganda were expected to kneel when speaking to a man. These women are responsible for childcare, subsistence cultivation and farming for cash crops.

Even Rwanda which currently boasts of largest number of women in parliament still faces major gender-related issues. Issues such as work-overload (multiple roles), less access to formal education, and gender-based violence still exist.

Although women in some Matriarchal society such as the Seychelles and some part of Ghana enjoy the same legal, economic, political, and social rights as men, mothers still tend to be dominant in household maintenance. Unwed mothers are societal norms in Seychelles unlike most countries in other parts of the continent. This is an unusual situation, since men are required by law to support the children. It is also important to note that the population makeup in the country is an exception to that of most African nations.

In many Moslem or Islamic Societies such as Libya and Morocco where the status of women is undergoing major adjustments however, these adjustments are largely based on Islamic values which places more restrictions on women rights. Islamic cultures and traditions tend to marginalize and seclude women from regular civic society. In these cultures (Mali, Niger, Burkina Faso), sometimes referred to as Nomadic lifestyles, women are expected to adorn themselves for men's (usually husbands) admiration only. They are mostly homemakers. Business or entrepreneurial activities focus on collection and dying of grass for making mats used primarily for decorating their homes while extra ones are sold in the local markets. These women also sell fresh milk and butter which they spend days producing from the livestock received from the dowry during the wedding. Wealthy women among these cultures are recognized by large collection of colorful plates, bowls, basins and jewelry most of which were received at the time of wedding (Wikipedia).

In Burkina Faso, families eat in groups and tradition demands that the men be served first while the women and children eat later together. This feeding procedure and grouping exemplifies the dominant role of the women for childcare. This situation reminds me (the author) of the video

I received on Mother's Day celebration (2019) titled **"Why Mother's Day is more popular than Father's Day**." The video depicts a rooster and a hen eating seeds from a bowl. The rooster was busy gulping the seeds as fast as possible while the hen was equally busy dropping seeds for the chicks, which could not reach the bowl. Mother hen did not swallow a single seed but was busy feeding her chicks.

This video not only typified the childcare role of women but also her responsibilities to the family including her spouse. She never complained about the spouse's unconcerned behavior about feeding the children.

Although evidence exists to show that in this modern time, husbands and other family male members tend to carry some of the household responsibilities formally carried out by the woman, the continuing existence of some traditions, social, and cultural dynamics in the continent still place the majority of the burden on women.

Dr. Sahar Nasr, Egypt's Minister of Investment and International Cooperation (2018), in an interview with the New Africa Woman magazine, stated that "as an economist, I also look at women's contributions at the household level as a critical element that should not be ignored." She explained this statement as follows "if a mother is mentoring and taking care of her children and helping them do their studies, that is productivity- it is work. If a woman is taking care of an elderly parent, this is a major contribution to the society and the economy- this is being productive." She therefore recommends the Gross Domestic product calculations take such activities into account because this is "an opportunity cost."

Consider an opposite of alternative situation where the woman choses to neglect her roles as a parent and a caregiver to focus on an income generating activities? The potential consequences of this alternate behavior are that the home becomes dysfunctional, children are not disciplined, and may become mediocre performers in school or at an extreme situation, drop out of school. Poor feeding and home care results in poor health, development of diseases that could have been prevented by clean and decent homecare, etc. In this situation, the children become a societal burden and misfits. In Africa, just as in other societies, the result is that most of these youth become public nuisance and sometimes criminals. What happens is that the value-added to the economy and society by the mother who wore her multiple roles effectively are devalued.

This may sound unreal to some but it should be noted that in Africa a common saying among men, educated and uneducated is that when a child is raised well or behaves well, the father refers to him or her as "my son or my daughter" but if he or she is a non-achiever the child is automatically referred to as the mother's—the father says to the mother, "you better talk to your son or see what your (referring to the wife) child has become."

> .... *women's contributions at the household level is a critical element that should not be ignored. If a mother is mentoring and taking care of her children and helping them do their studies, that is productivity- it is work..................this a major contribution to the society and the economy. (Nasr 2018)*

I (author) grew up in a family with eight siblings and about three to four house-helps at any given period. Most house-helps were relations including first and second cousins. Our mother, like any other woman of her time had very limited formal education—standard four (equivalent of JS 2 or grade seven in the USA). But Mama, as we all call her, was naturally intelligent, insightful, and very resourceful. She was a disciplinarian who scheduled home work sessions for after school hours. She could and did estimate the appropriate length of time to complete any home assignment.

I remembered one occasion when one of my younger siblings claimed to have completed an assignment because she wanted to play with her friends. Mama stepped in and asked her to show the assignment to another sibling who is in a higher grade to check and behold Mama was right. The assignment was incomplete and of course she would not allow my sister to play. We called her too strict then but as we grew up and realized that some of our friends whose parents especially mothers were more liberal and allowed them to engage in whatever they wanted never progressed in life as we did. Some became a burden not only to the family but to the society.

ENTREPRENEURS BY DEFAULT

Tradition and culture made the African woman a natural for entrepreneurial activities. With limited formal education, the woman's options for career employment in the early 1930s and beyond were non-existent. Be it at a micro or macro level, an African girl or woman was never idle. As a young girl, she is actively engaged in household activities with her mother—cleaning, helping in the kitchen, weeding in the vegetable garden or farm, fetching water from the stream, etc. In many situations, she is learning to balance these roles with a limited opportunity for formal education. Remember the story of Nneka—married at the age of sixteen with a junior high formal education. In addition to the domestic skills learned at home, Nneka's school extra curriculum included gardening, needle work or sewing, cooking and baking classes. Her "gendered" domestic skills and good character was a welcome gift to her married family.

Nneka had her first child in the tenth month following her wedding, but had started her sewing and dress making business six months after wedding. She was able to set up business in front (balcony) of their apartment. She had the tool (capital) in the form of the singer brand sewing machine she received as part of the wedding gift. She also had some limited sewing skills which she acquired from the needle work and sewing classes in her school.

> *Culture and tradition set up Nneka's roles—a wife, mother, parent, caregiver,* **etc.** *and by necessity a small business operator that brings the much-needed additional income to her new family.*

Phidora in Uganda quit school after standard four and got married. Her dowry included live stocks of which her parents shared with her when she left to her husband's house. She started a goat farm and occasionally rented a bull to produce calves with her cows (cows offered for dowry must be a virgin cow—must not have produced any calf). This is her means of raising her livestock. In the future she hopes to produce milk and butter from the cows for sale and consumption.

Dowry, tied to the items gifted to the new bride to help her develop and sustain her new family is a common cultural tradition across the regions of the continent. In most cases the major element of culture differentiating the requirements, type, and procedures for dowry or bride price was religion and sometimes the regional ecosystem.

Characteristics of a Traditional and Culture-Driven African Woman Entrepreneur

Mama (Anyansi) was as busy as any business woman of her time and beyond. As mentioned earlier in the introductory section of the book, many African women are rarely full-time stay-home mothers or spouses. Mama got married at an early age of fifteen and luckily through the intervention of her new mother-in-law was sent to a missionary domestic center where she learned the needed skills to become a viable, effective wife, mother, and parent. It should be noted that Mama was the only girl in her family of three. She lost her mother when she was barely two years old and was raised by her father and two older brothers. She joined her husband at his residence in the city after she completed the two-year training program and within months has started looking for ways to keep herself busy outside the normal household responsibilities. At the domestic center, she acquired skills in cooking, baking, knitting, crocheting, designing, sewing, and the importance of cleanliness for good healthy living.

Mama started a small retail business six months after joining her husband. She realized that the consumption of kola nuts and "burukutu" (a local drink made from millet) was very popular in the part of the country (North Central) where they resided. She set up a table in front of the house and retailed kola nuts of different sizes and colors. She brewed burukutu during the night going through the process of grinding, sifting, mixing, and boiling the mixture. The ready brew was ready for sale in cups or bottles as breakfast drink. With time she added other popular food items such as red pepper, crayfish, egusi (which she shelled by hand), aligator pepper, Ose-oji (local peanut butter) (the last two items are complementary items for kola nut), cigarettes sold by stick, roasted and boiled peanuts (groundnuts) and onions. Within four years she had added two children to the family, however, since her business operation was out of her home, she took time to maintain her domestic responsibilities of making sure the children and the husband were fed, and the home cleaned. On some occasions, she had the responsibility of taking food to her husband who was running a clothing materials shop in the city's main market.

Several years later Mama and her husband moved to Enugu (former capital of Eastern region of Nigeria), popularly known as the coal city. Enugu is about seventy-five miles away from Ogoja and with a different set of ethnic groups. At Enugu where most of her nine surviving children (out of twelve pregnancies), including me were born and at various grade school levels, Mama's relentless entrepreneurial pursuit continued. Increased family and domestic responsibilities could not and would not stop her rather she became what I may describe as a "seasonal" entrepreneur.

- *She cooked, roasted, and sold corn on the cob with side items (local pear and coconut) during the fresh corn season*
- *She switched to boiled guinea fowl eggs ("akwa ogazi") during its season*
- *She focused on fresh fruits such as oranges, mangoes, and bananas, etc. during the season.*
- *She designed and made children's dresses around Christmas and Easter seasons when most parents buy new clothes for their children*
- *Supported Papa (her husband) in his general contractor enterprise by keeping track of cement bags and blocks at the construction sites*
- Etc.

She had a kiosk in front of the house for non-seasonal goods including small firewood bundles and coal blocks. She never admitted to a customer about not carrying any items. She would tell customers that she just sold the last piece and hoped he or she would come back the next time. I used to think that she was being deceitful or actually lying to the customer (a behavior she will not tolerate from any of her children or the numerous relatives that lived with the family), until I went to college and learned more about fundamentals of small business and marketing strategies. We could not understand why she had to engage in all these business activities especially when husband's lumber and general contractor business were doing very well. As we grew older and asked subtly, she told us, especially the girls, that the worst situation you can be in as a married woman is to depend financially solely on your husband. "You need to have your own money for your women's organization membership dues, uniforms, change or pocket money for your children's extra curricula activities in school, and sometimes the school uniform." Mama belonged to several women's organizations including Abagana women organization, Sacred Heart Women Association, Ogbete Market Women Association, etc. She also held leadership position in many.

> *A woman needs to have her own money for personal use....... You do not always have to wait on your husband for every for every penny. (Mama)*

By the time the civil conflict or war affected the city (Enugu), mother's retail business had grown to a large "super store" of about 30–40 square feet with an "On and Off License Beer Store." The super market sold canned and bottled goods including tomatoes, corned beef, cereal, milk (powder and liquid), etc. you name it, she got it! The giant freezer and refrigerator took care of the beer, soft drinks, and other frozen or cold items. Her entrepreneurial venture slowed down and came to a sudden end in 1968 when violence from the civil conflict entered the city with the federal forces bombing of the city of Enugu. The family left and relocated to the home town of Abagana with minimal personal properties.

By this time, you must be wondering how these enterprising activities affected her traditional roles of a mother, parent, caregiver, etc.? How was she able to positively impact her family and community financially and otherwise? How did this African woman with equivalent of fifth grade formal education keep record of her sales, determine profit or loss, and manage her money? What were the forces driving her enthusiasm for business venture? [Full story in the profile section of this book, Chapter 12: **"Mrs. M. Anyansi Super Market."**].

The above is and could be the story of most African women. They are motivated to strive for self-sufficiency. They are resilient and although they could be generally characterized as necessity entrepreneurs, like Mrs. Anyansi, they seek and identify businesses that are trending and that will make their business venture viable given their limited formal education.

Some young women in the early 40s and 50s may be opportune to acquire higher education at the university level and attempted to build a formal career. However, the society or rather social structure labels them too academic (often referred to as "Acada") and with the tendency to be too independent, and very opinionated and therefore, "do not make good house wives." Remember the earlier statement about the "woman being defined by the status of her husband?" The stigma of not getting married early because of higher education follows the African woman as pressures begin to mount from parents and extended family, [recently depicted in the Netflix African movies—"Seven and Half Dates" and "Isoken"].

Now, how do we define an entrepreneur? Is Mrs. Anyansi, aka, Mama, an entrepreneur or just a mere market woman? Generally, an entrepreneur is depicted as an individual or group who takes the risk to start and operate business or businesses according to popular literature on the phenomenon. Classification of these risk-takers include but not limited to classical, serial, social, lifestyle, micro, etc. based on the practice and reason for taking the risk. A study that has taken the tradition, culture, and ecosystem as forces behind entrepreneurial ventures is yet to be seen.

In this book, an African woman entrepreneur is an individual who recognizes the need to act in the interest of her family survival and development toward self-sufficiency, then takes some actions by using the domestic skills and tools available to engage in some moneymaking activities such as designing and sewing (fashion), opening up a small roadside eatery or restaurant, selling extra vegetables from her garden, etc. This female entrepreneur aims to support and uphold her family especially contributing to the education and health of her children just as was identified in Mrs. Anyansi's case. Editors Moreno-Gavara and Jimenez-Zarco (2019) support this definition when they identified and defined entrepreneurship as a means of survival for the women in their edited book titled "Empowering African Women Entrepreneurs in the fashion Industry." They addressed the issues of sustainability, poor education, and lack of funding and found that eighty (80%) percent of African women entrepreneurs are in the fashion industry.

In addition to the African woman entrepreneur's motivation to support family income, she intends to be self-sufficient enough to buy her women's organizations' (where has membership) uniforms, pay her dues, participate (in) in fund raising activities, etc. without waiting on her husband. Further, the African woman entrepreneur does not only care for her immediate family but indirectly supports extended family and immediate community. The extended family is a common cultural phenomenon in Africa where a marriage is more a union of two families or communities rather than a man and a woman.

Summary

It is apparent that these African women are entrepreneurs and classification and characteristics in literature must be expanded to include seasonal and traditional. These women are self-driven, hard-working, motivated, and persistent just like any other classical entrepreneur. They are mostly necessity-driven rather than opportunity-driven. However, sometimes you can see some element of opportunity seeking many seasonal entrepreneurs. Culture and tradition certainly have influence on the type of business startup of many women. They see the needs and take risks with very limited resources to start and maintain their business. They are resilient and find ways to support each other and solve common problems through organizations such as Market Women Associations and groups (Famous Aba and Abeokuta Women Riots (1929–1930); "Wives on Strike" 1&2; Netflix 2019 African Movies).

In Kenya the women did not only protest but went a step further and set up a "women only" community. Led by Rebecca Lolosolu, "Umoja" (No man allowed) Community of Samburu tribe developed into a village where women who suffered domestic violence and other gender related abuse could relocate and find peace. The women organized themselves and provided security for the village. They built their homes and as many women arrived with children, a school building was erected and basic curriculum was introduced and taught by few educated members of the community. This matriarchal village grew to the point where arts and crafts made by the women, farm crops, and animal produce were sold and revenues applied to the maintenance of homes and schools. The community grew with the goal of becoming independent and financially self-sufficient. The leader met with Senator Hilary Clinton in 2015 to discuss women and gender issues in Kenya (YouTube.com).

African women entrepreneurs compete in business and several other situations but usually come together for a common cause especially when it relates to common gender issues and roles such as motherhood and caregivers. African women typify the saying that "It takes a Village to raise a child." The continent is possibly the only region in the world where it is okay to not mind your business when you see a neighbor or friend's child misbehaving. The African woman will chastise, correct, and if necessary, punish the misbehaving child prior to reporting to the family, especially the mother. In many situations the child, after taking the punishment from a neighbor will plead with her not to inform the parents, because parents, especially mothers, will likely double the punishment for the same offence.

African women entrepreneurs with limited formal education, enhanced domestic skills, and often marginalized by culture and tradition had no opportunities in corporate organizations or professional careers than to become entrepreneurs. Africa, according to World Bank Group study (2018) is the only region in the world where more women chose to become entrepreneurs than men. The bank study saw this as unusual and probably a phenomenon but further review and understanding of the cultures and traditions such as presented in this book will help explain the phenomenon.

This historical look at the social structure and the roles it placed on women is one of the major forces driving this entrepreneurial tendency. In addition to the above report, the same World Bank group concluded that female entrepreneurs are the future of the African continent. This prediction is supported by Entrepreneurs Watch List (2019) which described and characterized African women entrepreneurs as "breaking barriers, transforming industries, and inspiring change on the continent."

As much as these women micro-entrepreneurs were driven by tradition and culture to engage in business activities, the diversity of their activities has also been influenced by some nuances in regional and colonial cultures. The next chapter deals with a look at these differences and similarities among the five major regions of the continent.

References

Brooks, G. (1976). *Women traders in pre-colonial Senegal.* https://www.wikipedia/history-women-in-Africa.

Hayes, M. J. (1976). *How economic changes in pre-colonial Kenya affected Luo women.* https://www.wikipedia/history-women-in-africa.

Kadri, I. (2020). The Alchemist. 100 most influential Africans. *New African Magazine* (An IC publication), December 2019/January 2020, No. 599.

Moreno-Gavara, C., & Jimenez-Zarco, A. I. (Eds.). (2019). *Sustainable fashion: Empowering African women entrepreneurs in the fashion industry.* Macmillan-Palgrave Publishing company. ISBN 978-3-319-91265-3.

Nasr, S. (2018, November–January). Women need equal opportunities not equality. *New African Woman Magazine* (An IC Publication) Issue 44, pp. 23–40.

Okundayo, N. (2020, January 21). Personal Interview with author, at Nike Art Galleries, Lagos, Nigeria.

Oyewunmi, N. (1997). *Application of women cases in pre-colonial context.* https://www.wikipedia/history-women-in-africa.

Shilcola, A., & Prester, C. (1998 [1992]). *Role and status of women in pre-colonial versus colonial society.* www.wikipedia.com/history-women-in-africa.

Wikipedia. (2018). *Senegal women: Changes in roles during the colonial era.* www.wikipedia.org/Women-in-africa. Retrieved February 11, 2020.

CHAPTER 4

Regional Perspectives of Women Entrepreneurs: Similarities, Differences, and Contributing Forces

INTRODUCTION

Cultures and traditions which defined the African woman's status and gendered roles on the surface indicate more similarities than differences among women status across the regions. The tendencies for the first-generation women entrepreneurs and their multiple roles have more in common regarding the type of industries or businesses they operate. The potential impact of the culture-induced social structures in the five key regions of the continent and the implications for women entrepreneurial activities are explored in relations to the generally identified traditional characteristics of the African woman including limited access to education, marginalized, early marriage, family caregiver, denied property inheritance, and in most cases become vegetable farmers, small retail traders, with domestic skills.

My teaching career, especially my research focus on international business and issues of emerging economies provided opportunities for travel across the major continents of the world. My favorite thing to do in each country, outside the professional engagements, was to visit the local market and cultural centers. I always wanted to explore cultural differences and similarities as I assessed cross cultural management and communication issues. My travels in the African continent were special as I enjoyed talking to the local men and women. I inquired about the

© The Editor(s) (if applicable) and The Author(s), under exclusive license to Springer Nature Switzerland AG 2021
C. Anyansi-Archibong, *The Foundation and Growth of African Women Entrepreneurs*, Palgrave Studies of Entrepreneurship in Africa,
https://doi.org/10.1007/978-3-030-66280-6_4

cultures and the impact it has had on their respective lives including the food, religion, clothing styles, the roles created by the social structures, music, language, family relationships, cuisine, and colonial influence on cultures and traditions, among others.

Regional Markets and Culture

I never missed the trip to local open markets or what is known as the bazar market in some countries. This is where I shop for local crafts, especially hand-made items that are often specific to the diverse tribes and cultures.

In Morocco, Northern Africa for example, the Marrakesh (open market) presented local items such as local musical instruments, hand-made rugs and clothing materials, leader work, spices, and locally designed jewelry made with natural materials, all were representative of the majority Muslim culture. Street corner and kiosk cuisine displayed diversity of popular dishes such as couscous, beef and chicken-kabob, dates, olives, and numerous other fruits.

The south African market in the Zulu community presented variety of wood-carved items from ebony wood to soft-stone items. Local artisans displayed sculptures depicting images of families of various sizes, bowls with carved images prompting explanations and beautiful conversation, jewelry, musical instruments, and paintings depicting village scenes and cultural dancers and much more.

In the east African nations of Kenya and Uganda my shopping basket included items from the Massai open market and Kampala cultural market respectively. These items included colorful neckless, earrings, and bangles of various shapes and sizes. Most of these were made of local woods, native dye, and dried nuts.

Whereas the east provided me with colorful jewelry and shopping raffia baskets, the west satisfied my cravings for stylish dresses and materials ranging from Ankara textiles, batik, to cottage industry tie-dye. The colorful fabrics and designs had me and some friends spending money on shirts and dresses (long and short).

The central region's pottery and colorful bowls made of clay from mines in Democratic republic of Congo and Cameroon complimented the traditional weaved materials. The Cameroon art designs are unique and represent traditional paintings. These paintings form story lines of villages and their accomplishments.

It should be noted that most of the producers and sellers in these bazar markets were mostly women with the exception of the Marrakech market in Morocco which was dominated by young and middle-aged men. These shopping experiences in select countries of the major regions serve as a sage way of examining the similarities and differences.

The Moroccan market unlike the others was populated by men and few young unmarried women. I wanted some Moroccan jewelry which our host and other local staff were wearing. They indicated that these were made specially by women (mostly married) and who by societal norms and belief were not allowed to sell in the open market. Later we went to a secluded location where these married women displayed their products. The men in our group were not allowed to shop with us because tradition and beliefs did not allow men in this location. I had to buy some items for these men who wanted jewelry for their significant others.

The explanation was purely of religious values and norms which forbade any other man, besides the husband' to see a married woman's face. In such Muslim or Islamic society, attempt by women to engage in entrepreneurial or income-earning activities outside the home was frowned upon (Burkina Faso/YouTube 2019).

Regions and Countries of Africa

As much as it is not possible to itemize and discuss the fifty-four countries of Africa, an overview of its regions provides a backdrop to the cultural developments and the impact on entrepreneurial aspirations, status, and development of the women.

The five regions include 1. **Northern Africa** (Algeria, Morocco, Libya, Egypt, Tunisia, and Sudan), with the Atlas Mountains providing a route between the coast and the Sahara Desert. The Atlas slopes with dense forests with pine, cedar, cork, and oak trees, while the valleys provide pasture for livestocks.

2. **Western Africa** (Benin, Burkina Faso, Cape Verde, Cote d' Ivoire, Ghana, Gambia, Guinea, Liberia, Mali, Mauritania, Niger, Nigeria, Senegal, Sierra Leone, Western Sahara) with natural endowments of dense forests, vast desert, grassland and wetland areas grow some of the world's prized hardwood trees such as Iroko and Mahogany.

3. **Eastern Africa** (Burundi, Djibouti, Ethiopia, Eritrea, Kenya, Mauritius, Somalia, Uganda, Rwanda, Tanzania, South Sudan, Comoros), with its Great Rift valley including Lake Victoria, Mount Kenya, and the

Kilimanjaro, the region also presents the best coastlines in the world. The ecosystems of savannah grasslands are home to people and wildlife including the Serengeti and the Masai Mara.

4. **Central Africa** (Angola, Democratic Republic of Congo, Republic of Congo, Gabon, Chad, Central African Republic, Cameroon, Equatorial Guinea, Sao Tome and the Principe) is home to the great rain forest of the Congo River. Lake Chad, the fourth largest lake in Africa is an asset to the region because of its contribution to the much-needed hydrology and the diversity of flora and fauna it attracts (Nene 2009). Lake Chad is equally known for the role it plays in the trans-Saharan trade.

5. **Southern Africa** (South Africa, Namibia, Lesotho, Swaziland (E-Swatini), Botswana, Malawi, Zimbabwe, Mauritius, Madagascar, Seychelles), and its dominant land features such as the inland plateau, encircling mountain ranges, and coastal lowlands display variety of topography and natural resources. The Rand (Ridge of White Waters) is a ridge of gold-bearing rock. It is the site of world's largest gold deposit. The northern part is the open grasslands with trees and bushes called the Bushveld (Nene 2009) and is a treasure chest of minerals including chromium, copper, gold, iron, diamond, and platinum.

Cultural Elements: Similarities and Differences

Further reflection and examination of the items purchased from these various countries indicate more similarities than differences among the regions. Exhibit 4.1 presents major elements of culture, their characteristics, and the respective influence in determining the roles of women in the regions.

As shown in the above Exhibit 4.1 cultural elements and the induced traditions have influence on the status of an African woman, her roles in the society, and her tendency for entrepreneurship. While Africa's most common cultural characteristics could be summarized as that of inequality, male domination, hierarchical-oriented (association of birth place-royal), and respect for tradition, the details in the elements presented in the table influenced the roles, status, and the tendency of women to opt for entrepreneurship.

In general, the cultures seem to be more similar than different, however, elements such as **religion and belief** created more differences in its potential impact on women's status. The two dominant religions of Islam and Christianity in Africa present some dividing line in the status of

Exhibit 4.1 Elements of culture and influence on women wntrepreneurs

Key elements of culture	Meaning/characteristics	Potential Influence on Roles & Women Entrepreneurial Spirit [Significant & Insignificant & Moderate Influence]
• Beliefs/Religion	Tenets held to be true. Often based on religion and creates social control	Significant
• Values	Standards for determining good and bad include ethical decisions and attitude	Significant
• Language	System of communication and transmission of culture could be verbal and nonverbal	Insignificant
• Symbols	Gestures, signs, signals, logos, plaques, alphabets, shapes, etc.— forms of nonverbal communication	Moderate
• Norms	Informal laws learned by observation, imitation and general socialization	Moderate
• Mores	Moral views and lifestyles and "Folkways" which are norms without moral under-pinning	Significant
• Material Culture	Types of goods and services preferred including cuisine and fashion	Moderate
• Architectural Culture	Physical structures, building styles and materials, environment/ecosystem	Insignificant
• Social Structure	Family units, social groups, tribes, clans, etc.	Significant
• Colonial Culture	Imported culture and traditions including language, work ethic, social groups, etc.	Significant/Moderate

women. Social structures among Christian communities are more liberal and often encourage women entrepreneurial activities while Islamic societies with backings from the Koran and Sharia law does not discourage but frowns on such activities outside the home. It was regarded as a taboo for a married woman to work outside of her home. However, these same cultural components (**values, attitude, belief**) endorsed the roles of women as homemakers, child care, subservient to males and spouses. As indicated in the opening chapter, dowry or payment for taking a woman's hand in marriage spans across the continent.

The approach, the items demanded from parents of the bride, the negotiations, etc., differ in each region but this is one tradition that is similar and tends to define the African woman's identity. It should also be noted that as much as Muslim belief and values frown on entrepreneurial activities, research studies (Tlaiss 2014 [2015a]) show that Islamic work values and ethics are imbedded in the entrepreneurial activities. The study carried out in four Middle Eastern countries about how Islamic Business ethics impact women entrepreneurs found that the women seek well-being (falah) in their life and excellence (itqan) in their work. They adhere to the value of good and hard work (amal salih), honesty and truthfulness (sidik and amanah), fairness and justice (haqq and adl), and benevolence (ihsaan) and they perceived these values as instrumental to the survival and success of the business and career. In another study, the researchers saw Islam as enabler rather than obstacle to women empowerment (Madichie and Gallant 2012) and that many Moslem women entrepreneurs view the prophet Mohamed's first wife, Khadija, who was a trader and a business person as their role model and motivator (Tlaiss 2014 [2015a]). Several other research studies present the view that religion influences and is influenced by entrepreneurship (Henley 2016; Tlaiss 2014 [2015a]).

There are also similarities in the culture-induced forms of family units which were and still are more of extended families with tribes and clans living in communities. This situation promotes the woman's roles and responsibilities as the homemaker (cook, cleaner, healthcare giver, etc., and sometimes, a bread winner). In many African societies, culture and tradition require the African woman to bear and raise children including related extended families. These extended responsibilities tend to put added pressures on the women.

> *When it comes to Dowry Payment for marriage, the approach in negotiations, the items demanded by parents of bride-to-be, the voices involved in negotiations,* **etc.,** *is the only difference among the regions. However, the tradition of Dowry requirement is common to the five regions.*

Mores and values with their judgmental views on morality, lifestyles, good and bad, as well as attitude toward situation had influence on the woman's ability to grow and engage in economic activities. Attitudes toward women education (western formal education) is similar in both societies with dominant religious beliefs but for different reasons. Christian societies limit or discourage education for women because of family's limited resources while the Muslim societies do the same but because they believe that western education is bad. For example the "Boko Haram" (meaning- education is bad) movement in Northern Muslim region of Nigeria invaded girls' schools and continue to kill southerners for embracing western education. This denial or limitations of education for girls have significant influence on the ability of women to contribute economically to both their family and society through entrepreneurship.

Equally, the marginalization of women and the fact that young girls are not valued as much as young boys is common among African nations (girls are expected to get married, sometimes too early and be taken care of by their husbands) and undermines the African woman intelligence and potentials as a contributing member of the society. This culture and tradition are driven by the need for retention and extension of family names or legacy and since girls are expected to change their last name once married, also denies women the right to inherit and own properties especially land and building. It is sad to note that this tradition still exists in many regions and communities in this twenty-first century.

Also, with the limitation of education for girls, it became even more difficult for women to engage in growth entrepreneurial activity. Many were required by tradition to seek the permission of their husbands to leave the house at all times and for any purpose including engaging in any entrepreneurial activities. For example, Mama Nike's first break at growing her art business was delayed and the opportunity was almost lost because her husband would not give the permission to travel to an Art exposition to showcase her skills outside the country (Detail in Chapter 12).

Language, verbal and nonverbal are as diverse as the continent's nations and tribes. Sapir-Whorf Hypothesis states that "people experience their world through culture which is imbedded in their language which is also known as linguistics" (Swoyer 2003). Communication in the African continent is carried out within the tribes and as much as language did not influence the woman's interest in entrepreneurial activities, it limited their abilities to trade across tribes and borders. It should also be noted that with the introduction of colonial languages, women who were denied formal education came to a great disadvantage. This is one of the challenges for the first-generation women entrepreneurs.

Symbols, which are represented by gestures, signs, objects, logos, alphabets, words, etc., are more of a nonverbal communication. Symbols are as diverse as verbal and could be seen in tribal and national art work. These art works often represent ecological or ecosystem endowment and often drove the products of most traditional women entrepreneurs who had very limited resources for manufactured raw materials. Shopping experiences of the author in earlier paragraphs attest to these.

Material culture including **cuisine and fashion** represent the two most dominant industries where the first-generation women entrepreneurs feel at home. This tendency is not surprising given the basic skills acquired from parents and domestic training centers. Africa's **cuisine** is based mostly on starch often complemented with a variety of vegetable sources or stew.

The most common and essential food across the regions comes from yams, beans, lentils, plantain, millets, and cassava; meat is more of a flavor than meal and comes from cow, goat, and lamb; Wheat and rice came with colonial influence in addition to changes in tastes and flavor which came mostly from Arab explorers and European colonial masters.

As much as the above food items seem to be similar, preparations and flavoring differ across the region as will be seen in the paragraphs below. Steaming (in banana or corn husk leaves) is common form of preparing food in majority of the regions, and so are the processes of boiling, roasting in open fire, and baking in hot ashes.

Africa's Cuisine is based mostly on starch which is mostly complemented with a variety of vegetable source or stew

Summary of Regional Cuisines

- **Northern Africa**, with largely Muslim culture, major cuisine reflects the tradition of no pork nor any animal that is not butchered under Islamic faith. Morocco's signature meal- "Rusel Hanout" or Head of the Shop, has twenty-five to forty different ingredients including cinnamon and blackpeppercon. The same goes for the Egyptian Baharat, which is a meat-based meal while couscous (steamed semolina) is a national dish for Algeria and Tunisia.

- **West Africa**, major food in this region include rice, millet, lentil, corn, and cassava. Yams are important crops and are served in a variety of ways including "amala" pounded yam, with "egusi" or vegetable source/stew. Fish with palm-oil base is a staple for the coastal nations and Nigeria, with its variety of ethnic groups and culture presents diverse cuisine- Muslims in the North with faith-driven meals, Christian Igbos of the Southeast and "Yorubas" of Southwest eat "garri" and yam but with diverse stews or sources including okra and bitter-leaf sources.
- **East Africa's** unique cultural cuisine because of migration and relations with Arab and south Asia, especially around the coast, consists mostly of potatoes, rice, mashed plantain ("matake"). Cattle, Sheep, and goat are cash assets and are hardly raised for consumption. Spicy food is common in Ethiopia and Somalia and Kenyans' traditional food are of corn, potatoes, beans, "ugali" (corn porridge), with the Masai focus on food based on cow and goat by-products of meat, milk, and blood. The Kikuyis and Gikuyis who grow corn, beans, potatoes, and green mash all these together for the staple "irio" dipped in meat or vegetable stew.
- **Central Africa**, the use of edible leaves (collard green, kale, mustered green, okra, sweet potato, and pumpkin) in cooking is basic to Central African cuisine. "Saka-Saka" or "pondu" is a dish made from cassava leaf, onions, and dried fish. Sometimes another version is made with beans instead of fish. The use of red oil (palm-oil) is a distinguishing characteristic of Central Africa's cuisine.
- **Southern Africa**, South Africa, like Nigeria in West Africa has diverse ethnic settlers that came along with variety of cuisine based mostly on their occupation. The first settlers of hunters (sans) followed by cattle and sheep farmers (khoikhoi) and then the Bantus who farmed crops such as corn, sweet potatoes, squash, etc., prepared and consumed traditional dishes based on the basic food resource. There were also a mix of Asian-Indian and European dishes made of exotic spices. Meals made of corn are very popular in South Africa and Cape Maley's special dishes include "sosaties" (traditional kebabs) and "bobotie" (a curried pot meal with minced meat, brown sugar, apricot, raisins, milk-soaked bread, and curry).

Women whose fundamental roles include food preparation and feeding of the family often found ways to extend these skills and responsibility into an entrepreneurial activity resulting in the many roadside and micro-restaurants associated with traditional women entrepreneurs. Most of the ingredients are products of the woman's small farm especially, corn, potatoes, cassava, and vegetables.

Fashion and lifestyles are equally diverse across the regions mostly by preferred materials rather than style. This cultural element like cuisine is also affiliated with women who are responsible for clothing the family especially the children. This responsibility, like cuisine, are skills learned in domestic training centers or from mothers while at home, is again transferred into business operation, with the potential dowry item of sewing machine providing the capital (tool) this is also an industry dominated by traditional African women entrepreneurs and is being accelerated by the twenty-first-century women entrepreneurs.

Social Structure includes family units, community, kindreds, clans or tribes, and other forms of social groups. This element which is born out of the African cultures and tradition seem to have had the most impact on the status of the African women entrepreneurs. Social structures are responsible for "gendering" roles and thus the marginalization of women in the family and community. It defines and sets the marriage rites and position of the woman in her married home. It endorses the requirements for dowry payment (money or items given to parents of girl/proposed bride). The requirement for dowry is common across the regions however, it differs in terms of amount of money, type of, and number of material items negotiated.

Religious belief, values, and family units play major roles in the process.

Since most of Africa's family unit are extended, large units are made up of immediate children of the couple, other relatives of the man and wife, and sometimes all the children in a polygamous marriage. Mama Nike's case story includes her experiences in a marriage with fourteen (14) co-wives and over thirty-five children within the family.

This extended family unit puts additional pressure on women who in many cases have to help care for children of co-wives or husband's other relatives. In Muslim communities, extended care is an integral part of religious and social life. The commitment to this act is one of the five Pillars of Islam (Acknowledgment of one God (Allah) and Mohamed as a prophet, praying, fasting, almsgiving, and pilgrimage) and in this culture caring and giving to others is regarded as a unifying element of the community (Anyansi-Achibong, in Taylor et al. 2014).

In addition to the pressure of feeding multiple people, another social structural pressure on women is that of bearing children as soon as they are married and as many children as the husband and his family wanted. Young married women are expected to have a baby within the first year of their marriage. When this did not happen, the blame fell automatically on the woman who often got depressed and distressed. A combination of all the social structural forces created challenges such as the woman entrepreneur's aspiration to start her business, expand her business, or retain her profit if any.

Colonialism introduced changes and impacted work ethics, entrepreneurial activities, education, motivation, traditions, family units, relationships between man and woman, language, governance, etc.

COLONIZATION, COLONIAL CULTURES, AND AFRICAN WOMEN

In addition to the effects of local cultures and traditions on women entrepreneurs across the continent, colonialism, with its imported and enforced cultures created further diversity within the continent and the individual countries. The presence of multi tribes with diverse languages (estimated #) and dialects within nations created divisions, made communication difficult, and induced conflicts among the nations. Existing local languages were further complicated with the introduction of colonial languages.

The British colonies were forced to adopt English as the official national language, while the French, the German, Dutch, etc., colonies were equally forced to learn and adopt the colonial master's language as the official form of communication. These foreign languages further made it more complex for the continent's nations to negotiate or unite.

Colonial impact on Africa and specific nations changed the way Africa managed its affairs and developed economically and socially. It had a greater impact on women who were already denied formal education in pre-colonial era and were limited in engaging in the new official language. Colonialism introduced changes and impacted work ethics, entrepreneurial activities, education, motivation, traditions, family units, relationships between man and woman, language, governance, etc.

Evidence of the colonial influence on Africa's culture still exists especially in languages, and dress codes which is prominent in such countries like Kenya and Senegal. Family units and value systems were changed mostly for the colonial master's interests. For example, pre-colonial female chieftaincies eroded with colonial practices that forbade women to sit on local and village courts. These were older women who were selected because of their "experiences and wisdom" including wives of Kings or chiefs who could override the rulings of the chief in matters concerning women. This decision to remove titled women from councils and decision-making committees created conflicts, oppositions, and rioting such as the Abeokuta Women's riot in Nigeria (1930–1934). The most damaging act was that post-colonial era governments did not return power to the women who served as inspirations for what would be contemporary African women. Countries with titled women included but not limited to the following, to Senegal (Wolof Kingdom), Nigeria (Benin and Ijebu kingdoms), Ghana (Asante Kingdom), Ethiopia, Egypt, and South Africa (Zulu kingdom).

Exhibit 4.2 presents select countries from the five major regions of the continent. The table shows the dominant religions, the colonial master and official language, and the potential changes if any, for African woman's status. The selection of the nations also depicts the diversity in cultures and traditions created by indiscrete drawing of borders on a continent which used to be a landmass of different tribes with some larger kingdoms. There are limited studies on the impact of colonial policies on the tribal and national cultures, however, any policy affecting the African women status (stereotyping and "gendered") and roles had not been fully explored. In this book, the focus is on the effect on Women's entrepreneurial commitments, aspirations, and activities. The paragraphs below summarize identifiable colonial policies for the select nations and their impact on women status.

Northern Africa: In pre-colonial Egypt, Qur'anic law of inheritance provided women with a share of their parents, siblings, husbands, and children estates. The law stipulated that males get two-thirds while female children share a third. The same is applicable to a widow's share of her husband's estate (Rasod 2017). However, under the colonial era, Nashat in her essay—"Women in the Middle East" presented what she called a "double- othering" system in which the British, under the leadership of Lord Cromer, the Consul general, dehumanized Egyptian women on the basis of religion and gender. They discriminated between acceptance

Exhibit 4.2 Regions, select countries, colonial influence, and implications on African women status

Region	Select countries	Colonial master/language	Major religion	Change in women status/re colonization
North Africa				
	Egypt	British/English	Muslim	Limited impact
	Morocco	France/French	Muslim	Limited Impact
South Africa				
	South Africa	Dutch/Afrikana/English	Christianity	Reduced traditional rights
	Botswana	British/English	Christianity	Reduced traditional rights
East Africa				
	Kenya	British/English	Mixed	Reduced traditional rights
	Uganda	British/English (Some French)	Mixed	Reduced traditional rights
West Africa				
	Nigeria	British/English	Mixed	Reduced traditional rights
	Senegal	France/French	Muslim	Reduced Traditional rights
Central Africa				
	Cameroon	German/English/French	Christianity	Reduced traditional rights

(continued)

Exhibit 4.2 (continued)

Region	Select countries	Colonial master/language	Major religion	Change in women status/re colonization
	D R Congo	Belgium/French Plus…		Reduced traditional rights

of Christianity and staying with Islam. Several women rights such as the inheritance above, were taken away and replaced with British systems of governance that left women completely dependence on men. It should be noted there were Queens in Egypt such as Nefatari and Nefatiti even before Cleopatra.

In Morocco, pre-colonial women activities were biased toward urban and upper-class sectors of the society based on the Quran. Women were free to work and by no means powerless but benefits were appropriated by men and separation of sexes in the Ottoman empire, each sex acquired a separate hierarchy with its own system of decision-making. Women of ruling elite, in part through personal ability but through linkages to friends, kin groups, and patronage networks, at times gave the women control of entire state apparatus. In the face of multiple types of domination by the French, women resistance to colonialism and its effect on them was rarely documented (Pennel 1987).

The effect of Colonial cultures and policies on **West African** women as well as their strategic resistances have been documented in limited research (http://www.blackpast.org/global-african…/aba-womens-riots-nov-dec-1929). For example, in pre-colonial Nigeria, women held complementary rather than subordinate positions in indigenous societies. Power was based on seniority rather than gender. Identity of women was rooted in ethnicity and religion- Hausa-Fulani of the North Muslim society confined women to domestic roles and denied any type of western education; Kanuri women of north south labored in the farms and set up stalls to sell their crops; Yoruba women of southwest held important socio-economic positions; and Igbos of southeast had considerable socio-economic liberty and actively participated in politics of Igboland. Lord F. Lugard, first governor of colonial Nigeria described Igbo women as "ambitious, courageous, self-reliant, and hard-working." These women established law and order through the various group meetings of age, titled women, married women of a clan or lineage, daughters of the lineage even after they are married to another village (Songanga.inflibnet.ac.in).

The above characteristics of an Igbo woman from a British colonial officer remind me of "operation Affia Attack" which was a major challenge for the Igbo women during the Nigerian-Biafra war, 1967–1970. When the civil war disrupted the socio-economic activities and men and every young man, old enough to carry a gun in Biafra were recruited to fight the war, women became the bread winners. They were responsible for feeding the children and the older men. However, as in every war situation basic food items such as grains, salt, toiletries, fish, and meat proteins were scarce and children and older adults were dying of hunger and malnutrition. The scarcity of these items on the Biafran side overwhelming and these Igbo women Young and old organized themselves to engage in enterprise activities beyond the enemy line. They risked rape, death, and possible abductions to cross into the Nigerian side for trade. The women were gone for days and sometimes weeks to purchase the essential commodities which they brought back to families in the refugee camps.

> *Lord F. Lugard, first governor of colonial Nigeria described Igbo women as "ambitious, courageous, self-reliant, and hard-working." These women established law and order through the various group meetings of age, titled women, married women of a clan or lineage, daughters of the lineage, even after they are married to another village* (Songanga.inflibnet.ac.in)

Whenever my two sisters who and other women who were engaged in the "Affia Attack," which literally means "trading within the enemy territory," traveled, the whole refugee camp especially parents were in somber mood until they return. I remember one time when my sisters' group were gone for over three weeks and rumor had it that they have been killed or abducted by Nigerian soldiers. My parents and other families prayed nonstop and even organized a search team (another group of brave women) to look for them. The search team left before sunrise and returned in the dark every day for eleven consecutive days without success. However, in the middle of the 35th night the camp woke up to see the seven women. They were abducted, taken to the enemy military camp where they were locked up for what they believed was 20 plus days. They finally succeeded to escape and have been traveling only at night, getting lost at times until that memorable day.

The bravery, hard work, determination, and resilience of these women during the war is note-worthy. Driven by the need to save their families from hunger and diseases such as kwashiorkor, they risked their lives to fight another type of enemy who might be more dangerous than the military. They sacrificed their material possessions as they traded their jewelry, clothes, and anything that would attract the Nigerian legal tender so they could buy essential commodities for the family.

> *Arrival of Colonial rule attacked and attempted to weaken the "gender-neutral" Igbo culture with its establishment of "Victorian-value" system that stated, "women should be behind men." They created Warrant chiefs with authority to control women leadership and entrepreneurial activities. Missionaries established schools but with different curriculum for boys and girls.*

An attempt in 1916 to control the traditional village markets which was the center for women entrepreneurial activities, prompted the first open women protest against the colonial masters. In 1925, the British decided to levy direct taxes designed to "improve native structures" but with the notion that the cost of colonization should be paid by the colonized. Payments were made until 1929 when collection was tightened by introducing a census of household property, livestock, farms, and monetary wealth of the women. The women organized another major protest that spread throughout the country though started in the Igboland. Women resistance meetings funded by women were held and riots and demonstrations ensued. This six-weeks riot caused the death of over fifty women but resulted in end of taxation of market women and personal property, also warrant chiefs were eliminated as well as native courts that served only the interest of the British.

Other west African countries such as Senegal saw uprising of women in protest for inequality by the French colonial masters in voting rights and citizenships. During the French empire voting rights and citizenship laws ranked metro and imperial society along hierarchies of political "capacity" determined by gender, age, race, background, income, religion, place of origin, parentage, class, education, etc. This ranking curtailed the political rights of metro women. Options for females and non-white people were limited and new policies by the French questioned women rights.

Uprising and demonstration by women in targeted cities who were mostly non-Christians and non-white were effective enough to grant them equal voting status (Francee 2016).

Kenya and Uganda in eastern Africa saw equal colonial encroachments on their pre-colonial women rights. In Kenya for example, in Barona community of northern Kenya women herded small livestocks such as goats and sheep, processed milk, and skins. They exercised power and influence over the distributions and exchange of these products. In other parts, women also had important roles in not only raising families but in running farms; however, arrival of colonial British strengthened patriarchy and stripped women of many responsibilities and opportunities such as limited education relative to men, land ownership, and decision-making roles in government. When the British integrated pastoral institutions into the British economy, women lost their status as income and property owners. Ninety-nine percent of land was given to men, replacing the collective ownership of land with private property rights, and women lost access to natural resources as commercialization of pastoralism impacted gender relations. Taxation in-kind was introduced in 1901 30 herds of cattle plus 50 sheep per annum, however, in 1928 the tax system was changed to cash equivalent integrating men into the cash economy which replaced women control of milk, and other dairy products (Guye 2017).

Ugandan women suffered equal displacements from power and ownership of livestocks when the Colonialists arrive. Ugandan women further blamed the missionaries for their biased curriculum for women which focused on domestic training especially for children of believers who were also first to be employed in the missions. As much as the missionaries enhanced the education of women promoting marriage at a later age and possibly signaling shifts in power balance, they discriminated by religion and ethnic groups (Meier and Selhan 2014).

Botswanan women claimed that transformation of laws by the colonial leaders benefited them. However, it left them vulnerable to western individualistic lifestyle.

Botswana, in southern Africa claimed that transformation of law by the colonial leaders benefited women but left them vulnerable to western individualistic lifestyle. In pre-colonial era, girls herded sheep and goats while boys herded cattle. Although women could not inherit land or wealth, they were allowed to maintain the proceeds from the farm and small livestocks. The arrival of British rulers and missionaries transformed women rights by introducing the "Victorian-based notions of gender and moral ideology" and the slogan of "civilization by commerce." These two policies affected rural women by the establishment of educational institutions (by missionaries) that offered gender-biased curriculum. Girls' schools offered domestic-oriented training designed to transform roles of women in conformity with missionary's objectives of raising household servants, with some training for rudiments in sewing, knitting, and cooking. Boys curriculum included woodwork and agriculture. However, with the focus on commercialization and establishment of "Hut Taxation" by the colonial government, most men who had gotten training in new agricultural tools took over all farming for cash crops. With the need for cash for tax payment, many men migrated to South Africa with its colonial minority rulers for employment, leaving women stuck with subsistence farming opportunities and limited personal income. Women were systematically restricted from migration both for trade and work opportunities (http://doi.org/10.4000/etudesafricaines.7962/Mafela).

Colonization in select central African countries of **Democratic Republic of Congo and Cameroon** brought inequality with limited rights for women. Women in the urban area of D R Congo were considered to be legitimate if they were married, widowed, or elderly. Otherwise they were regarded as "femme libres" (free women) and taxed as income-earning prostitutes with or without proof. In pre-colonial era, women were required to obtain permission from husbands to apply and accept a job offer, open a bank account, rent or sell real estate but were not taxed for personal earnings. Most of the women entrepreneurial activities were informal with a focus on retails within local markets or stores.

Unlike the urban women, Lemba (a rural area) women had more power and decide what to grow, sell, or consume. These women, as others in different parts of Africa have banned together when necessary to resist imperial taxation- Tembo women growers of cassava and peanuts were successful in stopping "collectivity and market taxes" (en.m.wikipedia.org).

Pre-colonial Cameroonian women were more independent and had the power to extend influence on economic matters in and outside their households. Women were regarded highly and respected. However, the society was changed as the colonial capitalist structure was introduced. This structure moved women to domestic and small farm activities while integrating men into cash economy. As the colonial rulers expropriated the fertile lands for plantations, men were trained to use new agricultural tools and techniques of modern agriculture. These men were employed to work in plantations while women were left to manage and provide food for family. Changes in socio-economic functions of traditional Cameroonian family (shared decision making, managing family farm, independence for business activities, etc.) moved women to domestic responsibilities with little or no economic involvement (Nana-Fabu 2011).

Summary

Although African women were culturally and traditionally marginalized, many enjoyed some comparative rights and dignity relative to the men. As presented in this chapter, it is apparent that one cannot define nor identify an umbrella status of women across the continent. Forces such as ecosystems, cultural elements such as religion and traditional values, not to talk about different colonial policies and cultures, played major roles in the process.

Regional differences could be identified in religion, values, beliefs, preparation of food, lifestyles, languages, etc., of women. However, the African women seem to have some common tendencies including their ability to rise up and unite when pushed against the wall. Their resistance and protests against the colonial efforts to tax their means of livelihood and support for their family showed up in every region. These women were able to organize, fund, and carry out their protests as long as possible in order to achieve their objectives. Even today, the resilience of African market women can be seen in magazine articles and movies ("Women on Strike" Nollywood movie; YouTube.com/Kenya Women only Village). Another common or similar status of the women is the tradition of marginalization especially when it comes to level of education. Evidence shows that it is almost a continental tradition to deny women access to western formal education. This similarity is also seen in the tradition of requirements for "dowry" or bride price for the young girls as well as their inability to inherit property or own lands.

The above cultures and traditions significantly impacted the African woman entrepreneurial aspirations and success. They created several challenges, many of which were the result of limited education and lack of access to landed property and financial independence. However, these traditionally induced or "first generation" entrepreneurs, as shown in the protest to authority had the instinct and determination to survive, thus developed strategies (no matter how informal) to face the challenges and make the necessary decisions. The challenges and approaches employed by these women are explored in the next chapter.

References

Anyansi-Archibong, C. (2014). African entrepreneurs and their philanthropies: Motivations, challenges, and impact. In M. Taylor (Ed.), *Handbook of research on entrepreneurs' engagement in philanthropy: Perspectives*. Northampton, MA: Edward Edgar Publishing Inc.

Burkina Faso/YouTube. (2019). *Burkina Faso: Religion and family life*. www.youtube/burkina Faso. Retrieved April 10, 2020.

Francee, E. (2016). *Senegal: Gender and colonial legacy*. New Magazine of American Association of Historians.

Guye, F. B. (2017). Colonial and post-colonial changes and impact on pastoral women's role and status in Northern Kenya. *Pastoralism, 7*(13), 1–9.

Henley, A. (2016). Does religion influence entrepreneurial behavior. *International Journal of Small Business: Researching Entrepreneurship*. https://doi.org/10.1177/026624261656748. Sage Publishers Journals.

Madichie, N. O., & Gallant, J. (2012). Studies on Islam, muslim women, and entrepreneurship in context of restrictive culture. *Journal of Business Ethics, 129*(4).

Meier, F., & Selhan, Z. (2014). *Missionaries and colonial disempowerment in colonial Uganda: New evidence from protestant marriage register, 1880–1915* (pp. 74–112). http://doi.org/10.1080/20780389.2014.927110. Retrieved March 26, 2020.

Nana-Fabu, S. (2011). An analysis of economic status of women in Cameroon. *Journal of International Women Studies, 8*(1), 148–162. http://vc.bridgew.edu/jiws/vol8/issi/11. Retrieved March 27, 2020.

Nenes, M. F. (2009). *International cuisine* (pp. 501–542). Hoboken, NJ, Africa: Wiley.

Pennell, C. (1987). Women resistance to colonialism in Morocco: The RIF-1916-1926. *Journal of African History, 28*, 107–118.

Rasod, H. (2017). Impact of colonial rules on women's rights: Case study specific to Egypt under the rule of the British consul-general, Lord E. Cromer. *Journal of Religious Studies, 2*(2), 1.

Swoyer, C. (2003). The linquistic relativity hypothesis. In E. N. Zalta (Ed.), *The stanford encyclopedia of philosophy*. http://plato.stanford.edu/archives/win2003/entries/relativism.

Tlaiss, H. A. (2014 [2015a]). How Islamic business ethics impact women entrepreneurs: Insights from four Arab Middle Eastern countries. *Journal of Business Ethics, 129*(4). Also Available https://doi.org/10.1007/s10551-014-2138-3.

CHAPTER 5

Challenges, Opportunities, and Interventions for Women Entrepreneurs

INTRODUCTION

Dr./Mrs. or Chief/Mrs. Nike Okundaye or yet "Mama Nike" is used by most of the people who have come to know her and her work. One will think that with all the above titles that Mama Nike is one of the privileged African educated women, unfortunately, this is not the case.

Mama Nike was born in 1951 to the then, average-income family and in a small hilly village of about two hundred (200) people. "I lost my mother when I was 6 years old" she told me during a rare interview opportunity at her Art Gallery in Lagos, Nigeria (2020). Her story continued with her journey to her grand parents who raised her. "My grand- and great grand-mother raised me, helping me learn all the domestic skills necessary for a young woman." Nike was born into a family of artists. Her grandmother was an "adire" maker and designer. Her great-grandmother was a cloth weaver and her father worked with beads. He designed and made beaded hats and crowns for royalty and celebratory occasions.

As much as it may seem natural that with such family ties, Mama Nike would easily accomplish all she has today, the reverse is the case. Her childhood and early ages were full of challenges faced by many young girls and women of her time. She returned to her father's house at the age of ten to help manage the home but found she could no longer attend school because her father did not have the school fees for both her and her brother. However, she was lucky to win one of the missionary scholarships which paid nine-tenths of the fees while she had to gather and sell firewood to make up the difference. She smiled as she pulled up her beautiful "Adire Boubou" dress to show me the scars on her legs. "I walked through the bush on a daily basis, scratched by branches and bitten by insects." "It was not easy but I finished up to grade six schooling."

As things got harder for her father, he married her off as a fifth wife to a government officer who was almost as old as the father. "I could not stay and was able to escape about several weeks later," said Nike. "My father threatened to send me back since he has already spent the five-pound (British pound sterling) dowry for my brother's school fees" continued Nike. Luck smiled on Nike again as she got a call from the missionary principal of the school where she completed her primary six, telling her of a job as a baby and housekeeper for an Indian diplomat in Benin, about 22 kilometers from her home in Kaba. "I walked from Kaba to Benin with no money, wearing my old school uniform which is the only clothing I own at that time" said Nike. "I also prayed that no other person has made it there and taken the job," she concluded.

Nike got the job and was excited to learn that it pays one-pound sterling (20 British Shillings) per month even though she was required to sleep on the floor, in the balcony of the house. She had to go with her middle name—Monica, because the couple could not pronounce her full local name (Adenike). Nike taught herself some proper English language but at the early part of her housekeeping job, she communicated partly by gestures and signing with her employers.

Following her employment in Benin, Edo state, Nike who had learned the art of weaving, adire making and design from her great grandmother and her grandmother respectively, learned embroidery from her father, craft and embroidery for girls in her primary school. To make ends meet, she started with designing and drawing posters for sale. She took her paintings to markets, street-side stands, and art stores for sale. "I found that my Adire designs attracted higher prices and sold the most." Nike said with excitement. From there, she started recruiting other women to work with her. At this time Nike was married into a polygamous family of fifteen (15) wives. She worked with most of her co-wives whom she taught the art of Adire making and dyeing. She said they did not make much money but it helped her and all her co-wives sustain their respective livelihood and those of their children. By tradition, they were required to give all their profits to their husband.

She credited her trip to Oshogbo in her early years for shaping who she is today, simply because that was where her grandmother enrolled her in school for the first time. However, Nike feels her biggest break through came in 1972 when a group of museum curators from the USA visited Nigeria with the purpose of selecting African artists to display their arts and crafts at an international exposition. A government official who had seen my work called to tell me of this opportunity to "Showcase my Work," exclaimed Nike. She was not selected initially at that time because organizers were looking for educated artists and she did not have enough formal education. However, in 1974, another opportunity came because the curator insisted on having at least a female artist in the group. She was invited to travel to the USA to display and demonstrate her skills in arts-from paintings to sculpting.

She was very excited, however there was a major issue and challenge when the husband intervened and would not allow her to travel. He told the sponsors that she needed his exclusive permission and he was not willing to let the wife go out of the country. It was a challenge to find ways to convince him of the opportunities and benefits to the family which her trip will generate. He later persuaded the sponsors to include him in the trip and they did. Mama Nike with her limited education has been able to rescue over 3000 young street women and trained them to design, make Adire, and start their own self-sufficiency businesses [see more in her Case profile in Chapter 12].

Key Challenges

Nike's story underscores the challenges faced by the first-generation African female entrepreneurs including limited and inadequate formal education, gender discrimination, lack of business planning and organization skills, lack of fiscal resources and bookkeeping skills, male domination, control and marginalization generated by social structures that deny women ownership of property and inheritance of other assets, absence of networking and mentoring resources, pressure from family to get married and have children, stereotyping, etc.

Researchers have shown that these challenges existed across the continent and across cultures (Baradi and Tahir 2019) How Nike and many of the first-generation female entrepreneurs managed their challenges and succeeded will be discussed following the analysis of some of the key challenges.

Just as the tendencies for African women entrepreneurial activities originated from the culture and traditions that defined the majority of their roles and status, many of the challenges they faced in attempts to build and sustain their business were grounded in the same factors. These challenges could be grouped into "Education-induced" challenges and "Culture-induced" challenges.

Education-induced: The denial, limited, and inadequate education for the first-generation women entrepreneurs contributed to the women's inability to realize and demand their rights. These factors were also responsible for their inability to plan, organize, conduct market analysis, and grow their retail businesses. The effect of the limited and inadequate (selective curriculum that covered domestic skills, including how to be a good wife, cook, raise children, good housekeeping without any business training) formal education in pre- and during colonial occupation kept entrepreneurs such as "Mama Nike" with all her design and product skills from developing a viable and sustainable business until later and only with the support of a husband. The same limitation in appropriate education made it difficult for many women to keep systemic accounting records of their business activities.

Mrs. Mercy Anyansi (Super Market owner), served as the treasurer of two of the three social organizations where she was a member. I asked her how she could serve as a treasurer when she could not write and keep records of her business purchases and sales? She invited me to her bedroom and displayed a wall full of symbols. It looked like a code only she could read and interpret (see example in her case profile—Chapter 12). She confessed that it was easy for her to collect and record dues and other associations' spending than to keep a record of daily sales and other business transactions.

Many first-generation women entrepreneurs (1930s–1970s) counted themselves successful if they were able to generate enough income to feed, clothe, and sustain the family. Absence of adequate education was also responsible for the inability for effective marketing and organization of the business operations. Many could be classified as random or seasonal entrepreneurs who engage in buying or growing and selling produce of the season. In spite of the above-limited education-induced challenges, it should be noted that these market women were resourceful in banding together and organized successful protests and riots against colonial rulers who implemented flat taxes on their sales and domestic life stock. Individually, the women were incapable of developing an effective business structure. They remained small retailers who competed in open markets with some unwritten laws (norms) observed by each entrepreneur.

The issue of financial resources and the challenges it posed for the women had its basis on both limited education and traditions. The traditions or cultures that denied women the rights to own or inherit property made it difficult for them to borrow money without such needed collateral. In many cases, these women could not understand or complete the necessary paper work. Many needed the consent of their husbands as well as their (husbands') signatures on the application forms.

In addition to denying women the rights to own property or inherit family assets, **culture-induced** challenges included the pressure from families (immediate and extended) to marry early and have children.

During my recent trip (March 2019), to Uganda, East Africa, as a member of Rotary Vocational Training Team (VTT), I met a young lady who participated in my entrepreneurship education workshop. She was an active participant and raised thought provoking questions about developing an effective business plan as well as managing a successful small business in her community. However, at the end of the final session she approached me with a request for a private discussion. We set up an appointment to meet later that same evening.

The young lady started the discussion in an almost inaudible voice, "Chi (I had asked the group to address me by my first name to create an enabling environment for participation) I had to make a very important decision in the next six months. I have to either get married to a man twelve years older than I am or disobey my mother and my uncle again with a potential option of being asked to leave home. Although I have a job and have just started a small business, I chose to live at home to save more money to put myself through post graduate education. Another reason is that culture looks down on an unmarried girl who lives by herself." You see Chi, she continued, "I have rejected three other suitors and my mother and uncle are getting very anxious- my mother is concerned that at the age of 22, I am not married and she does not have grandchildren. She tells me that her neighbors with daughters younger than I have grandchildren. My uncle on the other hand is more concerned with the dowry or bride price which should be coming to him, since my father is dead. Both have the belief that my university education had made me a different person who no longer respect and abide by the culture and traditions of the people."

After listening to some more details on her childhood experiences and challenges, I smiled and told her that the solution to her so-called problem is simple. I was now thinking more like an American, when I said to her "What do you want?" her response to me was partially expected, however, I was thinking and hoping that this is the twenty-first century and with her diploma in community development from the African Rural University (ARU), she should be able to decide and live her own life. She told me it was not as simple as I was thinking because the pressure from her mother and uncle, and some other extended family members was becoming unbearable. She told me that although the current suitor was promising to help fund her small business idea, she did not believe him because "that was usually the case until you are in – married and expecting a child and sooner than later, you become the key bread winner of the family." "Your husband by tradition can collect your earnings for his personal spending and without your permission."

This young lady's situation is common in most of the 54 nations of the continent. Also remember that Ugandan culture and traditions required women to concede to the authority of men in the family including uncles, thus her situation is critical as she dealt with pressures not just from her mother but from her uncle and any other male figure in her life. Other internal forces defining a woman in Africa are imbedded in the nation's social structure including the married environment, child bearing expectations, (need to have a male child), plus other gendered roles which put enormous pressure on the woman and her entrepreneurial activities.

Culturally, a newly married woman was expected to have her first child within the first year of her marriage. Failure to do so, created pressure from her husband, his family, his friends, and some times her own family. This pressure got worse as the years go by without any pregnancy and birth. In many cases, the birth of female children only brought similar pressure on the woman. Her husband was never a suspect for inability to conceive nor for the birth of all female children although men supposedly carry the male sperm. Under this pressure many women lose their incentive and enthusiasm for their business operation. Others spent money on medical processes trying to conceive and to deliver a male child. This action often depleted the business capital since most traditional men would not fund this effort for the reason that "bareness'" is the woman's fault and she should be responsible for correcting the situation. This type of situation often led to polygamy as the man decides to take a second wife or third in search of children or male child. Mama Nike's story some how validated this issue when she talked about the situation with (told me that all) her 14 co-wives (have) who had female children including herself.

The traditional woman entrepreneur who later gave up trying (most times when the husband took a second wife) and focused on her business was still looked upon as inadequate and her success in business was credited to the assumption that "she was more of a man" since she could not bear children. She is expected to spend her money on the family and to raise the children of the second or co-wife. In some cultures, the birth of girls was tolerated as their father sees them as asset generators. The father looked forward to the time when they can marry them off for the dowry or bride prices they will generate. Lack of the ability to plan, organize, raise funds, grow, or create a formal network for entrepreneurial activities did not mean that the traditional women could not put together a viable small and medium business. These women were very resourceful and resilient in many ways as seen in their organized protest against colonial taxation.

Networking and mentorship of younger housewives were initiated and funded through a traditional form of micro-financing organized by the women. "Isusu" or "Isuzi" as it was known in west and east Africa. This is usually a small group of ten-fifteen business women who get together to create a revolving or rotating credit unit. Each member is obligated to contribute an agreed amount, for example, fifty dollars per month. The total is given to the scheduled individual to either expand her business or take care of a family issue. Another month the next member received the total and so on. This is a cyclic arrangement which is based on honesty, trust, and commitment of the members. Sometimes the amount contributed may increase as business operations became more successful. Isusu groups may be formed by members of similar trade group such as fish sellers, cassava sellers, clothing material and sewing center owners, etc.

Another form of networking and organization common among the women entrepreneurs was that of apprenticeship for young and newly married girls. Established fashion designers and seamstresses would accept newly married women into their sewing shops as apprentice. These ladies learned to design and sew until they make enough to be on their own. In Mama Nike's case, she trained, employed, or helped the young girls to be self-motivated and self-employed.

In so many other resourceful ways these first-generation women entrepreneurs were able to deal and manage the challenges they faced. The limitations caused by inadequate general and business education not only impacted the women but also the nations and the continent. The next paragraphs on the analysis of both the Millennium Development Goals (MDGs) (2000) and its extension, the Sustainable Development Goals (SDGs) (2015), provide some evidence of potential impact of educated women on the families and society.

Potential Benefits of Women Education

The importance of education for women and its implication for the continent cannot be over-estimated. The lack of access adequate education for women was behind most of the problems and challenges for these early women entrepreneurs and in many cases negatively impacted the socio-economic development of the community and country. For example, an examination of the United Nation's initial Millennium Development Goals (MDG) and the extended Sustainable Development Goals (SDG) reveal the relevance of female education in the world and especially in the African continent.

A discussion exercise in my global management class requires the students to;

1. Assess the goals (MDGs prior to 2015) and identify the roles that were related to women's roles and activities;
2. Renumber the goals in such a way that achievement of one will automatically impact or influence achievement of the next (some form of domino effect).
3. Following the announcement of the Sustainable Development Goals (SDGs) in 2015, the 3rd question requires the students to align the eight MDGs with the seventeen SDGs which was designed to "promote prosperity while protecting the planet."

The Sustainable development goals came with strategies that "will build economic growth and address a range of social needs including education, health, social protection, and job opportunity while tackling climate change and environmental protection" (www.UnitedNations.org).

Final analysis, discussions, and conclusions to the above questions included the fact that five out of the eight original goals directly and indirectly relate to women. Renumbering the goals show that achievement of universal primary education, especially for women, becomes the first goal, indicating that an educated woman will be most likely to undertake the improvement of maternal health by engaging in better pre-natal care and family planning (goal 5); thus reducing child mortality (goal 4); reducing extreme hunger and poverty (goal 1); and will be knowledgeable enough to help in the reduction of malaria by keeping home surrounding clean and dry enough to reduce mosquito breeding, HIV and other diseases by being able to read, comprehend, and take preventive measures to reduce infections (goal 6). Collectively, the above domino effect will reduce inequality as the educated woman learns to demand her rights and to make reasonable decisions.

Since Sustainable development Goals were built upon the Millennium Development Goals, it should be understandable that the above analysis and discussions are equally true of the importance of education for women. The similarities in the goals can be identified as shown in the table below:

Sustainable Development Goals	Millennium Development Goals
#s 1 and 2: No poverty and Zero Hunger	#1
# 3 Good health and wellness	#s 4, 5, 6
#4 Quality education	#2
#5 Gender equality	#3
#6 Clean water and sanitation	#6
#7 Affordable and clean energy	#7
#8 Decent work and economic growth	#8

SDGs #s 9 through 17 relate mostly to MDGs 7 through 8. It should also be understood that SDGs provided a better definition and expectations of MDGs through the strategies. For example, quality education (#4) qualifies the universal primary education proposed in the MDG.

The most significant lesson and understanding from the above exercise and analysis are the relationships of the impact of adequate education for women with the roles that societal and gendered structure imposed on African women. It is equally important to realize the impact on the women entrepreneurs' ability to better organize and grow their businesses.

Re-numbering of the goals show that achievement of universal primary education, especially for women, becomes the first goal, indicating that an educated woman will be most likely to undertake the improvement of maternal health by engaging in better prenatal care and family planning (goal 5); thus reducing child mortality (goal 4); reducing extreme hunger and poverty (goal 1); and will be knowledgeable enough to help in the reduction of malaria by keeping home surrounding clean and dry enough to reduce mosquito breeding, HIV and other diseases by being able to read, comprehend, and take preventive measures to reduce infections (goal 6). Collectively, the above domino effect will reduce inequality as the educated woman learns to demand her rights and to make reasonable decisions.

A statement by Dr. Moeti, of the World Health Organization (WHO) for Africa (2018) underscores the above analysis and findings. She stated in an interview that "Where women are more educated, the family tends to be healthier." She further explained this statement with the showcasing of the progress made by some African nations regarding the MDGs. She singled out progresses made in Rwanda, Eritrea, Mauritius, Seychelles, and Cape Verde. She indicated that these countries have made tremendous progress in the reduction of child mortality and other health-related areas such as HIV and malaria. Moeti attributed these successes to the fact that Africa has "seen some improvement in women education." She also predicted that as long as the continent continues to make progress in education of women or her people in general, there will be substantive improvement in health and development. She indicated that health is a good investment for social and economic development. This statement underscores the saying, "Educate a boy/man, you educate an individual; Educate a girl/woman, you educate a community or society."

There are other statistics and literature that lends support to the potential impact of education on health and socio-economic development. Statistical report from China shows an eighty (80%) percent reduction in child mortality with a 50% increase in women education and same 50% improvement for maternal health (United Nations.org/MDG country Report, 2018). Snyder (2015) an American social scientist, in her research publication titled "Farmers, merchants, and Entrepreneurs: African Women Grow GDP while Fostering Human Development" found that the purpose for women entrepreneurs was first and foremost the maintenance of family, followed by education of their own and other dependent children.

SUMMARY

Above findings give credence to the notion that most African women are social entrepreneurs. According to Alvord et al. (2004) entrepreneurship becomes a social endeavor when its activities transform social capital in a way that affects society positively. These authors argued that gaining a larger understanding of how an issue (or a set of issues) relates to a society allows social entrepreneurs to develop innovative solutions and mobilize resources to affect the greater good of the society and in this case the African society.

Innovation, it should be noted, could be radical (brand new idea or creation) or incremental (improving or adding value to existing product or service). In a recent posting, Tabitha Chepchirchir, Kericho County Trainer for Women Enterprise Fund (WEF)/Kenya was quoted as saying, "When you empower a woman, you empower a nation." She was discussing the joint training program (for women entrepreneurship) between Coca Cola, Central, East, and West Africa Ltd. And WEF. The program which was set up in 2014 claimed to have trained over one million women to run successful business enterprises in Kenya and disbursed over KS17 billion in loans to women (www.Techmoran.com).

In other studies, Baranik, et al. concluded that Muslim women entrepreneurs' successes in Tunisia depended on two major factors, social capital that comes from marriage and high levels of "Wasta," personal connections. The researchers explained the importance of marriage status (the adage that marriage defines a woman's status) and ability to make key connections or network in high-powered places. This was a major challenge for the African woman entrepreneur. This study found that religiosity showed no significant relation to entrepreneurial performance. In another study of States and women rights in Tunisia, Algeria, and Morocco, the authors cited the similarities such as common religious values (Islam and family law), heritage of "Maghrib," and kin-based societies as sources of success for women entrepreneurs, if only they could find ways to draw on them (Ahmed and Charrad 2002).

This book argues that most of the African women are social entrepreneurs whose number one goal was and still is to support family and community. They see family and community problems and seek and find business activities to solve the problems. Family and community self-sufficiency were at the heart of their respective business enterprise. The success of an educated woman entrepreneur is not only hers but that of the family, communities and society at large. It truly shows that when you educate a girl or women, you educate a community or society since women measure success holistically and not financially.

The need for encouraging growth of African women entrepreneurs through adequate business education and acceleration programs and training cannot be over emphasized. The impact of such programs on the continent could be seen in the analysis of the Development and Sustainable goals where educated women could have helped reduce infant mortality and the spread of diseases such as HIV/Aids and malaria. Evidence from the mid-term reports of countries where there was increase in women education attest to these.

Other reports such as the World Bank Group News stated that "female Entrepreneurs are the future of the African continent" (November 29, 2018) while the Conversation (January 8, 2019) reported that lack of access to entrepreneurial education is a major part of the reason African women entrepreneurs struggle to grow.

The next section of the book presents the second-generation of African women entrepreneurs. It explores the impact of education, technology, globalization, other interventions that influenced the growth of these entrepreneurs, the alignment of the African ecosystem to entrepreneurship ecosystem, and the impact of these women's activities on the continent's socio-economic development.

References

Ahmed, F., & Charrad, M. M. (2002). States and women rights: The making of post-colonial Tunisia, Algeria, and Morocco. *Contemporary Sociology, 3*(1).

Alvord, S. H., et al. (2004). Social entrepreneurship and societal transformation: An exploratory study. *The Journal of Applied Behaviioral Science.* www.Sagepub.com; https://doi.org/10.1177/002188634266847.

Baradi, E. M., & Tahir, R. (2019). Behind the veil: The challenges and impediments encountered by women entrepreneurs in United Arab Emirate. *Journal of Entrepreneurial Venturing, 11*(3), 258–282.

Moeti, M. (2018, November–January 14–20). Health is a good investment for development. *New African Woman Magazine* (An IC Publication), Issue 44.

PART II

21st Century Second-generation Entrepreneurs and Entrepreneurial Development

CHAPTER 6

Characteristics of Second-Generation African Women Entrepreneurs: Education, Technology, and Globalization Effect

Introduction

Research reports, publications, and magazines describe and attest to the resilience, courage, motivation, and other characteristics of the current generation African female entrepreneurs. And as much as the challenges of the first-generation and culture-induced entrepreneurs still linger into this present era, there have been notable improvements in female education, training, access to finance, mentorship and networking. These improvements came not only from new national government policies and programs for women but also from international and private organizations such as the United Nations' agencies, Forbes corporation, and Goldman Sachs to name a few. In her own words, Amina Mohamed, The UN Deputy Secretary General, stated "The new African woman is strong and is on top of her game in informing and shaping the future of Africa on every level; African women are closing the gap between the realities of today and our aspirations of tomorrow" (https://www.NewAfricanwomanMagazine.com).

Key characteristics of these female entrepreneurs could be identified from the diverse but consistent stories, reports, and studies in business and socio-political magazines as well as journals and social media. They have been described with terms such as very hardworking, resilient, industrious, determined, persistent, goal-oriented, risk-takers, driven, creative,

© The Editor(s) (if applicable) and The Author(s), under exclusive license to Springer Nature Switzerland AG 2021
C. Anyansi-Archibong, *The Foundation and Growth of African Women Entrepreneurs*, Palgrave Studies of Entrepreneurship in Africa, https://doi.org/10.1007/978-3-030-66280-6_6

courageous, inspired, motivated, innovative, dynamic, brave, resourceful, and many more. Many successful entrepreneurs as illustrated in the stories and examples below portray much of the characteristics identified above.

Credit is given to access to formal education and relevant trainings as well as technology and globalization for many of the successes achieved. With these driving forces, the new African women are able to face challenges of marginalization and limited opportunities created by traditions and culture—the social structure that placed women in bondage, subservient, and unable to challenge male-dominated households and communities. It was generally believed that women, especially married ones, have limited or lower intelligence than men. However, all that girl children and grown women lacked or needed in the traditional cultures were equal opportunities in all aspects of life. Armed with formal education, the new African woman was able to show her strength and determination in achieving her dreams.

On a personal note, thirty-nine years ago, I applied for and got admitted to a doctoral program after completing my MBA. I also got married and had indicated this in my application. However, three months later I wrote to the university regarding my intention to delay my admission to the doctoral program for eighteen months because I was expecting my first child. This notification I understood called for a review of my application and earlier admission.

The committee of five was about to overturn my admission until a senior and distinguished member intervened. From what I was told later, this professor asked for the nationality of foreign student in question. In response to this question, a member who was most opposed to the admission indicated that "she is from Africa, a female, and not only that, she is married and expecting child soon. There is no way on earth she will be able to handle the rigor of our doctoral program in Business and we are all about making sure we have 100% completion rate among our doctoral students."

The distinguished professor, whom I now regard as my advocate after learning of his role in my ultimate admission, then responded as follows: "Has any of you ever been in a program or taught an African woman in your career? They are the most resilient, determined, persistent, and goal-oriented individuals I have ever seen. I guarantee you that she will not only succeed, she will excel, and will do it on record time. And in addition, I just realized she is from Nigeria, to be specific; my personal experience on African woman's intelligence and determination was with a Nigerian." With this testimony, I got the opportunity to earn a doctor of philosophy (with a major in strategic management and minors in International business management and entrepreneurship) from one of the most accredited universities in the Midwest, USA.

I ended up with a career in university education, however, resilience, determination, persistence, and innovation are the middle names of most of the women entrepreneurs and leaders profiled in the following paragraphs. I also applied the above traits in my educational programs and training sessions I developed in my teaching career. It should be noted that entrepreneurship by definitions could be applied in all career including education-"edu-preneur."

Ilham Kadri, in a magazine statement (New African Magazine 2019/2020), said that she was driven by her grandmother who told her not to settle for the Moroccan saying, "that girls have two 'exits' in their lives – one to their husband's home and the other to their grave," but to seek a third one. She found her third exit in higher education and was inspired and encouraged by her as she worked toward her Doctor of Philosophy (Ph.D.) in Physical Chemistry. Dr. Kadri is currently the Chief Executive Officer (CEO) of Solvay, the Belgian Chemical Group with a market cap of 12 billion dollars.

Mama Nike equally credits her grandmother for not only teaching her the weaving and "tie-dye" skills but for sending her to school and encouraging her to study hard on her own. Although she never had the opportunity for formal higher education, her entrepreneurial activities and networking opportunities have taken her all over the world as well as earning her both national and international awards including an honorary doctoral degree in Arts. Her Lagos Art Gallery is among the most recommended site for visitors interested in Nigerian culture and arts (AFAM 2020). She believed that formal education, in her case as an adult learner, was the critical factor in her ability to survive as a micro-entrepreneur and transition successfully into the second-generation era. Nike is currently the managing director and Chief Executive Officer (CEO) of Nike Center for Arts and Culture, Oshogbo, where she offers training in various types of art including painting. The Center admits undergraduate university students for their Industrial Training (IT) in textile design and prints. In addition to the Lagos Art Gallery, Nike has been able to grow her business and is also the owner and curator of Abuja Art Gallery, Ogidi-Ijamu Gallery in Kogi state, and Oshogbo Gallery. Her textile (Aso-Oke) weaving center, established in 1996, is focused on training and empowering rural women to start own business. The Art and Culture Research Center and Textile Museum at the federal capital (2002) is the first of its kind in Nigeria. Nike's art corporations are as diverse as her entrepreneurial philanthropies (see case profile for details).

Tribute to **education** as a factor in the advancement and success of women entrepreneurs could be seen in the testimonies of many more successful African women entrepreneurs.

The listing of one hundred (100) most influential Africans (New African Magazine: December 2019/January 2020) included forty-two women of which twenty-one are in successful business activities and in diverse sectors of the economy. Others are serving in very high positions in national and international organizations such as United Nations, World Bank, African Union, and other civic organizations. Just as these women influence government and civic societies, the women entrepreneurs are impacting the continent's economies and societies by creating employment opportunities and other programs to motivate and enhance the future generations through better family and community development.

The Entrepreneurship Monitor (2019) reported that Sub-Saharan Africa has the highest rate of female entrepreneurs globally. Mckinsey, Inc. (2019) on the same line of thought and research indicated that the female economy is the world's largest emerging market with the potential to add twelve trillion dollars ($12T) to global Gross Domestic Product (GDP) and that twenty-six (26%) of adult females in Africa are successfully engaged and contributing to this emerging market. These statements should not come as surprise since most of the contributors to female economy (e.g., fashion/clothing, accessories, cosmetics, hair) are the sectors dominated by African women even at the micro-entrepreneurship level.

This finding is supported by a list of fifty (50) African women entrepreneurs which (experthub.info.com) included young females in their 20s and 30s and in diverse industries ranging from information technology (IT) to fashion and cosmetics. Although most of these businesses are at different stages of growth with many started between 2010 and 2016, analysis shows that the majority, twenty-three (23), are involved in the fashion and beauty industry. Thirteen of the businesses are in consulting, while six are engaged in manufacturing, and few are in agriculture, medical, or energy sectors. These women are located in all five regions of the continent which underscores the entrepreneurial tendencies of the African woman. Equally and very interesting, all of these women have earned a bachelor's degree and 40% of the fifty has a post graduate degree and/or professional certificate.

INTERVENTIONS AND CHARATERISTICS

Just as tradition and culture created a platform for the First-generation female entrepreneurs, education, technology advancement, and globalization influence the aspirations and successes of the second-generation females.

Examples include Fatima Haruna, Founder and CEO of Nisa Food and Bakery, who had multiple degrees and certificates from, State University of New York (SUNY). Fatima's childhood dream was to become a medical doctor. However, she ended up breaking all traditional and cultural bottlenecks and challenges to become a chef in her own restaurant and food business. Her journey, like that of every African girl child started from home where she and her siblings helped their mother in the kitchen and her small-scale restaurant. Realizing that Fatima was very talented and good with food preparation, her mother encouraged her to consider making that a career. But her father who was a civil servant, surprisingly wanted her girl child to (go) follow her childhood dream and go into medicine. Nisa Food and Bakery was born after Fatima's Masters' degrees and her success was the reason she made the top 50 successful African women entrepreneurs.

In a display of determination and focus on a goal, Zahida Jibril-Usman, with a university degree in International Relations, gave up her successful career in government and private corporation to start her farming business: Muzaif Farms. Zahida's interest in farming grew from her childhood's chore of helping her mother in the small farm located behind the house. Muzaif Farms is actively engaged in growing variety of cash crops, animal husbandry, hatchery, fishery, and exotic birds such as turkey and peacocks. According to the listing, Zahida wants to be the female Dangote (Forbes Magazine's richest African Businessman) whom she regards as her role model.

It is apparent, given the education levels of these young entrepreneurs, that access to formal education has not in any way diminished the African women's tendency to become entrepreneurs. They are still inspired and driven by childhood experiences and skills developed. Education has strengthened their resolve to challenge traditions and break bottlenecks created by these traditional social structures. Challenges of inequality, limited networking with role models or mentors, inadequate capital, limited job opportunity (lack of economic equilibrium), and the needs to balance work or business with family responsibilities. Driven, determined, and persistent, these African women have been able to invade and succeed in business and other sectors usually dominated by men. These women entrepreneurs are in information technology, oil and energy, mining, real estate, aviation, banking, and brewery, to name a few.

Forbes Magazine's (2014) report on top ten African women entrepreneurs and Weetracker.com article on "Top Five Business Women who are putting Africa on the World Map" presented individuals who have defied odds, broke traditions and culture, and managed to emerge as top female entrepreneurs. Prominent among this short listing is: Isabel Dos Santos of Angola, Njeri Rionge of Kenya, Folanronso Alakija of Nigeria, Sibongile, Sambo of South Africa, Bethlehem T. Alemu of Ethiopia, Salwa Akhannouch of Morocco, Hajia Bella Shagaya of Nigeria, Tabitha Karanja of Kenya, Maria Zileni Zaloumi of Zambia, and Bridgette Radebe of South Africa. These second-generation women entrepreneurs armed with access to higher formal education, hard work, and determination have built empires in diverse industries across the globe.

It would be remiss to talk about resilience, hard work, determination, and dedication with a focus on the prize without discussing Maria Zileni Zaloumis, also known as the "Zed Farmer," who transitioned from a dream career in cardiology to become a successful farmer. In an article titled, "From Fighting Depression to Amassing $2 million Fortune: The Zed Farmer's Extraordinary Journey" (Weetracker.com), the story of how this woman entrepreneur remained strong and determined in the face of overwhelming challenges including depression from loss of an only child, domestic violence, and divorce. Zileni left her medical career in Australia and returned to her home in Zambia to heal while taking care of her sick father. In the process of nursing her father, she decided to find some way of keeping busy and possibly earn some income to meet necessary expenditures. Her small family farm at that time managed by her father provided the platform. Zeleni put her challenges behind as she spent all her free time in the almost failing farm. She brought her medical knowledge into the business as she identified opportunities in growing assorted vegetables and berries. She equally organized forums designed to teach communities the importance of eating fresh vegetables and the health benefits associated with them.

Since her first encounter in a farm started when her mother assigned her the responsibility of taking care of a tomato patch in the backyard while she traveled, Zileni found a way to develop the production of tomatoes a major product of Tuzini Farms. In addition to being called the "Zed Farmer" (positive attitude to disaster and patience) she was also crowned as the "Tomato Queen" because she made the decision to streamline and specialize in this product. Tuzini tomatoes were known to be the best in the country and the surrounding markets. She credits her experiences and learnings about specialization to her medical background. Starting with improved ground restructuring to improve productivity, this thirty-three-year-old female entrepreneur has raised the failing Tuzini Farm Limited, to a profitable status. She now serves as its CEO and has become a reference point for individuals who have battled through challenges and rose to the top. The Zed Farmer's successes have earned her awards and titles such as the Director of Zambia National Farmers Union, the first ever and the youngest female member [www.weetracker.com/].

Further stories of African women entrepreneurs who are putting Africa on the world map by defying and challenging the social structures that attempted to and, in many cases, defined their "inabilities and limitations to start and succeed in in the formal business sectors" reveal these second-generation women's success in industries usually dominated by men. Top on this list is Njeri Rionge, who started her first business while at the university and at the tender age of nineteen. Hardworking and determined, Njeri found business opportunity on campus retailing yogurts to fellow students. Later, she moved on to selling clothes and accessories before moving on to information technology. She co-founded "Wannanchi Online," which by 2018 became East Africa's internet mass market. She has since expanded and grown her business into a conglomerate including consulting, healthcare, and business incubator, Insite. Insite is currently the largest consulting operation in East Africa.

Isabel Dos Santos with a net worth of over three billion US dollars (Forbes magazine) returned from Europe, where she received her university education to open the first night club in her home country. The night club located in Miami Beach, Angola, grew fast, and she expanded into transportation business initially designed to serve the club and later became a revenue generator from other nearby businesses. Isabel later diversified into oil and energy industry as well as diamond mining, a business she co-started with her mother. She is successfully affiliated with several international investment companies including operations in banking, mobile network, and investment services.

In another story of goal orientation, opportunity recognition, and persistence, Folaronso Alakija, saw the growing interest and growing demands among women socialites in Nigeria where she had built a career as an executive secretary in a government ministry. With aspirations to be her own boss, Foloronso resigned from her executive position in the 1980s to attend a fashion and design college in the United Kingdom. Upon her return to the country and continent, she started a high-class fashion and design business exclusively for the elite. In 2016, Forbes listed this sixty-five-year-old business woman as one of Africa's wealthiest woman with over $2 billion in net worth. Alakija did not build her wealth from the fashion business alone, her instinct for business coupled with her networking with individuals she knew during her secretarial days opened up an opportunity in the oil and energy industry. Alakija expanded into oil and real estate industries where most of her current wealth comes from.

In a story that presents the epitome of persistence, independence, and achievement orientation, Sibongile Samba is a breed apart when you talk about an African woman. She is the first female to start and own an aviation business. Inspired and challenged by the South African Airways' denial of a job offer because she did not meet their height requirements, Ms. Sambo was pushed to start her own aviation company. Her company SRS offers services in tourism, VIP Charters, Cargo Charter, and medical evacuation services.

The traditional drive that leads the African woman toward business activities that will help them support family and community is still found within the second-generation of women entrepreneurs. Social and philanthropic entrepreneurship abound among many African women. Examples include Bethlehem T. Alemu who started her business, Sole Rebels, with a focus on applying and improving community skills and employment for the youth. Her eco-friendly foot ware manufacturing operation has created hundreds of local jobs. Ms. Alemu's business has expanded internationally with operations and sales to Spain, Switzerland, Austria, USA, Singapore, Japan, and others.

In the same social consciousness, Devine Ndhlukula of Zimbabwe has created over 3500 jobs in her community as she dived into the male-dominated Security industry with her company "SECURICO," a major security company in the region. Tabitha karanji challenged and successfully competed in the Brewery industry in Kenya. With perseverance and hard work, she fought and dared to compete with foreign brewers to establish "Keroche Brewers," the makers of spirit, wine, and beer. Under the brand of Keroche beer, Summit is currently the most popular and fastest selling beer in Kenya and surrounding countries.

With improved access to education and knowledge about rights and opportunities, Hajia Bela Shagaya broke traditions and culture, even in a Muslim society, when she started and grew Bolmus Group International. This is a conglomerate with operations in oil prospects, real estate, banking, communication, and photography. Shagaya said she believed in continuous search and study of the environment to seek out business opportunities and that once she sees potentials,

her interest is awakened and the rest is history. Hajia Bela's story exemplifies the new African woman who is educated, semi-independent, out-going, strong, and shaping the future of Africa.

She is "closing the gap between the realities of today and the aspirations for tomorrow" (Amina J. Mohammed 2018). Her foundation is one of the largest female-founded and focuses on females, especially single mothers, who are selected and trained for entrepreneurial ventures.

> *[The Second-Generation African Woman Entrepreneur has access to formal education;*
> *She is education, Media, Computer, and Information Literate;*
> *She explores equal opportunities and Exploits opportunities in all sectors of development;*
> *She is resourceful and finds ways to improve the quality of life and standard of living in her Society;*
> *She sets goals, perseveres, and works hard to achieve them;*
> *She is ready to disrupt status quo and make a difference to her society]*

In another history making story, Salma Akhannouch is creating a sensation in a Muslim dominant society, Morocco, with her international floor materials distribution company: Akwa Group. With fortitude and resilience, Salma has grown and expanded Akwa Group operations into other sectors including petroleum products distribution and a wholly owned subsidiary, Akasai Group. This subsidiary is a major Moroccan group that deals in luxury goods, department stores, and malls. While Salma is making news in Morocco, Bridgette Radebe is breaking barriers with her success in the mining industry in South Africa. Ms. Radebe is the first black female entrepreneur in mining. Her company, Mmakau Mining has growing interests in gold, platinum, coal, ferrochrome, and uranium.

It is apparent that access to formal education at all levels offered the second-generation entrepreneurs the ability to start, expand, and grow their business activities with unimagined success even in sectors usually dominated by men. Just as tradition, especially dowry, which provided the basic capital for the first-generation entrepreneurs and guided their seasonal and social activities, education provided the second-generation the skills to organize, acquire, and analyze the necessary information to grow and diversify into various industries. Nike who has been on both sides of the proverbial coin testifies to the same fact—that education and exposure through opportunities to travel are the reasons her conglomerate of businesses is in existence today.

WOMEN ORGANIZATIONS AND NETWORKING INTERVENTIONS

The dynamic nature or characteristics of culture has significantly moved the compass needle in favor of the African woman. Although some traditions are still practiced in some places (e.g., male dominance, domestic violence, child marriages), gradual but steady changes in tradition have given women opportunities to make decisions concerning their lives. Access to education has provided these second-generation women entrepreneurs a better platform to decide, organize, network, participate in national and international policymaking, and organizations.

They are able to learn, communicate, engage in technological advancement and globalization processes. International organizations, advanced nations, and global private corporations are playing major roles in changing the status of the African women. International programs such as the US Department State Exchanges' African Women's Entrepreneurship Program (AWEP), designed to assist women entrepreneurs across Sub-Saharan Africa, Master Card Sponsored programs; World Bank; Goldman Sachs; Forbes Company; Coca-Cola joint program for Women Enterprise Fund (WEF), etc. These programs are focused on diverse training and workshops for women in such areas as accounting, fundraising, collaboration, management, marketing, and other necessary success factors for their entrepreneurial growth.

In addition to the above support from international and global organizations many postcolonial national governments have created programs designed to support women socially, politically, and economically. Equally, women have rallied together with formation of nongovernmental organizations (NGO) in an effort to promote and improve female status in all sectors. Examples include the Alliance for Arab Women (AAW) in Egypt, founded in 1987 by a group of highly educated women led by Dr. Hoda Badran, a university professor and former United Nations' (UN) Women Development officer. AAW operated under six key objectives including review and documentation of studies on women issues and needs, organize training programs to improve socio-economic status of women, and establish relationships with other organizations that deal with women issues.

[The dynamic nature or characteristics of culture has significantly moved the compass needle in favor of the African woman. Although some traditions are still practiced in some places, (e.g., male dominance, domestic violence, child marriages), gradual but steady changes in tradition have given women opportunities to make decisions concerning their lives]

With the growth of entrepreneurial spirit among Arab women, AAW's earliest activity (1988) was to secure funds for two income-generating projects for needy families in a suburb of Cairo. The first project made children's toys while the second was engaged in the revival and production of traditional jewelry. Both projects were funded by Netherland and Canadian organizations making good in one of their key objectives. Similar collaborations with international groups were created across nations of the African continent with the sole purpose of improving women's socio-economic status.

In Eritrea, East Africa, the National Union of Eritrean Women (NUEW) was initially established (1980) by men of the Nationalist Revolutionary Forces on an exchange for participation of women in the fight for independence and with the promise of post-independence equality with men (Leisure 2002). However, with disappointments from the Eritrean People Liberation Forum (EPL F) promises (abolishment of feudal marriage system, granting equality to women, abolishment of child betrothal and dowry payment, free choice of marriage partners, and equal participation in productive labor), the organization became increasingly committed to specific struggles of Eritrean women. The NUEW then declared itself an independent NGO with a focus on women's equality and rights.

Women are working together in West Africa to make a difference. They have built formal and informal organizations to solve problems and explore opportunities. They build a spirit of solidarity and purpose, learning and supporting each other in opening up business prospects, creating access to credit, and ensuring that families get better education and healthcare (Fick 2006). West African Businesswomen's Network (WABNET) is a regional organization with national chapters in each of the thirteen-member nations of Economic Community of West Africa (ECOWAS). Amina Hassane Wangari who is the president of this organization and two other national women institutions (Niger network of Women Business owners and Credit Union for Women Enterprises) believed that the internet is a major force for empowering women in business. As west African business women continue to go wireless and get online, Wangari calls it "revolutionary" and went on to found several technological training centers in collaboration with a college of general education in 2002.

Strong association with the West Africa International Business Linkages program (WAIBL) funded by US Agency for International Development (USAID through the West Africa Regional Programme (WARP) has made it possible for business women like Ms. Wangari to attend some US-Africa business education and training summits in Philadelphia (2001) and New Jersey (2004). This linkage program has been a catalyst for women in trade and investment, including import/export, joint ventures, and equity partnerships with the USA (email exchange between Amina H. Wangari and David Fick 2004).

Nationally, Ghana Association of Women Entrepreneurs (GAWE) was developed on a program with a focus to Build, Operate, and Transfer (BOT). GAWE planned to establish a factory starting with 1000 industrial machines for weaving, knitting, sewing, and packaging ready to wear clothes. This plan was designed to help members and the organization take advantage of AGOA and EU/ACP programs. BOT was also set to tap into the twenty million US dollars project in agriculture and its related activities in Ghana. In 2002 it proposed a project for commercializing subsistence farming and off-farm activities for women and youth. The project succeeded in training over 70 groups of women and youth involving 3,500 individuals in functional literacy (Apraku 1991; Fick 2006).

In South Africa women's right was tied to education and women used programs in adult education in its structured and unstructured forms as a vehicle for liberation (Rajuili and Burke 2002). It was believed that literacy and "numeracy" helped in the ability to function better in the economic and changing global society but its conservative approach did not promote women's liberation. The Learning for all Trust program, an NGO developed for early childhood (ECD) literacy and adult education facilitated informal education for the participants through support groups called Care Clubs where women learned skills, earned some income, and helped support family. The major problem with the program was the development of diversity of the interest of the learners. Also, these groups were mostly part of the National Reconstruction and Development Programs (NRDP). The absence of comprehensive formal education processes left many women wanting in many skills needed for effective liberation and development.

[Many modern women say that they are not seeking equality but are only asking for "equal opportunities," opportunity to get education, skills, and knowledge to compete at all levels and sectors of the society and where possible add values and help build a stronger economic society]

A common issue often found and always a point of discussion in both national and international women forums or summits is that of equality. Equality of rights of women to own property, participate in policymaking, acquire formal education, choose life partner, etc. As much as these issues still exist, it should be noted that they are not discrete, but in many ways interrelated. A woman with formal education is more likely to recognize and demand her rights in all socio-economic areas. Many women today say that they are not seeking equality but are only asking for "equal opportunities," opportunity to get education, skills, and knowledge to compete at all levels and sectors of the society and where possible add values and help build a stronger economic society. They want opportunities, "that way everything is based on merit and performance" (Nasr, Sahar; New African Woman Magazine). Dr. Nasr continued to say that the African woman needs an environment that does not marginalize her just because she is a woman. She called this decision "smart economics" not a feminist or woman's issue considering that women account for over 50% of the population and the government has invested in their education and healthcare, thus making them productive human capital with potentials to be tapped.

The impact of formal education on African women entrepreneurs include giving them the ability to read, analyze, plan, seek opportunities, organize a start-up, grow enterprises, connect with national and international groups, gain knowledge, and understand the environment that affects their well-being. When I think of my experience in South Africa during the HIV epidemic in the country, I wonder how women have been able to survive without effective education literacy. Both international and local NGOs in the country had giant billboards promoting the importance of "safe sex" and key guidelines for avoiding infection. These messages were written mostly in English with local language translations below or beside them. Interestingly an opportune discussion session with a local group of women show that most of the women were not literate enough to read and comprehend the messages even those in local languages. They could speak the local languages fluently and some minimal English but could not read the words and information in either language. This inability significantly undermined the impact of the messages. The same could be said of the millions of pamphlets and leaflets distributed to stem and control the disease.

Literacy by definition is the "ability to identify, understand, interpret, create, communicate, and compute, using printed and written materials associated with varying contexts" (UNESCO 2018). In another definition, Literacy Education/Encyclopedia.com, explained the concept as "a process by which one expands one's knowledge of reading and writing to develop one's thinking and learning for purposes of understanding oneself and the world." This concept of literacy education, the encyclopedia continued to explain is fundamental to achieving competence in every situation, including self-esteem and self-actualization, especially for women.

> *Literacy is critical to economic development as well as individual and community well-being. Economies are enhanced when citizens have high literacy levels.* (https://projectliteracy.ca.projectlit…)

African countries when compared to other nations of the world recorded low literacy rates. And African women, prior to gaining access to formal education had the lowest rate of literacy within the countries. It is apparent from the above definitions that literacy offers individuals the ability to seek opportunities; understand information; and find, confidence to make decisions, for oneself, and learn about community and the world. Studies show that literacy leads to greater self-reliance and civic engagement (https://www.litworld.org.blog). For the African woman, it is fundamental to her efforts to achieve self-esteem and self-actualization.

Literacy teaches people to own and value their own person as shown in the report of "All Global Monitoring," which stated that there a clear link between literacy and self-image. An example is Nike's (Nike Art Galleries) statement about how "humiliated and inadequate" she felt after she dropped out of middle school and was offered a babysitting job at the home of a highly educated couple. They were so concerned about her illiteracy that they did not want her to speak to the child. "You should only wash the clothes, dishes, pots and pans and feed the child in silence, etc." were the instructions she received. She remembered that she could only communicate to the adults by "signs" because she could not speak English, which was the official language. She was able to understand spoken instructions after a few months but could never read nor understand written instructions.

Other studies in Litworld.com show that people who write down their goals are 80% more likely to achieve them. It empowers them to seek and understand information leading to the achievement of the goals. In another article, Ehigiamusoe (2006), founder of LAPO, Nigeria, underscores the impact of illiteracy on African women. The study indicated that "women are poor because they are largely illiterate and so do not participate in the decision-making processes of the country. They lack access to assets, health information, other welfare services, and thus are poor and that leads to material deprivation, loss of self-esteem, and powerless."

The second-generation African women entrepreneurs may still face some challenges experienced by their predecessors (first-generation microentrepreneurs), however, access to formal education at any level has armed most with the opportunity to seek and access information. Information to identify economic and income-earning activities, assess the environment, start and organize viable business operations, dare to move into business and political sectors formerly reserved and dominated by males, engage with local, national and international organizations designed to uplift women's status, participate in decision-making, make choices, raise healthier and educated families, etc.

Adequate formal education, fortified with literacy, is the platform on which this new set of African female entrepreneurs embraced their challenges and built business conglomerates. It is equally safe to say that education is a major critical success factor for women enterprises as well as the driving force behind their engagement in technology and global activities. It expanded opportunities for women to develop self-esteem and to some extent self-actualization. The door has been cracked open and it is now the responsibility of all women to use their natural instincts, resilience, bravery, persistence, resourcefulness, and so forth to widen the door by taking advantages provided by technology advancement and globalization process. In addition to education, the dynamic nature of culture has moved the compass needle in favor of women by giving them some voice on who to marry, when, and rights in their married homes. Ability to seek opportunities, be creative, and innovative is the trend.

Take for example, the tenacity and dedication to research shown by a 26-year-old Kenyan woman in an effort to achieve her dream of making a difference in the society through a start-up in the waste management industry. Nzambi Matee found her opportunity when in 2016 the Kenyan government allocated 1.5 billion Kenyan Shillings for waste management. Nairobi, capital of Kenya produced 2000–3000 tons of solid waste daily. With her college degree in physics and material science, Nzambi quit her job at the national oil company just to give full attention to her research. She discovered through research that plastic could be converted into polymer concrete which could be used for building houses and other structures (Nayantra 2018). It took two and half years of determination, commitment to ideas, persistence, moving back to her parents' house because she lost all of her savings and could not raise funds from banks nor other investors, for her to get a break through. Her breakthrough came when her fifth prototype was approved. She was selected for the Lynn University, Colorado, and Watson Institute Incubator for a four-month program. From there she made connections with mentors and investors and today Gjenge Makers Ltd., with Ms. Jha as the CEO and co-founder, is producing bricks from plastic waste. Gjenge is a product born out of persistent research and innovation and the co-founder and CEO represents the new African woman entrepreneurs who are ready to take risks, endeavor, and challenge barriers until she achieves her objective.

Educated African women, such as Nzambi, are becoming innovative and more opportunistic as they attempt to engage in start-ups in the tech sector. The United Nation's Magazine, African Renewal, reports that women-led tech start-ups are on the rise in Africa but it equally cautions that most of the start-ups do not show growth potentials. They are mostly single founder-employee operations with challenges of inability to raise funds from venture capitalists and equity investors. Another study by the

Africa Technology Business Network (ATBN) stated that in many cases men often receive 90% while women record only 2% of all venture capital investment per 100 start-ups in the tech sector. Also, a Netherland-based organization, Venture Capital for Africa, reported that only 9% of tech start-ups in 2016 are women led.

Eunice B. Ball, the founder and CEO of ATBN whose business (that) is based in England promotes access to resources that creates gender-inclusive "innovation ecosystem" in Africa, believes that with the right incentives, African women can unleash their potentials in the growing tech sector. Some African countries have started to develop tech start-up ecosystems that support women. Morocco, for example, is home to dozens of ambitious female-led start-ups including Ways to Cap, a Casablanca-based cross border commerce platform. At the forefront of these new developments are Kenya, Nigeria, and South Africa. The CEO and co-founder of Piggybank.ng, a Lagos based online platform, Odunayo Eweniyi, believes that culture and traditions are at the root of women's hesitation to engage in tech start-ups. She sees tech start-ups as a high risk, unsafe, and more difficult to operate than usual entrepreneurial activities carried out by women. Thus, African women who have been groomed from young age to believe that these kinds of activities are not for them and were not encouraged to aspire to high-end operations such as tech start-ups.

Ms. Eweniyi's statement and belief suggests that culture and traditional forces still haunt and create barriers for the African woman in the twenty-first century. It could also be argued that limited entry into the tech sector has a lot to do with women's inability to secure the needed capital, tech mentors, and networking support group. Other factors may include lack of training and inadequate infrastructure designed to support telecommunications and advanced technology in the continent. Venture capitalists, investors, and financial institutions still see women-owned business or aspirants as high risk especially for the tech sector. They still regard the traditional roles of women (e.g., mothers, nurturers', homemakers) as a factor that will always keep women back from growing and operating successful business especially a tech enterprise.

All the same some African women with guts and determination have created successful tech start-ups including Uche Pedro who has revolutionized Nigeria media Landscape with her e-zine bellanaija.com. This online entertainment, fashion, and lifestyle online magazine has changed news consumption in the country by taking advantage of the boom in internet connection. What started as a blog hobby in 2006 while Uche was studying for her master's degree in Canada has become an internationally recognized platform for latest news and celebrity updates with over two million viewers per month (GLAM Africa Magazine 2017). Mariamme Jamme is regarded as one of the handful of African women in tech. This founder of technology consultancy company, "Spot On Global Solutions" helps technology companies break into markets in Africa, Europe, middle East, and Asia. Clients include Google, Microsoft, and HSBC. Mariamme is also co-Founder of "Africa Gathering" one of the leading platforms in Europe that enables businesses, governments, entrepreneurs, etc., to share ideas about Africa for positive change.

Olatorera Oniru, Founder and CEO of Africa's Amazon-Dressmeoutlet.com, a leading Nigerian online fashion retailer is revolutionizing the retail landscape with digital innovation according to GLAM magazine which interviewed her. The e-commerce website offers fashion, health and beauty products, and home-goods. Olatorera who received her first and master's degree in the USA spoke of the challenges of starting and running an online business in Africa and in Nigeria in particular. As she listed corruption, slow internet connection, and unstable energy supply, among others, she cautioned that nothing great can ever be achieved by focusing on challenges without developing strategies for growth. On funding for female entrepreneurs in Africa, she advised of the need to bootstrap and maximize resources available locally. "We must create greatness out of what seems like nothing" and believes that "once significant traction has been established, investors will come around" (GLAM 2017).

Summary

The future promises growing opportunities for African women entrepreneurs as advanced technology-driven globalization creates international and national women networking groups. Organizations such as the United Nation continues to create and host women's forums across the world. African women are elected to serve in high positions in world and international organizations such as World Bank (WB), International Labor Organization (ILO), World Trade Organization (WTO), and World Health Organization (WHO). Women are also being appointed by African Union to serve as ambassadors to other world nations. The point is not being appointed to high positions, the encouraging news is that most of them are speaking up and encouraging other women to aspire to engage in positions where they can add value to the society and the continent.

The former African Union (AU) Ambassador to the USA, Dr. Arikana Chihombori-Quao in an interview with a Voice of America Reporter, stated that "Africa needs capacity building and freedom from exploitations by foreign multinational corporations." She continued by challenging African women to develop "mindset of no apologies (for being a woman), strength in each other, take care of neighborhood and communities, and go for leadership positions in both economic and political sectors." Dr. Arikana, offered an example of an event in colonial era Ghana when women held significant leadership positions. She told the story of Nanaya Asantua, caretaker of the "Golden Stool," the spirit of Ashanti people who challenged the British and refused to give up the Golden Stool in exchange for an exiled Ghanaian king. The men of the village agreed to the British demand in return for their king, but Nanaya stood firm and said to the British representatives, "I shall call upon all my female sisters and we will pick up arms and fight the British rather than give up the spirit of our people." The moral of this story according to Dr. Arikana, is that African women have an important role to play as mothers, grandmothers, sisters, etc., and should work together to build stronger and economically viable Africa. She also challenged the African Union to elect a leader who will be an enforcer, who can bring change with disruption, think outside the box and not just act like a diplomat.

In another positive proposition for the future of African women given by the former Lead Economist and Manager at the World Bank (2018). Egypt's Minister of Investment and International Cooperation, Dr. Sahar Nasr, predicted a more inclusive socio-economic development in Africa, which will only happen when women are given equal opportunities in all aspects of the society. Dr. Nasr claims that "women's empowerment is smart economics." She believes that Africa can only achieve sustainable and inclusive growth by giving women an equal opportunity to play an active role in the economic, social, and political sector. She continued to say that the Egyptian government has fully endorsed gender empowerment and UN Sustainable goals of which gender mainstreaming is key. Women and girls should have equal access to education, skills development, labor force, political participation and all social services, if the continent really want to be inclusive" reiterated Dr. Nasr.

Sandie Okoro was the first black woman General Counsel at the World Bank and prior to her move to the bank in 2016 was the general counsel for HSBC Global Asset Management. Ms. Okoro did not make the 2019/2020 list of Most influential Africans because of her position at the World Bank, but because she is a vocal defender and champion of women's empowerment and gender equality. She is very proactive in engaging in campaigns around gender-based domestic violence, sexual harassment, child marriage, and women's access to justice.

In her own words, The UN Deputy Secretary General, Dr. Amina J. Mohammed, declared that "men have to recognize that in every home, the woman has a right to participate in the economy." She said she was gladdened to note and strongly believed that the new lady heading the Economic Commission for Africa, Vera Songwe, would bring a different kind of vision for supporting Africa's agenda by making sure Africa integrate the economy: women's issues, youth issues, and technology across the continent. She is confident that the future looks promising and rhetoric is about to be turned into actions. She predicts and hopes that the dynamic nature of culture and the evolution of society which gives women the opportunities to engage in economic activities will not happen to the detriment of the home. Like other African women in similar positions, Dr. Mohammed believes that there is a light at the end of the tunnel for women. She warns that "men aren't just going to step aside" but that with gender parity at the top of the United Nation's Agenda, the future is encouraging for African women's equal opportunity policies.

Dr. Matshidiso Moeti, the WHO Regional Director for Africa underscores the importance of supporting, educating, and training women for better African development in her statement, "Health is a good Investment for development." She credits women for healthier families and communities in another statement saying that, "Where women are more educated, the family tends to be healthier." She encourages the continent's leaders to invest in the education of women as well as developing policies that will create equal opportunities for all.

The new African women are in media and movie production. Stream African movies in Netflix or YouTube to experience the dynamic nature of African culture and the roles of women in the society. Many of these movies are based on realities of life in both the rural communities and the cities. They reflected societal norms and events. Examples include Women at War depicting struggles of women to end child marriage; marginalization of women, and "Mortal Inheritance" which sheds a spotlight on the stigma associated with Sickle Cell Anemia in Nigeria. Veteran and popular African movie actresses such as Omotola Jalade-Ekeinde, Oge Okoye, Genevieve Nnaji, Tonto Dike do not only act but they are producing and directing own movies. Many like Omotola (are) also own other private enterprises in entertainment and fashion industries [full story in case chapter].

There is a lot of work to be done in the continent to develop an inclusive and viable entrepreneurial ecosystem which allows women to explore and engage in all aspects of business sectors. Recognition of the significant and impactful contributions of women entrepreneurs is paramount to the development of the continent.

The African woman is very resourceful, resilient, courageous, brave, persistence, concerned, focused, daring, etc., when given the freedom and opportunity to contribute to the socio-economic environment. The need for development of entrepreneurial ecosystem in Africa is overdue and needs a model that is inclusive of women in all sectors of the economy especially entrepreneurs. Discussions and development of a model for an African ecosystem is next. A systemic model that is not just an adoption or adaptation of developed economy's culture and tradition is needed for the continent.

REFERENCES

Academy of Management (AFAM) 5th Biennial Conference. (2020). *Globalization, pan Africanism, and the African business climate.* Hosted by Lagos Business School, January 8–11, Lagos, Nigeria. https://www.africaacademyofmanagement.org.

Apraku, K. (1991). *African émigré' in the United states: A missing link in Africa's social and economic development.* Westport: Praeger Publishers.

Ehigiamusoe, A. (2006). Impact of illiteracy on women. In D. Fick (Ed.), Africa: Continent of opportunity (pp. 73–75). Johannesburg, South Africa: STE Publishers.

Fick, D. (2006). *Africa: A continent of economic opportunity.* www.realafricanpublishers.com/most-popular/business/africa-continent-of-economic-opportunity-detail.html; www.amazon.com/books/dp/1919855599.

GLAM Africa Magazine. (2017, December). *The digital innovator in GLAM Africa: The GLAM powerlist of Africa's most influential entrepreneurs.* London: Quarterly Publication by GLAM Africa Ltd.

Kadiri, I. (2020). Moroccan saying, girls have two exits in their lives: One to their husband's home and one to the grave. *New African-Pan-African Magazine*, December 2019–January 2020, #599, p. 23.

Leisure, S. (2002). Exchanging participation for promise: Mobilization of women in Eritrea. In J. M. Bystydzienski & J. Sekhon (Eds.), *Democratization and women grassroot movements* (pp. 95–110). Bloomington, Indiana and New Delhi, India: Indiana University Press and Kali for Women.

McKinsey Inc. (2019, August 10). *The female economy is the world's largest emerging market with potentials to add $12T to global GDP*. https://mckensey.com; www.pleasuremagazine.com.ng.

Mohammed, A. J. (2018, November–January). You cannot put a band-aid on the world's problems. *New African Woman Magazine* (An IC publication) Issue 44, Interview by Regina Jane Jere, pp. 6–11.

Nayantra, J. (2018). *This 26-year-old from Kenya is churning out bricks from plastic waste*. http://www.weetracker.com.

Rajuili, K., & Burke, I. (2002). Democratization through adult popular education: A reflection on the resilience of women from Kwa-Ndebele, South Africa. In J. M. Bystydzienske & J. Sekhon (Eds.), *Democratization and women's grassroot movement* (pp. 111–128). Bloomington, Indiana and New Delhi, India: Indian University Press and Kali for Women.

UNESCO Literacy Definition. (2018). https://www.litworld.com/unesco/definition.

Wangari, A. H., & Fick, D. (2004). Women working together in West Africa. In D. Fick (2006), *Africa: Continent of economic opportunities/Niger* (pp. 105–107). Email correspondence between David Fick and Amina Hassane Wangari. Johannesburg, SA: STE Publishers. ISBN 1-919855-44-0.

CHAPTER 7

Africa: Prospects for Entrepreneurial Development

Introduction

Aliko Dangote, Africa's richest man and industrialist cautioned African leaders about its constant blame on lack of financial capital as a major hindrance for its development. Commenting on Planning and development at a session on "Powering Africa" (Davos World Economic Forum 2017), the industrialist stated that "Finance or capital is not the issue in a business start-up nor economic development. If you come up with a well-planned and credible project, funding agencies will be ready to work with you."

In response to his reasons for investing in the largest refinery in the continent, he explained that energy is key to not only economic development but needed for building quality of life and standard of living for Africa's citizens. He emphasized that the current energy situation lacks credible pipelines for supplying natural gas and oil, the absence of innovation and appropriate infrastructure in energy, and concludes that the major problem is the fact that governments lack credible planning and most significantly, implementation strategies. He encouraged the leadership at both the national and continental levels to develop a more appropriate program to growing start-ups for better development.

© The Editor(s) (if applicable) and The Author(s), under exclusive license to Springer Nature Switzerland AG 2021
C. Anyansi-Archibong, *The Foundation and Growth of African Women Entrepreneurs*, Palgrave Studies of Entrepreneurship in Africa,
https://doi.org/10.1007/978-3-030-66280-6_7

National Development Planning in Africa

Self-study, resource assessment, and especially community and national needs assessment are rare occurrences in African nations' economic development plans. The regular Five-Year Economic Plans (FYDP) are inadequate and ineffective as they are based on the simple allocation of funds to government officials identified and select programs and projects. For effective development planning, it is imperative that the African Union (AU) and the nations of the continent conduct comprehensive self-study and strategic analysis of resources designed to achieve productive economic development. This assessment will serve as a premise for enacting the desired and appropriate entrepreneurial ecosystem for effective development.

Africa has made some progress in its socio-economic sectors in the past 50+ years following the post-colonial era, but is still very far from what it could achieve given its abundant and diverse resources. It has allowed years of cracks in its planning systems which tends to underscore the statement that a bad plan could be worse than no plan. The continent has an urgent need to identify and assess the critical success factors of socio-economic production relative to her resources in order to become truly the next economic renaissance.

In her publication, Planning in Developing Countries: A Strategic Assessment, Anyansi-Archibong (1995), reviewed and compared government planning processes in China and Nigeria. She argued that China's seventh Five-Year Development Plan (FYDP) was the pragmatic move by China that built a new socio-economic system. This plan unlike its predecessors was developed following a comprehensive assessment of the environmental factors and feasibility studies of potential programs, projects, geography, and topology, such as the determination for locations of the Special Economic Zones (SEZ). This 1986–1990 plan was debated, and programs were analyzed by a wide variety of officials, citizens, scholars, and technical experts within and outside the normal planning mechanisms of the past. In contrast, Nigeria's FYD plans were the sole responsibility of the Central Planning Office (CPO) or the Ministry of National Planning (MNP). This office is responsible for developing the policy framework and resource projections which serve as guidelines for articulating programs and projects as well as drives the planning for the enterprises.

There were no environmental analyses nor feasibility studies done in the Nigerian national plans, unlike China's where socio-economic environmental factors such as culture, education, religion, geography, land topology, and status of economic variables like agriculture, energy, transportation, etc., were systematically assessed as a premise for a more dynamic and pragmatic development planning. While Nigeria planned to fund most (80%) of her programs and projects from the "fluctuating" petroleum revenue, China's plan included the establishment of Special Economic Zones (SEZ) in 1989 designed to encourage entrepreneurship and private enterprise start-ups by indigenes as well as foreign investors. This effort is designed to support and sustain planned programs and projects while generating foreign exchange reserve for the society. Investors in SEZ received generous incentives such as tax breaks and cheap labor. As much as this study is almost 25 years old and between two countries with different cultures and in different continents, effective development planning process is universal so long as the planners build a premise based on its ecosystems and ecology. China's economic growth and status among superpowers today are evident of its major pragmatic planning many years ago while Nigeria's poor plan has not moved it any further from an economy which is still depending on oil revenue for sustenance.

Entrepreneurship and National Development

Given the above example, the author argues that, "entrepreneurship is an environmentally driven phenomenon and a major factor of improvements for socio-economic conditions." Although several other factors contribute to economic development, the governments play not only the lead factor but are responsible for positioning other factors of production for sustainable growth and development. It is the role of the government to create an enabling environment for entrepreneurial spirits and actions as seen in China's moves. Government roles need to be redefined by moving it from focusing on regulating and maintenance of public institutions to a focus on creating and facilitating, enabling entrepreneurial environment for problem solving and innovation. Just as it was presented earlier that entrepreneurship spans across entities, it is time for Africa to lean toward "entrepreneurial governments," governments that will reexamine and redefine traditional structures and roles (including the gendered roles of women) in attempt to promote values of innovation and entrepreneurial behavior.

African Union (AU) and national leaders need to become more visionary and develop entrepreneurial thinking behavior. There is a need for leaders who would be courageous enough to disrupt the status quo and be game changers. Leaders who are knowledgeable, understanding, and would take the challenges of economic and societal development seriously. This development calls for promotion of more intensive and advanced economic activity with restructures in such areas as education, improved tools, and techniques, finance availability, energy, other infrastructures, etc., to spark entrepreneurship and support the scaling of existing businesses especially the microenterprises of women in the informal sectors. It is a process that challenges leaders and respective governments to improve the standard of living and quality of life for its people and the recognition of the roles of private and public institutions, resource producers, agencies, individuals in and outside of the continent in the process. Emphasis is on revamping of Africa's lackluster development and growth where research studies have shown that poor governance, policies, mismanagement of resources, abuse of power, and absence of appropriate functioning institutions inhibit development.

Ghatak, in his 2001 publication defined development as a sustainable increase in the standard of living that integrates material consumption, education, health, and environmental protection. He argued that this definition supports the fact that development must involve more equality of opportunities, political freedom, and civil freedom. Cypher and Dietz (2004) defined it as an "advancement in technology, varying of institutions, adjustments in ideologies, that are imperative for achieving expansion and brighter opportunities." In another study, Mafimisebi calls specifically for a conscious effort directed toward diversification and increased productivity in agriculture as a necessary move in Africa's sustainable economic development. He cites low technology development as the reason for poor productivity and equally calls for Africans to see technological advancement as an indispensable and necessary investment. In a similar note of concern, another researcher, Sanyang et al. (2010) indicated that agricultural technology development and transfer is a major driving force for development in Africa. He recommends the establishment of research institutions, extension services, farmer organizations (cooperatives), and public and private participation to achieve the needed reduction in hunger and poverty while creating employment. In addition to creating employment, reducing hunger, and reducing poverty, improved agricultural productivity will improve quality of life and standard of living by adding value to human life. This is an area where the roles of women (in agriculture and small farming) should be a major factor for consideration and acknowledgment.

> ....it is time for Africa to lean towards "entrepreneurial governments," governments that will re-examine and re-define traditional structures and roles (including the gendered roles of women) in attempt to promote values of innovation and entrepreneurial behavior. (author)

Most African leaders tend to maintain the status quo concerning plans, policies, and institutions established by colonial rulers. Africans must learn to innovate and reimagine existing processes in order to make the continent a viable competitor in this changing technological and global society. In their publication Igbokwe and Ozor (2007), challenged the sustainability of agricultural programs such as the "Green Revolution." They claimed that the Green Revolution and the early technology applied to it were not sustainable and continue to result in food shortages and widespread poverty in many developing countries of Africa. They called for the governments to develop public and private sector policies, establish partnerships between the two, and develop appropriate infrastructures, especially in rural communities. This recommendation supports the possible creation of infrastructures that will provide enabling tools and support for women in rural agricultural business.

As much as the above studies have done a great job of identifying diverse areas of the environment that are driving national development, they are very limited in the identification of key resources and effective processes that support sustainable development. These processes have worked for China, India, South Korea, and other emerging countries of Asia. Although Nigeria, the largest economy, and South Africa, another growing economy in the continent, were mentioned in both MINT (Mexico, Indonesia, Nigeria, and Turkey) and BRICS (Brazil, Russia, India, China, South Africa) as fast emerging nations respectfully, the nations of the continent still have a long way to go. Sustainable development as proposed in this book includes the following components—improvements in citizens health, access to education, equal opportunities for participation in public and private sectors, provision of clean environment, and promotion of equity that are transgenerational in nature (Human Development Report 2006; UNDP 2007).

Africa's entrepreneurial and sustainable development plan must start with and incorporate a comprehensive assessment of all the elements of productive society including human, especially women, socio-economic resources, institutional elements, and infrastructural elements in thought and planning processes.

With respect to the focus of this book, it is imperative that all institutions (commercial, educational, political, etc.) and infrastructural assessments include recognition of the impact of female entrepreneurial activities in the society and therefore their prospective roles in more sustainable development planning. The continent cannot afford to develop a viable and sustainable development without the support of 55% of its population, especially when 21% (World Bank data) of this group are within the productive age of 25–29 and still growing while the male equivalent of this age group is on the decline (www.UNICEF.org; www.WorldBank Group.org/data). It is also noteworthy that the life expectancy for women (65) is higher than that of men (61).

African nations and the continent's union (AU) must take some page from Asia's emerging nations, especially from China and India. Development planning efforts must start with the creation of a group of diverse individuals and organizations including academia, especially economists and strategists, business men and women (entrepreneurs), technicians, innovators, financial analysts, diaspora, inventors (indigenous and foreign), etc.

Indigenous authors such as Osabushien wrote about the significance of technological innovation and Africa's quest for development in the twenty-first century. He claimed that the low levels of technological innovations in Africa are one of the major reasons the continent is lagging behind in economic development compared to other regions of the world. Although emerging technological innovations for development exist, which can be achieved in many ways such as governance, education, health, and communication among others, it is even more imperative for the global and technological economy. The importance of restructuring education technology is most relevant for developing human capital in this era of knowledge and entrepreneurial economy. The need for the African nations and the continent to restructure and develop more functional and goal-oriented educational systems must be addressed.

Considerations must be given to not only an appropriate education technology innovation but to relevance with Africa's ecosystem and its needs. Edoho (1997) for an example, calls for an emerging technology "nanotechnology" (technology innovation with prefix nano) which has potential faster applications across various sectors of the global economy, including consumer goods, healthcare, transportation, energy, agriculture, education, and improvement in management, and environmental control (Bello 2009) all of which are needed for effective development, yet the issue is absence of inclusive and "Afrocentered" technological planning.

It is not surprising that even in recent discussions and forums involving Africa's leading business men and policymakers such as Dangote, Ibrahim, & Adesina of African Development Bank (ABD) topics revolved around economic development with recommendations and the need for an all-out war on fighting corruption and reducing conflict. Dangote in an interview with Aljazeera Studio emphasized the need to fight corruption among African national leaders while indicating that restructuring of systems to encourage and improve interstate trade is a must. In another discussion at Mo Ibrahim forum (governance weekend 2019), emphasis was on Africa's youths, job creation, and immigration. Touting Dangote Group's operations in 18 African countries and the creation of over 150 K jobs in two years, this wealthiest African promoted the need for "Africa to be developed by Africans," and that the development plans must "involve everyone." This statement reiterates Elumelu's promotion of "Africapitalism"—a capitalist system created by Africans for Africa. This demands that African leaders learn to engage all hands-on deck in the process of developing the continent with a platform for equal opportunity for youth and women in all areas of economic and political activities.

WOMEN AND SOCIO-ECONOMIC DEVELOPMENT

Should women, educated, semi-educated, and experienced in family and community resources management be considered and included in national planning decisions? These are human resources have been ignored and are still being ignored among others in Africa's discrete planning efforts. An earlier chapter discussed the conceptual exponential effect of restructuring and prioritizing the United Nations' Millennium Development Goals (MDGs) to induce other desired goals by starting with female education which indirectly lead to achievement of reduced child mortality, increased maternal health, disease reduction, and decreased hunger. Equally, Anyansi-Archibong (2006), identified entrepreneurship and knowledge as the two missing factors of productive development for Africa. And again, Dangote (2017) reiterated that finance or capital is not needed to start a business but is only needed to grow and expand a business.

Consideration must be given to the restructuring of the education systems to become more functional and goal oriented, creating a system with a focus on developing entrepreneurial thinking individuals irrespective of the type of socio-economic sector they select. This means developing individuals who are not only generally literate (literacy define), but equally media, technology, and information literate. Exhibit 7.1 presents thirty plus characteristics or traits usually associated with an entrepreneurial individual or group including an entrepreneurial leader, entrepreneurial philanthropist, entrepreneurial manager, to name a few. The most significant thing is the development of an education system that is functional enough to raise Africa's human development capacity

Exhibit 7.1 Characteristics and traits of entrepreneurial individual or group

1. Risk-taker (Calculated)	19. Dedicated
2. Internal locus of Control	20. Determination
3. Innovator/Innovative	21. Self-Confident
4. Persistence	22. Adaptive
5. Perseverance	23. Energetic
6. Social/Networker	24. Low-Uncertainty-Avoidance
7. Creative	25. Works well or calm under pressure
8. Hardworking	26. Analytic Skills
9. Driven (by goal/need)	27. Industrious (hard work)
10. Achievement – Oriented	28. Dynamic
11. Goal-Oriented	29. Courageous
12. Independence	30. Visionary
13. Assertive	31. Critical Thinker
14. Persuasive	32. Inspired
15. Resourceful	33. Resilient
16. Tolerance for Ambiguity	34. Knowledgeable
17. Optimistic	35. Self-Esteem
18. Future-Oriented	36. Highly Motivated

and index. This new educational infrastructure must have an inclusive curriculum that integrates health, technology, entrepreneurship, and innovation process education.

An examination of the above list shows that many of the traits and characteristics have been and could be associated with African women entrepreneurs without access to equal opportunities in education and property ownership. This situation is almost parallel to the efforts made in South Africa to transform education and land distribution in the post-apartheid era where researcher Irogbe (2003), concluded that the task of analyzing the complex processes including continuous resistance from "economically well-established elite whites" made it difficult to achieve success. The researcher, however, recommended free education at all levels with government scholarship and fellowships as a key to bridging the gaps between the education of whites and blacks in South Africa. Resistance to change and inability to adapt to changing environment by the "establishment" are the major issues limiting development in Africa.

Compare the above situation to the broader picture in Africa, where women with limited education and inability to own or inherit property continue to achieve. Male-dominated environment in all sectors as well as the traditional gendered roles are equally making it very difficult to tap into the resources and skills available among women. Appropriate education and training programs for all will not only bridge the gaps between men and women but will also enhance Africa's capacity to harness its other productive resources (land, labor, capital) for sustainable development. The challenge is what and how to develop curricula that will teach and enhance the spirit of entrepreneurship as well as capture the traits and characteristics. Some characteristics could be taught such as creative thinking, persuasion, innovative processes (radical or incremental), critical thinking, etc., but traits such as self-esteem, self-confidence, resilience, and optimism are difficult to teach, although they could be developed with time and practice.

To realize the above traits, there has to be an enabling environment, programs, and training centers designed with the purpose of achieving these goals. Take a look at women entrepreneurs who are the focus of this book; they are resilient, determined, persistent, driven (Affia attack women of Nigerian civil war), achievement oriented, and feel a need to improve the health and standards of living of their family, especially their children. Researchers such as Kirzner (1973) believe that the lack of economic equilibrium is the basis for entrepreneurial aspiration. This conception is true in Africa, especially with women who are marginalized relative to men. Evidence exists to show that the spirit of entrepreneurship is already there and all that all which is needed is to find ways to "fan" and support this burning desire.

Testimonies regarding the positive impact of African women entrepreneurs on the socio-economic development of the continent continue to grow. Adesina, the president of Africa Development Bank gave credit to the survival of families and sustenance of standards of living to women who traded and worked hard during the financial crisis of 2008–2010. In his comments at the Davos 2019 World Economic Forum, "Achieving a Single African Market." he emphasized the need to involve women and youth in the planning process for Africa Continental Free Trade Agreement if for the program to be a success. Yamor, a young entrepreneur on the panel reiterated that Africans are entrepreneurs by nature, however, there is an urgent need to involve women and young entrepreneurs in planning or giving them the opportunity to help in designing the architectural blueprint for development.

Note that the term "economic development" often connotates GDP growth while "development: in general, includes improvement in standards of living and quality of life." By definition Standard of Living (SL) is referred to as "degree of wealth and material comfort available to a person or community measured by Gross Domestic Products/population = goods and services available and includes improved health services, increased jobs, reduced inequality (Wikipedia.com/quality-of-life)." On the other hand, Quality of Life (QL) is the well-being of individuals and societies and consists of expectations of individual and society for quality goods and services including health facilities; infrastructures such as roads, airways, clean and consistent energy; education; security; etc. (https://www.investopedia.com>terms) Simply defined, SL is the amount of goods and services available in the society which an individual can buy with his or her income while QL depends on the availability of facilities and institutions for health, education, and other amenities often provided by the government. Women's contribution to the QL or SL cannot be overlooked or ignored in development planning since their major driving force and achievement orientation are and have always been to enhance family well-being, especially the children.

Summary

African Leaders must learn to Disrupt the Status Quo; Embrace Entrepreneurial Government and Economy; Develop a Pragmatic and Visionary-Oriented Development plan that enhances its citizens Quality of Life and Standard of Living.

The Continent has great prospects for creating a favorable environment for the entrepreneurial economy. Poor planning that lacks details of implementation strategies and enforcement policies have created challenges for the continent. As much as A.U. and national leaderships are making strides in creating Africa Continental Free Trade Agreements (Kigali, Rwanda 2018), there is still the need to take some steps back and maybe some lessons from China: Assess the economies' costs and benefits of past planning processes, identify the limitations, and develop a more meaningful goal-oriented planning. For example, prepare a pre-planning self-audit of the resources, regional climates, geography, topology of lands, distribution of capital/tools, human resources (skilled and unskilled), etc., as a prelude to effective pragmatic development.

Knowledge of resource locations or acquisition will guide a plan that will promote not only comparative advantages of nations but also competitive advantages. This one example will guide a more effective continental Free Trade Agreement. Barriers such as transportation infrastructures, energy, intra-continental politics, and conflicts must be addressed as well as development of knowledge, technology, media, and information literacy to organize the resources and create opportunities for sustainable socio-economic development. This task is an obvious and complex process but is also feasible. It requires a continuous process that cannot be in any form related to the historical Five-Year Development (FYD) plans.

Most importantly effective planning requires a diverse task force (not committees) at all levels of the process. Diversity of men, women, youth, Africa's diaspora, planning experts, national and international, academia, etc. It is time for African nations and the continent to develop pragmatic, cyclic, inclusive, and long-term, goal-oriented, and sustainable development. An attempt at a framework and potential model for an inclusive entrepreneurial ecosystem for Africa is the focus of the next chapter.

References

African Union (AU) meeting in Kigali, Uganda. (2018). *Establishing the Africa continental free trade agreement*. www.youtube.com. Retrieved August, 2020.

Anyansi-Archibong, C. (1995). *Planning in developing countries*. Chicago, IL: The Planning Forum.

Anyansi-Archibong, C. B. (2006). Entrepreneurship as the missing factor in the economic development of developing nations. *Global Entrepreneurship Monitor*.

Bello, D., et al. (2009). Exposure to nanoscale particles and fibers during machining of hybrid advanced composites containing carbon nanotubes. *Journal of Nanaoparticle Research, 11*, 231–249. https://doi.org/10.1007/s11051-008-9499-4.

Cypher, J. M., & Dietz, J. L. (2004). *The process of economic development* (2nd ed.). London: Routledge.

Dangote, A. (2017). *Discussions on powering Africa*. World Economic Forum. www.weforum.org; www.youtube.com.

Davos World Economic Forum. (2017). *On powering Africa*. www.youtube.com. Accessed April 14, 2020.

Edoho, F. M. (1997). International technology transfer in the emerging global order. In F. M. Edoho (Ed.). *Globalization and the new world order, promises, problems, and prospects for Africa in the 21st century* (pp. 99–126). Westport, CT: Preaeger Publishers.

Human Development Report. (2006). *Beyond scarcity: Power, poverty, and global water crisis*. New York: United Nations Development Programme.

Ibrahim, M. (2019). *African youths: Jobs or migration?* Speaking at the governance weekend forum, Abijan, Cote d'Voire, West Africa. www.youtube.com. Retrieved May, 2020.

Igbokwe, E. M., & Ozor, N. (2007). Roles of biotechnology in ensuring adequate food security in developing societies. *African Journal of Biotechnology, 6*(14), 1597–1602. In N. Ekekwe (2010, ed.) *Nanaotechnology and microelectronics: Global diffusion, economics, and policy*.

Irogbe, K. (2003). Transformation in South Africa: A study of education and land. *International Third World Studies and Review, XIV*, 11–28.

Kirzner, I. M. (1973). *Competition and entrepreneurship*. Chicago: University of Chicago.

Sanyang, S. E., et al. (2010). The impact of agricultural technology transfer to women vegetable production and marketing groups in the Gambia. *World Journal of Agricultural Sciences, 5*(2), 169–179.

UNDP. (2007). *Human Development Report. Fighting climate change: Human solidarity in a divided world*. United Nations Development Programme. New York: Palgrave Macmillan.

CHAPTER 8

An Inclusive and Diverse Entrepreneurial Ecosystem for Africa

INTRODUCTION

The African Union (AU) and its allies have been holding series of discussions on the need and potentials of achieving a single African market, Africa Continental Free Trade Agreement (ACFTA). Discussions are ongoing with a focus on the benefits of this single market for Africa's economic development and job creation, especially jobs for over 400 million Africans under the age of 15 has been vocalized as these discussions on a potential borderless Africa continue. It is also believed that this historic Africa Continental Free Trade Agreement (ACFTA), when established, will be the world's largest, relative to E.U. and other free trade blocs.

Other issues surrounding the development and enactment of the ACFTA are the fact that Nigeria, the continent's largest economy has not signed on in addition to issues surrounding regulations and tariffs policies. Logistics and infrastructural considerations have received very limited attention. Other factors of importance were being raised including the need to ensure that key participants are involved in the planning and implementation of the free market. Adesina, president of African Development Bank (ADB) presented this issue when he stated that "the day that Africa gets it right with women entrepreneurs is the day it will fly with two wings economically" (Davos 2019). He recommended the inclusion

© The Editor(s) (if applicable) and The Author(s), under exclusive license to Springer Nature Switzerland AG 2021
C. Anyansi-Archibong, *The Foundation and Growth of African Women Entrepreneurs*, Palgrave Studies of Entrepreneurship in Africa,
https://doi.org/10.1007/978-3-030-66280-6_8

of women and young people in the planning of the free trade and the need to create a bridge between large and small businesses as a road to better economic development.

Decision-Making and Planning Process

As much as the issues of the Africa Continental Free Trade Agreement (ACFTA) is not the focus of this book nor the chapter, it provides an inroad into the discussion of the process of decision-making and development planning in the continent. Group decision-making literature abound and in many cases the issues of complexity, potential delay in reaching an agreement, and inefficiencies as attempts to compromise drive final decisions. The popularity of the theory of bounded rationality, which promotes the idea that in decision-making rationality of the individual or group is limited by the information they have. The cognitive limitations of their minds and the limited amount of time to reach decisions (en.m.wikiquote.org) have been criticized for their use of short cuts and relations (heuristic) to produce good enough but not optimal decisions. An alternate to Bounded Rationality is Ecological Rationality defined by Gigerenzer and Todd (2012) as to how cognitive strategies exploit the representation and structure of information in the environment for purposes of making reasonable judgment and decision. Ecological rationality is also referred to as Practical Rationality.

In his research publication, Dekker (2018) discussed two types of ecological rationality (ER) or how best to combine psychology and economics. The first type (ER1) is closely related to bounded or heuristic defined above and type two (ER2) is the work of Vernon Smith (2003) referred to as the "Rationality of cognitive systems consisting of multiple individuals, institutions, and social norms." "It is an un-designed ecological system that emerges out of cultural and biological evolutionary processes; homegrown principles of actions, norms, traditions, and morality." Gigerenzer (ER1) argues for more heuristics, psychology, and modern decision-making while Smith's ER2 argues for more of an institutional environment, social systems, and processes of social interaction. This concept relates more to the roles and status of African women. Smith's definition of the best approach is closer to Adam Smith's [no relations] (1937), The Wealth of Nations, on how socially beneficial results emerge from actions that are initially self-centered and based on limited knowledge. This conception could easily be tied to the situation of female entrepreneurs in Africa. Entrepreneurial activities meant to help raise family's self-sufficiency end up benefiting communities across the country.

Ecological rationality, especially Smith's approach (ER2) has significant implications for leadership, learning, and decision-making. It is more applicable to Africa's leadership and development planning. It involves analyzing and understanding of three key elements of the environment (natural, social, and institutional) and their interactions in building sustainable socio-economic development. The potential of ecological rationality approach to learning and decision-making in Africa is paramount as it considers the total environment of the decision-maker and attempts to identify many possible courses of action in an uncertain and diverse environment. This characteristic defines Africa and its nations of diverse cultures, traditions, political ideologies, intuitions, natural resources, etc. Similar diversity is seen with nations including conflicts among tribes' land disputes, leaderships, etc.

Evidence of the environmental uncertainties and conflicts in Africa is the reason AU goals, such as the ACFTA/Single Market Project is yet to start and even without the endorsement of the largest economy in the continent. The ecology impact on business and development of nations is underscored by Anyansi-Archibong (1987) in her book—<u>Strategy and Structure of Enterprise in a Developing Country</u>. The study identified the elements of ecological factors—social, family constellation, and economic milieu. The study showed that ecological elements of social (family structure, culture, religion, norms) and economic status influenced the strategic patterns of firms' evolution, while family constellation, (partially influenced by the social milieu), influenced the structural patterns. The study argued that it was impossible to separate the influence of ecologic elements and governmental programs, (education, health, and industry projected programs), meaning that social, economic, and governmental factors interact and operate simultaneously with family constellation relationship in several ways to affect the development of the eight forms in this study. There was only one company in which family form did not influence structure as a result of religion—Muslim/Islamic beliefs discouraged the intensive pursuit of wealth, especially by women.

There are significant relationships between Anyansi-Archibong's study and the ecological elements of the ER2. Although her study focused on Nigeria, Africa's largest economy, the findings could be applicable to the

Exhibit 8.1 Ecology in decision-making

Environmental factors of ecological rationality[a]	Ecological factors of firm's decision making[b]
– National Economic Resources – Social Norms – Institutional	– Economic – Social norms – Family Constellations (societal institution)

[a]Smith, V. (2003) Constructionist and Ecological Rationality in Economics
[b]Anyansi-Archibong (1987), Strategy and Structure of Enterprise in Developing Economies

continent especially in the need to include elements of social environment in development planning.

Exhibit 8.1 presents two empirical studies providing evidence of ecological factors and its relevance as well as impact on decision-making and business growth. The need to consider societal issues in decision-making and development planning means that governments should think of culture and traditional norms, and its impact on the citizens. In Anyansi-Archibong's study of the business environment in Nigeria—societal norms and traditions were found to influence not only the type of family constellations (extended family, nuclear family, village structures and the relationships), it significantly influenced the private firm's organizational structure and conflict resolution approaches. The study also indicated that the participation of female members in management of the private family firms was rare. They were rarely allowed to serve on the board relative to the male children. This situation of course is the result of the social-environmental structure that created different roles for women.

THE NEED FOR ENTREPRENEURIAL ECOSYSTEMS FOR AFRICA AND ITS 54 NATIONS

A review of past economic development plans may provide reasons for Africa to move toward a more pragmatic entrepreneurial ecosystem. Compare to another term, national development plan which in many situations is used to reflect socio-economic development. Economic development is generally measured by resource output such as the national Gross Domestic Product (GDP). With its focus on the production of goods and services produced in the country, this measurement approach usually fails to take into consideration the standard of living and quality of life of its citizens and as such does not include input from the informal sector where the African women dominate. It is incomplete in that it fails to capitalize in all its resources, especially its human capital.

Nobel Prize winner Amartya Sen, argued that GDP measurement is very limited and proposed a more contemporary approach to assess emerging nations' development. He argued that development could be better assessed by "Capabilities and opportunities that people enjoy rather than by resource output – GDP." He equally stated that development is not just an economic process but a socio-political one. He proposed that governments provide opportunities in basic healthcare and education, especially for women, as he reiterated that society or people cannot develop their capabilities and contribute to society if they are sick or illiterate.

Based on Sen's thesis the United Nations developed the Human Development Index (HDI) designed to measure the quality of life. HDI is based on three factors including life expectancy at birth (healthcare), educational attainment (adult literacy and enrolment in educational institutions), and average income based on Purchasing Power Parity (PPP) estimates (adequate food, shelter, and affordable healthcare). The U.N.'s index promotes literacy, infant mortality, women equality, eradication of disease, sustainable development environment, etc. All these factors or variables aim to enhance literate & healthy society with equal opportunity to contribute to the socio-economic development. The significance and positive impact on society of equal opportunities for African women were discussed in Chapter 4. The above thesis and recommendations for real and sustainable development justify the call and the need for an inclusive and broad entrepreneurial ecosystem development.

Ecosystem Frameworks/Models

Isenberg's 2014a entrepreneurial ecosystems model which was proposed and adapted for Johannesburg, South Africa entrepreneurial ecosystem development plan, a biodiversity and ecosystem-based planning centered around game reserves and cultural global markets, identified 13 major factors including culture, leadership, financial capital, government, infrastructure, human capital, economic factors, education, etc. The factors in this model are similar to the eight pillars of the successful entrepreneurial ecosystem identified in a panel discussion at the World Economic Forum (2015).

These pillars include Human Capital development mentors, advisors, and other support systems, education and training, cultural support, and universities as catalysts. These factors, especially human capital development, education and training, culture, and societal norms, appear to support the need and necessity for inclusion of women and units which seem to be lacking in current development planning efforts in Africa.

Exhibit 8.2 presents detailed elements and potential actors on the factors proposed by Isenberg (2014b). The breakdown of the proposal shows some specifics regarding recommended players or actors but did not explicitly indicate the need to consider roles of women and youth in the planning process such as how they fit into human capital development, education and labor. His recommendations for elements listed educational institution programs for general and professional degrees as well as specific entrepreneurship training include skilled and unskilled labor, serial entrepreneur and later generation. (while) The element of labor was expanded to include skilled and unskilled labor, and serial entrepreneurs.

Suggested impactors or actors for these elements were universities, leaders of training centers, and service professionals and falls short of mentioning experienced women entrepreneurs who may not be professionals. There was no mention of potentials of women entrepreneurs such as serial or seasonal entrepreneurs who by their efforts and roles in the family support the economy and human development. This suggestion indirectly excludes women as potential impactors who have limited opportunities for university education. The potentials of these seasoned women entrepreneurs as invited speakers in the university entrepreneurship courses would make great impact on the youth especially young girls who could see them as role models and mentors especially in South Africa where women entrepreneurs are on the rise.

The same could be said of the details for culture, where the model (Isenberg's) presented cultural elements such as tolerance of risks and mistakes, creativity, innovation, experimentation, social status, ambition, drive, and hunger for achievement. The proposed impactors on the other hand include journalists, popular cultural icons such as athletes, social media, and informal opinion leaders. This list of impactors for culture and traditional roles in entrepreneurial ecosystem planning is questionable especially when you think of the ecological impact on effective decision-making. How does the journalist impact cultural norms such as tendencies

Exhibit 8.2 Model of ecosystem: factors and actors/impactors

Factors/(word)	Elements	Elements	Proposed Actors/Impactors
Policy: Government internship	**Government** -Institutions & Investment -Financial support for R&D/Startup -Regulations & Tax break	**Leaders** -Solid support -Social legitimacy -Open door for advocates -Entrepreneurial mindset & strategy	-Policy Makers -Elected mayors & governors -Legislators -Regulators -Govt. Research Director -Innovation agencies -Econ. Dev. Director
Finance: Financial Capital	-Micro Loans -Angel Investors -Venture capital	-Private equity -Public capital markets -Debt	-Bankers -Venture capitalist -Leasing Mgrs. -Non-Bank lenders -Grant givers
Culture: Social norm Success stories	-Tolerance of risks, failure, mistakes -Creativity, Innovation -Ambition, Drive -Social status of entrepreneur	-Visible success -Wealth generation -Reputation	-Journalists -Pop Culture Icon -Social Media -Informal Opinion leaders
Human Capital: Educational & Labor	-Education institutions -General & Professional degrees -Specific Entrepreneur training	-Skilled & Unskilled labor -Serial Entrepreneur -Later generation family	-University leaders -Training center leaders -Service professional
Support: Infrastructures & Non-Environmental & Professions	-Professions -Legal -Accounting -Tech experts/advisors -Infrastructure & Telecommunication -Transportation & Logistics -Energy -Zones -Centers, clusters	-Promotion of Soc. Entrepreneurship -Bus. Plan center -Entrepreneur Assocs. -Conferences	-Event organizers -Incubator director -Mentors -Foundations -NGO Managers
Market: Early Customers & Network	-Reference customers -Distribution channels -Local Bus. Networks -Diaspora Network	-Multinationals -Entrepreneurs Network -Early adopters	-CEOs -Distributors -Export agencies -Trading Cos.

Source Adapted from Isenberg 2014 and #Ecosystem

to become entrepreneurial, creative, ambitious, resourceful, driven with a purpose, etc.?

Socio-cultural environmental elements such as tradition and norms support the informal sectors which are dominated by women in Africa. The impactors for culture should include the women who can make relevant input for enhancing the growth of the informal sector. The value of the informal sector in Africa's economic development can no longer be ignored. It is said that "he/she who wears the shoe knows where it hurts." Besides, the African woman carries most of the entrepreneurial traits identified in the model including creativity, innovation, driven, hardworking, energetic, and many others. Once more the model seems to ignore the presence and potentials of women who are making impact in the society, even with their limited formal western education.

Contrary to Isenberg's suggested impactors, Nnadozie (2020) in his review of Africa's progress four years after the adoption of the 17 Sustainable Development Goals (SDGs), cautioned that although progress was being made, "most African countries lack the political will to see national development strategies through to the end, they involve too few nonstate actors in decision-making, they fail to **engage youth and women** in implementing actions related to SDGs and rely too much on foreign financial support and technical assistance." In his introduction of the report, he reminded the continent leaders that "Africa's transformation agenda requires strong leadership and political visions; effective regional, sub-regional, and country institutions, competent staff; and inclusive multi-stakeholder collaboration' to achieve its goals. His proposals underscore the proposed GIV model and its impactors as he indicated the need to strengthen for major capacity building area-operational capacity for organizations, change and transformative capacities, composite capacities (planning, facilitating, managing, and financing), and critical, technical, and sector-specific skills. Emphasis was on skills audit or assessment so as to identify deficits in the number of professionals required to promote an effective agenda for change.

The central point in designing an appropriate entrepreneurial ecosystem is to have a visionary leader who thinks entrepreneurial. One of the benefits of an entrepreneurial ecosystem is its ability to transform communities of different sizes. This effort starts with identification of the resources, humans, and materials available to the society. The society's demography, socio-economic contexts, and geography with connection to other pieces create a more sustainable economy and overall development.

Building an effective ecosystem for entrepreneurship requires that leaders include all human resources with different roles, skills, perspectives, knowledge, etc., without exception. It implies cooperative and productive relationships among the different institutions, political, economic, and social. It requires the adaptation of ecological rationality thinking and decision-making.

According to Isenberg (2011), an ecosystem can be intelligently designed. It is more of an intelligent evolution, "a process that blends the invisible hand of markets and the deliberate helping hand of public leadership that is enlightened enough to know when and how to lead as well as when to let go the grip to cultivate and ensure (relative) self-sustainability."

This definition of the phenomenon (ecosystem) puts the onus of creating a sustainable development ecosystem on the community, national, regional, or continental leaderships. In this book, it calls for African leaders to become more entrepreneurial and broad-minded in creating an inclusive, African-focused development ecosystem. It is time for leaders to move toward an entrepreneurial-oriented governance.

The creation of a dynamic, self-regulating network of different types of actors including women with diverse skills and roles are needed for Africa's development. The action needs effective use of Africa's resources, both natural and social, and appropriate institutions for its unique development ecosystem. It is possible to describe an ecosystem under the six major domains (culture, support services, finance, policy, human capital, and markets) or four major capitals (cultural and intellectual, strategic, network, and economic). Each is different and is dependent on the results of the interactions of elements in a "complex and idiosyncratic way." For example, Israel's ecosystem in the 1970s evolved successfully without natural resources and the country was located far from markets for its products. The system was built on a deliberate effort to train participants of defense sectors to become entrepreneurs at the time they complete their national service commitment (Senor and Singer 2009).

The Generic Incremental Value-Added (GIV) Model

The African continent with its abundant natural resources and diverse culture has all it needs to create a sustainable development ecosystem. A Generic Incremental Value-added (GIV) model is proposed for

Exhibit 8.3a Generic incremental value-added (GIV) framework for entrepreneurial ecosystem entrepreneurial ecosystem

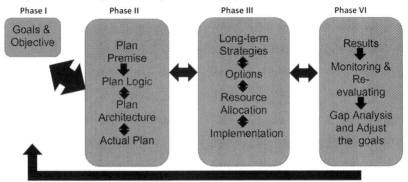

Note Two head arrows indicate the need for congruency among the planning phases and elements
Adapted from: Anyansi-Archibong (1995). Planning in Developing Countries: A Strategic Assessment

entrepreneurial development planning in Africa. Exhibit 8.3a presents a four-phase model that includes the Goal Setting, Plan Technology, Strategy, and Implementation phases. This framework/model is based on the adaption of ecological bounded rationality thinking and decision-making as well as the need to lean toward the concept of HDI as a measure of more sustainable socio-economic development. The framework equally subscribes to the need for explicit inclusion of women and youth of the societies given the growing population of these in the continent's demography-women represent 57% (World Bank, 2019) of Africa's population and trending up with 21% of the same population under the productive age of 25. *This model underscores the earlier statement by Isenberg that "an ecosystem can be intelligently designed. It is more of an intelligent evolution, a process that blends the invisible hand of markets and the deliberate helping hand of public leadership that is enlightened enough to know when and how to lead as well as when to let go the grip to cultivate and ensure (relative) self-sustainability."* The African government should recognize the invisible hands (informal market) of women entrepreneurs and the impact they make in the societies and therefore include them in both development planning and measurement of the gross domestic product.

This model is inclusive because it identifies areas where several stakeholders, especially women, entrepreneurs were left out in the past planning efforts of African nations and continent.

Phase one deals with the assessment of the community, nation, or continent needs for purposes of determining the mission, goals, and objectives of the development plan. As used in this book- the HDI measure looks at the capabilities and opportunities that people in the country enjoy. Thus, the assessment should involve every stakeholder group and institutions and aim at capacity building and equal opportunities for all. Capacity building activities for sustainable development should in many ways include the development of knowledge, skills, attitudes (societal, entrepreneurial, patriotic, etc.), and finding ways to motivate citizens with key objectives of strengthening government, economy, institutions, and all other stakeholders through appropriate education, training, mentoring, effective management of resources that effect stable and sustainable development. This phase is responsible for establishing the premise for development as it has input from the people to be impacted. Women in general as well as entrepreneurs could and should be able to make several input in this phase. Their resourcefulness in identifying and managing scarce resources for family and community is an experiential learning in planning and government should harness this knowledge.

Phase two is the Logic and Architecture stage with focus on resources development, technology assessment, and selection. Phase two is responsible for creating the blueprint and infrastructure for socio-economic development and sustainability measures. It is charged with identification of opportunities and threats in the external environment (e.g., political risks, economic risks, corruption, absence of transparency, opportunities for trade relations, partnership potentials). This phase focuses on conducting a comprehensive SWOT analysis and identifying the strengths, weaknesses, opportunities, and threats in the country and most importantly prioritizing them for appropriate strategy formulation. Again, the need for inclusion of women in a pragmatic planning and at this phase is important. Their capabilities for identifying trade needs and potential partnerships between large (formal) and small firms (informal) cannot be overlooked. It is important to develop a positive relationship between large and small businesses as this bridge has potentials for small and medium business acceleration and ultimate development. *Capacity building for sustainable development hinges on adequate and diverse skills acquisition. An appropriate education system that offers equal opportunities for women and youth should be taken seriously.*

Phase three bears the responsibility for building relationships among institutions and stakeholder groups. This is the strategy formulation phase charged with developing both long- and short-term strategies by use of resources and strengths to take advantage of opportunities for development. The phase actors provide approaches for developing or acquiring needed technologies (process/product, knowledge, skills, techniques) for achieving goals and objectives. Formulated strategies must be assessed and ranked, including alternatives and short-term policies and procedures. Resource allocation and implementation strategies are also formulated and vetted in this phase. Implementation and enforcement are major issues for planning in Africa. Lack of transparency and commitment to development are major issues and should be addressed by getting stakeholders involved early in the planning process. Timeframes for completing implementation of programs and projects must be set at the time of approval so that evaluators and auditors in phase four will have a premise for their actions.

Phase four is responsible for monitoring and evaluating the results of implemented programs and projects. Phase actors conduct gap analysis, reevaluating performance to ensure achievement of intended goals and objectives. Gap analysis is critical given the fact that the environment is dynamic and may change so much as to make goal achievement difficult.

GIV framework calls for systemic and cyclic processes where all elements of the phases are congruent and consistent with each other. For example, congruity exists when goals are consistent with objectives, and objectives are consistent with available resources and planning technology. These in turn, should be consistent with the recommended and implemented strategies. It is a pragmatic entrepreneurial ecosystem planning process defined as a continuing process of creating the vision and mission statements, scanning the environment (internal and external), formulating and adapting strategies, rearranging and maintaining desired goals (value chain) in the face of a fast changing and technology-driven global environment. The model challenges respective nations, regions, and the continent to set constructive, inclusive, and achievable goals designed by all stakeholder groups to motivate sustainable development and growth. The possibility of achieving results is enhanced when all stakeholders are involved in planning and implementation of the programs and projects.

8 AN INCLUSIVE AND DIVERSE ENTREPRENEURIAL ... 135

Exhibit 8.3b is an extension of the phases in Exhibit 8.3a and attempts to present a more detailed plan of action including participants and executors of the development plan. Emphasis is on identification of appropriate agencies, institutions, stakeholder groups, partners and alliances, etc., who, with adequate training and appropriate environment,

Exhibit 8.3b Elements of GIV model: visions for a sustainable development

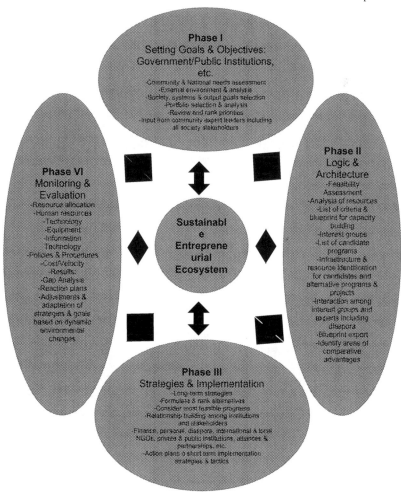

will be charged with crafting and implementing the development plans. Incremental and value-creation cannot be achieved without all related institutions and agencies working on the plan continuously to minimize unnecessary abandonment or discontinuation of projects because of changes in leadership or ruling political parties. Continuous and consistent development which includes input and enlisted commitment of women entrepreneurs, especially the "market women" who control the informal economy will help the nations and the continent grow as well as sustain the economic development.

With access to education and increased literacy in technology, media, knowledge, and engagement in politics, financial institutions, and international representations African women are in excellent position to play effective roles in all the phases of the GIV sustainable entrepreneurial ecosystem planning Model. In phase one which calls for community and societal needs assessment, experiences of women from past society-structured roles and current knowledge-base place them in a very good situation to lead input from community experts and also help with the ecological bounded rationality decisions.

In phase two, it will be remised on the part of planning organizers to disregard the potential contributions of women in areas of identification of candidate programs and projects, resource identification, and areas of comparative advantages. Women not only have a natural but also have developed skills in finding and managing scarce resources. Their entrepreneurial tendencies and courageous, resilient, goal oriented, persistent, characteristics and pragmatic approach to measure success holistically places them in a very good position to help craft a sustainable blue print for development of the community nation.

African women's tendency for analytic thinking and negotiation will be appreciated for their contributions in phases three and four where the need for formulation and prioritizing strategies are needed. The same could be said about potential contributions for building relationships among individual and group stakeholders. They are action oriented and could contribute to the implementation and evaluation processes. Adaptive and innovative tendencies of women entrepreneurs could come handy in the final phases where gap-analysis, adjustment, and adaptation plans resulting from the dynamic environmental changes are needed.

> *GIV framework is a pragmatic entrepreneurial ecosystem planning process defined as a continuing process of creating the vision and mission*

statements, scanning the environment (internal and external), formulating and adapting strategies, re-arranging and maintaining desired goals (value chain) in the face of a fast changing and technology-driven global environment (author)

Capacity building for sustainable development hinges on adequate and diverse skills acquisition. An appropriate education system that offers equal opportunities for women and youth should be taken seriously. Technology education and training of personnel with entrepreneurial attitude, ethical, and ecological rationality thinking, and decision-making are needed for the nation's and continent's sustainable development.

Emphasis is on embracing and building an entrepreneurial ecosystem for development through systematic analysis and selection of appropriate skills, necessary infrastructure (transportation channels, energy, telecommunication, clean water sources), institutions (commercial, legal, finance, education), and explicit commitment to restructuring education and training (technical, knowledge, entrepreneurs, leadership, engineering, technology, sciences) as a foundation for developing the necessary human capital.

As the African proverb states "If you do not mend the cracks, you will soon be rebuilding the wall." Africa and its 54 nations seem to have neglected mending the broken institutions, most of which were set up by colonial rulers and have since become obsolete in the global economy; the economic or national plans of past years, a planning that left many relevant stakeholders out of the process.

It is time to reconstruct, minimize, and possibly eliminate inhibiting factors in the development efforts such as ethnic and political difference, religious differences, social division and conflicts, discontinued and incomplete economic programs and projects, corruption, and non-visionary leadership. It should improve leadership effectiveness and transparency as well as relationship with Africa diaspora.

Most significantly, the nations and the continent can no longer afford to exclude over 57% of its population who embodies most of the entrepreneurial attributes and traits including creativity, energetic, innovative, hardworking, resilient, perseverance, resourceful, and recently, knowledgeable and future oriented. These steps will help the nations and continent to achieve the ultimate goals of improving the standard of living and quality of life of the African citizens.

It is time for the continent and its nations to mend the cracks on their policymaking, development planning, and the individuals or stakeholders they invite to the table. African women are value-added resources and are critical elements in mending the cracks.

References

Anyansi-Archibong, C. B. (1987). *Strategy and structure of enterprise in a developing country*. Avebury: Gower Publishing Company Limited, England. ISBN056605471X

Anyansi-Archibong, C. (1995). *Planning in developing countries*. Chicago, IL: The Planning Forum.

Davos. (2019). Africa Union (AU) on discussion of the potential benefits of proposed Africa continental free trade agreement. *World Economic Forum*. www.youtube.com.

Dekker, E. (2018). Two types of rationality: Or how to best combine psychology and economics. *Journal of Economic Methodology, 26*(4), 291–306. https://doi.org/10.1080/1350178x.2018.1560486. Accessed June 13, 2020.

Gigerenzer, G., & Todd, P. M. (2012). Ecological rationality: The normative study of heuristics. In P. M. Todd & G. Gigerenzer (Eds.), *Ecological rationality: Intelligence in the world* (pp. 487–497). New York: Oxford University Press, Cross Reference/Google Scholar.

Isenberg, D. (2011, May). Nature or nurture; Born or made?—Do ecosystem evolve naturally or can they be intelligently designed? *Forbes.com*.

Isenberg, D. (2014a, May 12). What an entrepreneurship ecosystem actually is. *Harvard Business Review, 5*, 1–7.

Isenberg, D. (2014b). *Entrepreneurial ecosystem and growth-oriented entrepreneurship* (p. 6). In Mason and Brown (Eds.).

Nnadozie, E. (2020, January). Capacity imperatives for the SDGS: In line with the African Union Agenda 2063. In B. Ankoma (Ed.), *Some progress on SDGs, but still a long way to go—ACBF Report*, New African, An IC Publication.

Senor, D., & Singer, S. (2009). Start-up nation: The story of Israel's economic miracle. Twelve: Hachette Book Group, New York. www.HachetteBookGroup.com.

Smith, A. (1937). *The wealth of nations, editor, Edwin Cannon*. New York: Modern Library.

Smith, V. L. (2003). Constructivist and ecological rationality in economics. *The American Economic Review, 93*, 465–508. https://doi.org/10.1257/000282 9803322156954.

World Economic Forum. (2015). Entrepreneurial ecosystem around the globe and company growth dynamics.

CHAPTER 9

Africa's Diaspora: Prospects for Women Entrepreneurs

INTRODUCTION

It is interesting to note that as much as Africa is not fully developed (economically and socially) nor free of the ever-present political conflicts, its citizens in the diaspora are always thinking of her, especially the women. Women think of parents, sisters, brothers, and other relatives they left in the quest for higher education and better quality of life and standard of living. In addition to sending Dollars, Euros, Pounds, Yen, Yuan, etc., home to support family, many are investing in businesses and social ventures to improve the immediate communities and the continent as a whole. Trending is the efforts of Africa's diaspora women to minimize and lighten the burdens of the society, especially for women through attempts to establish projects that impact rural community dwellers. Many diaspora men and women have embraced the Arab proverb that says that "he who dares finds a way, but he who fears finds an excuse" (Africa Missionaries Calendar 2004).

In 2019 I had lunch with a mother and daughter who migrated from South Africa 40+ years ago. Tizzy, the daughter who has a doctoral degree in leadership, introduced her mother and then proceeded to tell us (two other rotary friends) of her mother's plan to go back home and help build "Micro-flush" toilets to serve a community of over 5,000+ people. They have heard the discussions on our trip to Uganda regarding a similar project and are already raising funds for this project. They needed more information on the "Micro-flush" toilet, such as costs, structures, sustainability, and other details that we could share from our experiences. They both knew it will help enhance hygiene practices as well as reduce diseases such as diarrhea, and other housefly and water borne diseases. Most importantly, it will improve overall health in the community, especially for women and children.

In a similar story, a group of four women (two Nigerians, and two American friends) initial objective was to financially support each other's business ventures by agreeing to monthly contributions of a fixed amount. Any member could borrow a limited amount for emergency and without interest charges. However, last year, they decided to do something to help in their respective villages in Nigeria. Upon inquiries as to the primary needs, clean water topped the list in the two communities. Plans were put into action and by January 2020 there was a borehole in each of the villages with two more planned for completion before the end of the year. The American members of the group have been convinced of the need and impact of clean water in the developing communities and are therefore helping to raise extra funds for the project. Mrs. Kakhu, the secretary of the group, enthusiastically described the gratitude of the women in the community. She shared the messages of gratitude from the community leaders for, "making life better and minimizing their burden of walking long distances to fetch water that may not be clean enough to cook with, not to talk about drinking."

The group plans to continue working with each village with prospects of supporting women in micro-business including farming. Immediate in this plan, according to the leader, is the collection and shipment of the second-hand or newly used clothes for sale. The second-hand clothing business in Africa is a booming enterprise and has earned many nicknames such as "Okrika," "bend-down boutique," and "hand-me-down". The names differ in each country and according to the languages, but this is an example of how diaspora women can make connections and use their relationships with internationals to impact their home country.

Although the above seems a low-level effort by diaspora women, it is creating opportunities and positively impacting women in rural communities in a positive way. Other enterprising activities are making inroads into the continent such as "IKE's Café and Grill" in Kumasi, Ghana (Wado Maya 2020). This authentic African cuisine spanning acres of property was founded by an African diaspora woman who lived in the USA for over thirty-six years. In her interview, she spoke of how she had retired from a successful career in Atlanta, Georgia but has always dreamed of opening a restaurant in Ghana (her home country) where both visitors and Ghanaians can have authentic, quality African meals and drinks in a scaled and comfortable restaurant.

This business is currently scaling up with a five-story hotel within the premises. The restaurant boasts of fresh items for the menu including a fresh fish pond. It currently employs over 25 individuals with the hope of doubling or tripling this number when the hotel opens in the year 2021. The founder still faces many of the challenges that women entrepreneurs encounter in Africa (e.g., funding, networking, inconveniences of macro environmental infrastructures, etc.), but she is ready to grow with the new Africa and is hopeful about the future.

Africa's diaspora is a major resource that needs to be tapped and encouraged for the development of Africa. A commentary on the African Diaspora Initiative (ADI) calls on Africa's experts and diaspora organizations to help and educate the African governments on their importance and how to set the tone of engagement with their diaspora, finally understanding how overall worldwide diaspora has become a core part of most countries' journey to development. The article also stated that governments should understand that **diasporas are experienced and highly motivated resources who are a prerequisite ingredient on the national strategic development efforts** (www.pambazuka.org/feb-2019/).

Google Search of Africa's diaspora produced several links to Africa Diaspora organizations including Africa Diaspora Initiative Web Portal; African Leadership and Progress Network (ALPN), a network of African and non-African professionals who are strongly dedicated to utilizing innovative and entrepreneurial approaches for fostering growth in Africa; Africa Diaspora in Asia (ADIA); and Association for the Study of Worldwide African Diaspora (ASWAD) (www.library.stanford.edu). Among the many links, only the Diaspora African Women Network (DAWN) and Pan African Diaspora Women's Association (PADWA) show specific links for women. However, my few years on the board of North Carolina African Services Coalition (NCASC) in Greensboro, exposed me to several national African diaspora organizations including some which are women specific organizations.

African Population in the Diaspora

The following exhibit show top seven countries with the highest African population in the diaspora. Although the numbers and percentages were more in developing economies similar to many in Africa, the populations in developed economies such as the USA (46 million) and France (5million) did not include most of the developed European nations such as England, Germany, Spain, etc., who colonized the continent and houses of many diasporas. Most Africans in these developed economies went there for higher learning and are professionals in diverse sectors of these economies. United Kingdom's population (England, Wales and Scotland) for example includes over 5% of Africans (https://www.ons.gov.uk>aboutus)

Country	# of African Diaspora/m	% of Country Population
Brazil	83 million	40
USA	46 million	14
Haiti	11 million	95
Colombia	5.5 million	11
France	5 million	8
Venezuela	3.5 million	5
Jamaica	2.9 million	92

Source Youtube.com/African Diaspora (Accessed 7 March 2020)

There is an urgent need for African governments and institution leaders to provide an enabling environment for diaspora engagement and commitment to the continent's development. Diaspora investment opportunities could come from many sectors including education and training, youth programs, mentoring, capacity building, and networking.

As a young Assistant Professor of Strategic Management, International Management, and Entrepreneurship at North Carolina Agricultural and Technical State University (NCA&TSU) in the USA, I chartered the university's first Students in Free Enterprise (SIFE) program. This is a co-curricular program currently, known as ENACTUS (**En**trepreneurial **Act**ions for better world through **US**, students, academia, business leaders, etc.). The mission and objectives include "Engaging the next generation of entrepreneurial leaders to use innovation and business principles to improve the world." It is also regarded as the world's largest experimental and practice-oriented learning platform. With over 72,000 students, in 1,730 campuses impacting on over 1.3 million lives as of the year 2019, Enactus.org/home, describes the organization as "a community of students, academic, and business leaders committed to using the power of entrepreneurial actions to transform lives and shape a better, sustainable world." The organization's logo for its 20th anniversary [1975–1995) reads as follows—"**college students teaching free enterprise in order to better individuals, communities, and countries**" is still true today.

This logo motivated and encouraged me to make a daring move at that 1995 National Competition in Kansas City, Missouri. As the faculty advisor and a Sam Walton Fellow for my school's program, I saw firsthand the impact the program is having in our communities as well as on the student members. My students confessed that they learn more by being involved in identifying, developing, teaching, and implementing projects in the surrounding communities. In the 12 years I advised and coordinated the SIFE (ENACTUS) program, the team participated in the annual regional competition and qualified for the national competition which equally exposed the team to other great projects from other schools.

The international (later the World Cup Competition) brought student teams from Europe and Asia but none from Africa. I got an opportunity to meet a member of the SIFE National Board, Mr. Tom Moser of KPMG, during the international conference in 1998. I told him that I would like to take SIFE to Africa, "both university students and several communities will benefit from the SIFE program." I pleaded, Mr. Moser promised to get me into the board meeting the following year (1999) since they just ended the year's meeting. He was the Vice President for KPMG, Inc., as well as the Board President-Elect for 1999. With this promise and information, I committed to take SIFE to Africa even if it meant using personal contacts, funds, and starting from my home country, Nigeria.

I collected all literature on SIFE, scanned them, and sent them to my older brother Peter in Nigeria. He had a part-time lecturer position at the then Enugu Technical College, and I asked him to share the idea with his students. Very limited progress was made. However, I went into the SIFE national board meeting in 1999 with the only other African student in a team from Florida University, Silvester John, and I made our **"elevator speech,"** which I concluded with the following statement, **"Give African students the opportunity to compete in SIFE** and I promise you they will win world competition within three to five years." I was told later by Mr. Moser and Bernie Benny Milano, the KPMG Foundation Chair, that my statement was made with such confidence and convincing voice that KPMG Foundation, which has been a major sponsor of the SIFE US program, decided to help in establishing SIFE in Africa, starting with Nigeria and Ghana, where John had contacts at the university. They would later introduce me to the Director of KPMG Lagos. I also got an endorsement from the Vice President of Blue Bunny Ice Cream, who was at the board meeting and happened to have a subsidiary plant in Lagos, Nigeria.

But the major support and driving force for SIFE Nigeria came in 2000 when a gentleman by the name of Dr. Isaac Nnadi then director of Scientific Equipment Development Institute (SEDI) in Enugu, Eastern region, approached me in Abuja, following my presentation at the 5th Africa-USA International Conference on Manufacturing Technology. My presentation was on "Promoting Community Economic Development through University Partnership Programs: A Service-Learning Approach," which reflected the SIFE program. Dr. Nnadi invited me to come and speak at SEDI when I was in Enugu. He was very enthusiastic about the program and told me he shared my passion for creativity among students but also in increasing entrepreneurial thinking across the campuses. In the following two weeks before I returned to the USA, I spoke to 300 plus students at the University of Uyo, in Akwa–Ibom state, and 200 plus at SEDI which invited students from three other local universities.

Peter Anyansi, whom I had tapped in 1999 and supported with personal funds and resources, became the mouthpiece for SIFE. He worked with Dr. Nnadi and SEDI to organize the official launching and inaugural Nigeria National SIFE Competition in May 2001 with six university teams in Abuja. The National Champion, University of Uyo, could not be in London for the International World Cup Competition because of delay in visa processing at the British Consulate. However, the 2001 World Conference in London, England, opened another door when SIFE board decided to appoint an African continent-wide executive director, the rest is history.

In 2020, 10 (out of 37 worldwide) African countries are actively participating in ENACTUS programs, including Nigeria, Ghana, Kenya, South Africa, Morocco, Eswatini (Swaziland), Zimbabwe, Senegal, Tunisia, and **Egypt which won the 2020 World Cup, in the Netherlands.** Egypt beating USA, Canada, Germany, England, etc., with their innovative project, "Rosie," an eco-friendly and affordable, self-sufficient social enterprise offering high-quality organic pad made by women for women. This project according to the source (enactus.org) is impacting 50,000 plus women in rural communities of Egypt. This is the result of one person's daring action in one country and it clearly indicates the impact that could be made if we dare.

Usually, I shy away from talking about my initiatives or achievements. However, the narrative on the process of founding SIFE Nigeria and indirectly SIFE Africa serves the purpose of creating awareness of what diaspora women can contribute to the development of the continent. It did not take a lot of personal financial investment to impact this learning approach. I did not create nor innovate a business. I am a teacher (or learning moderator/facilitator) who saw the potentials of a new learning approach for the African society, one community or country at a time. **Entrepreneurship is not only about starting and growing businesses, but it is also about process. It spans across sectors including education, health, arts and crafts, transportation, technology, etc.** It does not require the physical relocation of the diaspora to affect society. "It is about positively impacting communities and nations" as noted in Philimena: Liberia (Wado Maya 2020).

In the article "African women in the new diaspora: Transportation and the (Re) creation of Home" Osirim (2013), explored how intersections of gender, class, and race affect women's contributions to civic society and business development. He found that transnational ties lead African immigrants to make a significant contribution to community revitalization and that African women immigrants are most transnational in their civic lives. They differ from their male counterpart in a strong commitment to improving the lives of their families and communities at the home. These findings support many of my experiences with immigrant communities I have met in the USA. It is usually the women who think of the need to send money or clothing and other items home to families. A close friend told me how she usually had to take extra luggage when she travels back home, one for herself, one for her family, and the third for the in-laws (husband's family). It is estimated that Africans in the diaspora send millions of dollars per year to families, mostly through Western Union and Money Gram. Cash sent home through friends and relatives are not included in this estimate. Nigerians in diaspora alone were projected to have sent $24 billion home in 2018 (Zakaria 2019).

Diaspora Women Organizations

In another article titled "Change Makers: Women of the African Diaspora," author Salami (2013) indicates that although the recognition of Africa's diaspora, by the African Union (AU), as the sixth region of the continent met with some hesitations among members, AU still acknowledged that women of the African diaspora are contributing to positive social changes. Examples provided include Fatoumata Diowera, an advocate of peace, and women's rights. Erinma Bell, who received recognition (Queen's Golden Jubilee Award) for founding the organization, CARISMA [Community Alliance for Renewal of Inner-South Manchester Area (UK)]. The study characterizes the African woman's history for "stepping up to social responsibility with creativity and commitment" (www.newint.org>blog). It concedes that there is a huge sense of "Social Contract" in a lot of work by women of the African diaspora as well as within the continent with early examples in the 1915 women's right activists in Sierra Leone followed by the 1926 women demonstration against taxation in Gambia, and 1928 Nigeria women's fight to participate in colonial government policy decisions and revolt for unfair taxation of market women. These are major foundations of women activism, demonstrating bravery, determination, and perseverance.

Evidence shows an increase in women's organized movement in the diaspora, including the Nigerian National Council of Women's Societies, founded in 1958 and launched its diaspora branch in 2013. The council is designed to promote women's participation in leadership and policy-making especially on issues concerning women's affairs. The Diaspora African Women's Network (DAWN) founded by Semhar Araia, focuses on investing in the next generation of African diaspora women leaders. With its core principle as S.E.E.D.S (Sisterhood, Excellence, Empowerment, Diversity, and Service), DAWN offers leadership and professional development training as well as networking avenues. The organization has membership in four continents and twenty-four US states. Its motto, "Because change starts with women" forms the basis of its activities.

The "Social Contract" embedded in most of the women's work and the impact on societies' development is equally underscored by the commentary on CNN (2013) titled "Africa's Secret Weapon: The Diaspora." There is a large population of highly educated and career professional Africans all over the world. In many discussions, these are often referred to as brain-draining from Africa since most of these experienced professionals rarely return to their respective home countries, but many young people retain the interest of the continent at heart, especially if the African parents discuss their roots in the family [story: www.cnbc.com/2020/07/12/facebook-ime-archibong-head-of-npe-top-black-product-vp.html]. However, as mentioned earlier in this chapter, diaspora women seem to never sever the "umbilical cord." They are most likely to stay connected with home countries and make continuous efforts to improve the quality of life and standards of living for immediate and extended families.

According to Wangari Maathai, Nobel Laureate, "We (women) must make our choice, or others less sympathetic will make that choice for us." Women's work has been closely associated with social issues and philanthropy which impacted the much-needed human development. Since entrepreneurial thinking and activities span across sectors, the development of appropriate social entrepreneurship ecosystem and enhanced involvement in entrepreneurial philanthropy rather than the current diaspora practice of "giving a man or woman a fish rather than teaching him or her to fish will somehow turn the brain drain" concept into "brain repatriation concept." This concept of "brain repatriation" could easily be achieved when you think of the number of Africans with advanced degrees all over the world. CNN's Zakaria (2020) in his analysis of Nigerian diaspora in the USA alone estimated that 59% of several thousands of legal residents have advanced degrees with 54% in white collar and professional positions.

Lessons and experiences gained by diasporas (just as with the ENACTUS program for students and possibly for high school) could go a long way to scale up development opportunities for the continent. The success of this type of effort needs partnerships with governments and business leaders to create an enabling environment with motivations for the diasporas! Africa could take pages out of Israel, India, China, etc., proverbial books on their various use of their diaspora to develop the respective society. Cooperation, alliances, networking, and partnerships are highly recommended for successful and sustainable development.

Times are past when it was simply necessary to donate money to society for community development. Most of the time the projects were not completed and donors' intentions were not met. Reasons for the lack of enthusiasm by beneficiaries could be the result of the non-inclusive determination of the communities' needs. The above table shows the elements

Exhibit 9.1 Conceptual Ecosystem for Social Entrepreneurship & Entrepreneurial Philanthropy

Elements	Favorable Environmental Factors
Social Orientation	Transparency in Legal & Political
Need Recognition & Assessment	Ethical Socio-cultural
Innovation	Technological Infrastructure
Market Orientation	Ecological rationality thinking orientation
Impact and Outcome Measures	Values and Community norms
Sustainability Plans	

Adapted from "Dialogues of Sustainable Urbanization" Press book

of entrepreneurial social activities that could be applied or integrated into the appropriate environmental factors. Collaboration is the key to successful philanthropy in any society. The new African diaspora, especially women, are encouraged to move the focus from (one project focused on) social entrepreneurship to the trending entrepreneurial philanthropy defined as "the pursuit of big social objectives through active investments of economic, social, cultural, and symbolic resources" (Harvey et al. 2011). It is important to involve local communities in determining their needs and build effective relationships that ensure implementation and sustainability. The assessment of the respective culture, ecology, values, and norms of the beneficiaries must be done and clearly understood. Roles of the government and its agencies in implementing and sustaining the designed project are critical, and appropriate technology must be considered for both implementation and sustainability. The bottom line is to set up appropriate groups for designing an ecosystem for an impactful project.

My children learned early in their young lives to differentiate between "need" and "want." They learned that Mom and Dad would not discuss any request that starts with "I want" and even when they learned to use the word "need," they also figured out the subsequent questions of why and for what purpose. My husband and I, though they will probably say mostly mom, discovered that when you discuss the purpose and how to acquire the needed item with them, the tendency to take care of the item is usually very high, relative to when we just bought something simply because we thought it will be good for them.

In another and more expansive example, The Rotary International (TRI) and its foundation which is known worldwide for its social good have equally understood the importance of starting a project with community needs assessment as a means for inclusive planning. For both local and global grants, Rotary (it is more like the saying) requires evidence community assessment including names and signatures of leaders involved, implementation plans, and sustainability and maintenance plans. In addition, a Vocational Training Team (VTT) itinerary designed to oversee and train the local maintenance committee must be uploaded with the résumé of team members.

Rotary seems to be adapting to the old saying, **"Tell me, I may forget; show me, I may remember; involve me, I will learn and commit to goal accomplishment."** Beneficiary or learner involvement in determining, designing, and implementing a project is critical to the project's success. Just as with my experience with the ENACTUS (SIFE) program, I found that when my students were actively involved in identifying and designing a project, they were more committed and enthusiastic in completing the project. They were equally more passionate about presenting the said projects at competitions because they owned it. They knew it and could relate their results to the judges as well as answer any questions relating to the project. Women are usually in the best position to understand and acknowledge family and community needs which are the subjects of social entrepreneurship and philanthropy entrepreneurs.

Potential benefits include potentials for positive "exploitation" of international organizations for networking, venture funds connections, relationship building for investments, etc. An example of a relationship with an international organization is Folorunsho Alakija, a business leader and philanthropist who co-founded along with other African philanthropists, the African Philanthropist Forum, an associate organization of the Global Philanthropy Forum headquartered in San Francisco, California State, USA. The forum's mission is to assist donors connect with programs that fit their interests and with each other (Dolan 2013). Although this may sound more like the traditional philanthropy as opposed to entrepreneurial, Alakija's philanthropic interest include empowering widows through scholarships and business grants (Wilson 2012; Folade 2011).

According to Morino (2007), the social sector is different from the private sector where most benefactors of philanthropy come from. He reiterates that the focus of social entrepreneurship as well as entrepreneurial philanthropy should be on relationship and not on the process. The context is more important than the content, and that social complexity comes with diverse nuances. Morino also warned that challenges for philanthropists may include identification of the real needs, abuse of funds, and other environmental factors such as government regulations. He warned that these entrepreneurs must learn to be patient, practice empathy and respect, noting that they are about to engage with a different set of stakeholders and the need to work through formal and informal systems.

The diaspora entrepreneurs seek to teach beneficiaries how to be self-sufficient and financially independent, and the diaspora with her experiences and knowledge seeks out income-earning opportunities for relatives by providing training for a trade or business activities, as well as the seed fund for the start-up. The trend should be engaging the beneficiaries in entrepreneurial activity rather than the traditional form of sending young and productive-age relatives' money for feeding. The apprenticeship program in Africa is a system that has provided individual men and women (men in trade, carpentry skills, welding, etc., and women in fashion design, sewing, cooking, baking, etc.) skills needed for self-sufficiency.

I remember growing up and seeing three to four young men at a time, some living in the household, others from other places but all were engaged in the building materials market where my father had his lumber and sawmill enterprises. I was not sure how well they did, following their four to five years residency or apprenticeship until I heard testimonies during my father's funeral ceremonies and my mother's 100 years birthday celebrations. Testimonies included stories of how they succeeded in life and raised their families because of the training and mentoring received from my father. A young man testified during my mother's birthday celebration that his late father told him that he was able to attend college because of my parents' support. His father's experiences during his apprenticeship made him an honest businessman and that this value which he learned from my parents made him successful. He told my mother that his father said she (my mother) treated all the apprentices like her sons! Some older ones told my siblings and that they were serving as young apprentices when most of us were born.

Testimony to the benefits of the apprentice system was recently presented in a discussion titled "Igbo Apprenticeship System makes People hate Igbos" (Yesufu 2020). In her tweeter opinion of the Igbos of Nigeria, the author stated that the "age long Igbo apprenticeship system has produced a lot of multimillionaires of Igbo extraction to the wonder of many from other tribes." The Igbo apprenticeship system allows a businessman or woman to take a young person to learn about his or her business and eventually get settled, meaning the young man or woman will be given a start-up capital upon completion of the agreed time of apprentice under the master or mistress. During the period of apprentice, the younger persons serve the master or mistress while they learn the business.

According to popular opinion, the Igbos have used the system to build themselves and relatives into renowned business men and women even where the apprentices have little or no formal education. Another twitter commented that the "Igbos' apprenticeship program is the only 'MBA' class in the world that teaches the real intricacies of running a business, the practical application of SWOT and PESTEL analysis. And when you graduate, they'll give you seed capital to start a business."

The problem, many non-Igbos say the fact that the system is focused on Igbo youths and usually the business man or woman never recruit apprentices from other tribes in the country. Many recommend the inclusion of other tribes or groups in the system; however, the issue is a question of trust and it is easier to trust someone you know than the one you do not know. They also likened the Igbos' approach to the Jewish trait of helping each other grow family business making others feel like outsiders are not allowed to share the goodness. This apprenticeship program echoes the recommendation that diaspora support for family moves toward entrepreneurial philanthropy by engaging the beneficiaries in entrepreneurial activity rather than the traditional form of sending young and productive-age relatives' money for feeding and accommodation.

Several diasporas have told discouraging stories about the dishonesty of families and friends with whom they have tried to set up business transactions. Some speak of close relatives' abuse of funds remitted for business start-ups or construction of buildings. Again, this relates to planning to fail; when you do not plan well you cannot provide funds for an individual who has not been trained or have adequate experience in business, for example, opening a provision shop for someone who does not understand costing and pricing issues nor bookkeeping processes. Besides, because the funds came easily, the likelihood of failure is very high. The need to promote training or apprenticeship is necessary. Funds will be better used if sent to the individual to the Trader who will train them in the arts of the trade.

Corruption and deceit are part of life everywhere and worse in some places. They just need to be managed and controlled. The nurturing characteristics of women, in general, will not disappear because of corrupt people. Just as an African proverb **"we will water the thorn for the sake of the rose."** Consider the potential positive impact a successful diaspora investment will make. Success breathes success and with enabling environment and effective planning, Africa's secret to socio-economic development could still be her diaspora. Morino's suggestions of being open-minded, willing to learn (things might have changed since you traveled out), be collaborative with purpose, and have a positive attitude for a meaningful impact could help the diaspora make an impact. The goal is to ensure that the impact is positive and sustainable. The large number and diverse professions of Africa diaspora have potentials for making positive and sustainable impact if government will create a motivating and enabling environment for entrepreneurship.

Africans in the diaspora are all over the world and in every type of professional and business sectors. Most are doing very well and have established successful business and professional organizations such as medical clinics (dentistry, optometry, OBGYN, Pediatrics, nursing homes, home care, etc.), Accounting and financial firms (Investment, tax, Personal financial management, etc.), marketing organizations both online and brick and mortar operations including restaurants, etc. Diasporas need to dare and dare bravely to replicate their successes in the African continent.

It is equally encouraging to note that many diasporas are investing in Africa. Many are starting with investments in home country which is not bad. Since it is said that the devil you know is better than the one you do not know. I did that with "SIFE Nigeria" and actually started with my brother whom I could trust with personal funds. High-class restaurants, Amusement Parks, Medical Clinics and hospitals, etc., are being set up by diaspora returnees (Wado Waya 2020). Others are focusing on entrepreneurial philanthropy that organize, fund, and network with established youth and women training programs across the continent. These programs and sponsorship are usually connected with diaspora relationships with foreign organizations such as the United Nations, Goldman Sachs, Social Media giants such as FaceBook, Google, etc.

Diaspora Africans should join many who have dared and who have found ways to connect and made the lives of the people better especially those in the rural communities. Their courageous moves have impacted entrepreneurship among the youth. Most important, Diaspora women have a mandate to connect with African women entrepreneurs and philanthropists through networking relationships and with broader objective to develop innovative and pragmatic strategies for sustainable development of the continent. African governments support with enabling environment in this call cannot be over emphasized.

References

Dolan, K. A. (2013, April 18). African charitable giving gets a boost with new launched African philanthropy forum. *Forbes.com*, p. 1.

Folade, K. (2011). *Fashion icon-Foloronshe Alakija at 60.* http://www.thenationonline.net/2011/indes/php.

Harvey, C. M., et al. (2011). Andrew Carnegie and the foundations of contemporary entrepreneurial philanthropy. *Business History, 53*(3), 425.

Maya, W. (2020). *Show case Africa.* www.youtube/ghana/liberia. Retrieved July 8, 2020

Morino, M. (2007, September 28). *Business entrepreneurs and philanthropy: Potentials and pitfalls, keynote Speech-Legacy.* National Philanthropic Trust Forum.

Osirim, J. (2013). *African women in the new diaspora: Transnationalism and the (re) creation of home.* https://repositorybrynmawr.edu/cgi/viewcontent.cgi/article=1005andcontent=soc.pubs; www.researchgate.net/publication.

Pocket Planner. (2004). *Missionaries of Africa*, 1622 21st Street, NW. Washington, DC 20009–1089.

Salami, M. (2013). *Change makers: Women of the African diaspora.* www.newint.org>blog>2013/o8/01>women-of-the-africa.

Wilson, J. (2012, December 5). Richest black woman in the world, Folaronshe Alakija was a major fashion designer in Africa. *Huffington Post.* http://www.huffingtonpost.com/2012/12/05/folaronsho-alakija-richest-blac-woman-fashion-designer-n-2245703.html.

Yesufu, A. (2020). *Igbo apprenticeship system makes people hate Igbos.* www.ne.np.facebook.com>posts>igbo-.

Zakaria, F. (2019). Nigeria-Americans' contributions to the US economy. www.cnn/GPS/nigeria-american-economic-contributions

Zakaria, F. (2020). *Analysis of Trump's controversial travel ban list*. https://www.cnn-africa/GPS/february/17/2020.

CHAPTER 10

Future of Women Entrepreneurs in Africa

INTRODUCTION

Chisolum was not sure what the future will be when she lost her husband at the age of 35. They had four children with the oldest barely celebrating her seventh birthday and the youngest barely five months old. Her future and that of her young children at that moment of unforgettable tragedy were bleak and almost non-existent. Her husband died unexpectedly from a fire outbreak at the petroleum company's rig where he worked as an engineer.

As she mourned her beloved husband, she was trying to figure out how to raise her four young children who barely knew what fate has done to them. Sooner than later, this young and beautiful widow started receiving suitors for second marriage. Friends and even some family members were encouraging her to remarry so she could get help to raise her children.

Before her culture and tradition required one year of mourning was over, she summoned the courage and made the decision to go at it alone. She knew she had to create the future for her and her children because there was no guarantee that a new marriage would help her raise her children at the standard she had anticipated. She and her husband often discussed the future of the children, especially as it related to their formal education. Her husband, according to her, had wanted all their children, especially the girls, to complete a minimum of first-degree university education before they even thought of marriage. She wanted that dream

© The Editor(s) (if applicable) and The Author(s), under exclusive license to Springer Nature Switzerland AG 2021
C. Anyansi-Archibong, *The Foundation and Growth of African Women Entrepreneurs*, Palgrave Studies of Entrepreneurship in Africa,
https://doi.org/10.1007/978-3-030-66280-6_10

and goal for her girls and baby boy in honor of her beloved husband. Besides, marriage without love was not an option for her. She knew that the best way to predict the future she wanted for her family was to create it.

The future she wanted for her four children was a good college education. It would be a 15–20+ years journey but she had to work toward it. She believed she had to create this future for her children. She continued to work at her job and concurrently engage in micro-entrepreneurial activities outside the hours of her official job. She credits God, family, friends, self-determination, persistence, and perseverance for her accomplishments. By 2018, her four children had achieved master's degree education, and her oldest daughter graduated with a doctoral degree in early 2020. She built a two-story duplex in the city and another in her hometown. In her nonstop credit to God, she often exclaimed "I can't believe I am a landlady- God you are the Greatest." The claim to being a landlady came from the fact that she rented out one of the four-bedroom duplexes.

In 1990, Rebecca Lolosoli co-founded the village of "Umoja" (meaning no man allowed), in the Samburu District of Kenya, East Africa. In one of her numerous interviews with journalists and media stations (e.g., www.Shewillsurvive.com; www.vitalvoicesglobalpartnership; www.youtube.com; www.nbcnews.com), Rebecca indicated that her marriage at the age of 18 was full of heartache, emotional, and physical abuse. She recalled that tradition did not allow her as a woman to return to her family after marriage, even when she is physically abused over time. One of the village residents underscored that statement with the following emphatic and explosive statement, "Your husband could literally kill you and get away with it. You will not get support from your family or community because you are his property." Reasons include the fact that the man could demand the return of his dowry which in most cases has been expended by the woman's family.

She knew she had to create a better future for herself and other women when a number of fellow abused and battered women met with her to discuss a way out of their situations. She also knew she needed a lot of courage to accomplish the task just as the African proverb that says that "if you want honey, you must have the courage to face the bees" (African Missionaries, 2004).

Soon after the village started with about sixteen women, who built their own shelters and hunted for food, challenges continued as husbands raided the camp and sometimes raped their wives. The women reorganized and trained each other on how to fight the men. They schedule teams of security guards around the village. With time, Umoja village came to be known as a refuge for abused women, a community where women ruled, made their own decisions, and could find freedom. This all female matriarch village later became entrepreneurial out of necessity as the need to raise funds for new structures such as a schoolhouse became necessary. (At this point, several fleeing women had arrived with their child or children.) They made colorful beads for sale to local and foreign visitors. They built a school for the children that arrived with their mothers. According to the cofounder and leader, Rebecca, it is important to open a school to educate the children so they could have a better future than they did. She claimed that the women of Umoja were in this continuing abuse because they lacked the necessary education and the rights to question the male authority. She believed that the younger generation of women, armed with reasonable and appropriate education, could fight for equal opportunities in marriage as well as in the larger society.

In its current thirty years of existence, alumni of the village have moved on to found two other villages. Nachami (Love) village and Supalaky, which unlike Umoja allow male residents; however, women are in charge and are responsible for setting the rules and regulations in the village. Men are mandated to share chores or leave.

The courage, determination, resilience, and entrepreneurial attitudes of these women predict and promote a positive future for women everywhere just as Rebecca said, "We did this for all women, black and white." This quest for equal opportunities in education and economic sectors continues to drive growing efforts seen around the continent such as seen in the vision, mission, the educational approach of African Rural University (ARU) for women as well as the Uganda Rural Development and Training (URDI) program for girls in middle and high school, provide evidence of some positive steps which are being taken not only to recognize the potential impact of women entrepreneurs but show that with systemic, holistic training, and equal opportunities, women could be the most significant catalyst for sustainable development.

ARU's vision statement—"African Rural University is a value-based all women university that offers a professional discipline in Rural Development and enables students, staff, and supporters have a shared vision and **purpose;** An institution that has governance and management systems that nurture and promote participatory decision making, transformational education, training, and endogenous knowledge development; products which include community practice, grounded in the principles of the creative process, disciplines of a learning organization and holistic development." "ARU has a sustainable resource base and collaborates with public, private, and academic institution, civil society organizations that share philosophy of empowerment of rural people for self-reliance."

In ARU's mission designed to "provide transformational education, to create effective change agents within an African development context, it applies theoretical and innovative learning instructions so that ARU graduates can awaken leadership skills and increase their capacity for self-generating and sustainable change."

With the above vision and mission for human development, and the motto of "Awakening the sleeping genius in each of us," the school which was started by Ashoka Fellow, Dr. Mwalimu Musheshe has developed an education and learning ecosystem for developing women entrepreneurs and leaders. The educational program embraces the Ubuntu philosophy of "**I am because we are.**"

This is the future of African women. It is an example of what people can do if they are not afraid. It is an example of developing the courage to face the "bees in order to get the honey" or succeed (Exhibit 10.1).

Appreciation for the above program's success can only be complete when one understands the impact these young girls are having in their respective families and communities. I had the opportunity and pleasure of visiting URDT/ARU in Kagadi, Western, Uganda. The enthusiasm and commitment of both staff and students were contagious and before I knew it, I was wearing a rubber band on my wrist which I understood was a symbol for the "structural tension" between "your vision and your current situation." These female students are taught to always think strategically including how they could uplift the family and the community. Parents of the young students are required to participate in a monthly weekend program where they interact with their respective daughters and learn new and creative lessons they have developed for the benefit of the family.

In a conversation with one of the parents, he (a father) assured me that his daughter is the most brilliant person in the school. He claimed that the knowledge she has acquired from the school has enabled her to develop a vision for the family farm and that implementation of some of these identified plans has significantly improved their quality of life and

Exhibit 10.1 ARU educational model for rural transformation

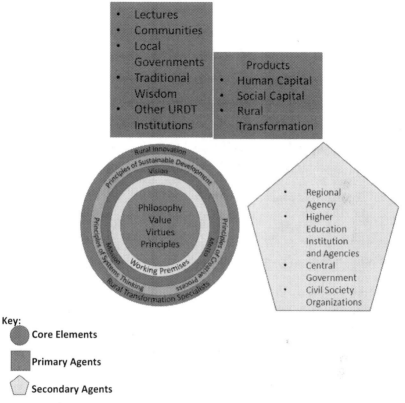

Source www.urdt.net

standard of living. "We have found new ways to increase our farm produce in addition to diverse marketing approaches."

This statement from a Ugandan father is noteworthy since Uganda is one of the societies where girl children are marginalized and women were required to kneel when they speak to a man. You could imagine the pride on the faces of both parents. They were both beaming with pride and the appreciation for their daughter's knowledge and impact on their lives was described as overwhelming.

By extension, the surrounding communities are benefiting and the traditional marginalization and disregard for girl child and women are diminishing.

For more information, see documentary titled—RJF Production (2019) presents The Uganda Project: The New Direction in World Development; http://Fritzfilm.docx.

The education ecosystem in URDT/ARU model could be related as mini model of the GIV framework proposed in Chapter 8. The model not only focuses on producing entrepreneurial human capital but also specifically on female development and social capital. It has a significant impact on rural transformation, a sector mostly dominated by women. Think also of the indirect impact on minimizing potential urban migration which is a growing issue for Africa. This model also underscores the phrase "Educate a girl/woman, you educate a community."

These young ladies during and after graduation are the future of women entrepreneurship in Africa. Replication of such purposeful education and training programs across the nations, regions, and the continent will bring hope, and some solutions to the key challenges for women entrepreneurs even in the twenty-first century. The three stories (Chisolum, Umoja Village, and the URDT/ARU program) present some evidence that African women entrepreneurs can create their future and resolve such challenges as inappropriate entrepreneurial education and training, own property, and other assets to obtain loans and scale their businesses, create enough social network locally and internationally through effective organization and association memberships.

An enabling entrepreneurial ecosystem created around the following elements with purposeful goals and objectives [Cultural and Intellectual Capital (norms, attitudes, knowledge, and experience); Strategic Capital (logic road map, leadership and entrepreneurial government); Network Capital (relationship building: national and international, Diaspora connections and social transparency); and Economic Capital (resource accumulation finance, skills, appropriate infrastructures, etc.)] will provide the necessary framework for a positive future of women entrepreneurs. However, just as one of the African proverbs at the beginning of the chapter predicts "if you want honey, you must have the courage to face the bees." The African woman entrepreneur must dare bravely and not just explore opportunities but must invest in them in order to achieve.

Challenges associated with limited or denied education, for example, have improved. The entrepreneurial woman should find a way to get into programs which enhance her chances of becoming independent and self-sufficient. This does not mean that every female child gets equal opportunities for education. No, there are still so many places on the continent where girls cannot complete primary education because of family financial resources. Where they could, higher education opportunities may be limited to training in programs such as nursing, teacher education, fashion design, with limited admissions to engineering, technology/computer sciences, sciences and mathematics, and entrepreneurship.

It is disturbing to know that the few females who dared and succeeded in the technology and engineering programs find it difficult to get positions in both private and public engineering organizations. The "potential" roles of motherhood and homemaker even with university education still serve as inhibiting factors to employment and grants/funding for start-ups.

In one of my visits to Kenya, I stopped at a roadside kiosk to buy phone credit (before WIFI and WhatsApp). This kiosk also hosted colorful shopping baskets made of locally dyed materials; however, in my conversations with the two young ladies in the kiosk I found they were university graduates with bachelor of science degrees in electrical and civil engineering. They graduated two years ago then, had applied for jobs without success, while their male counterparts were hired within the year. Excuses include lack of experience and practice with equipment in labs, etc. I was told that they started designing and weaving baskets for sale as a means of survival. Further discussion with the young ladies, revealed that the civil engineer had a secondary (or what you may call a minor) certificate in Landscape Architecture. So, we started a discussion on shifting the entrepreneurial activity of designing the baskets with possibilities for designing landscapes for home, offices, etc., since construction projects were going on all over the capital city.

As the young ladies got excited, they admitted that they never even thought about the entrepreneurial option, thereby underscoring the need for an entrepreneurial ecosystem that will restructure education and training programs: an educational system from primary to the university that teaches strategic and entrepreneurial thinking and training programs that develop skills through laboratory experiments and internships. An appropriate and purpose-oriented education and training facilities with equal opportunities for all create the premise for developing effective human capital—intellectuals with traditional knowledge and experiences for entrepreneurial development. For women, appropriate education and training opportunities will awaken and catalyze their natural tendencies for entrepreneurship and enhance commitment to societal development.

An article by Krotz (2017) finds that "women in business tend to define success holistically in contrast to men who typically use financial yardstick for measuring success" and claims that as a result of this, women often gravitate toward social entrepreneurship with the tendency to find purpose in a project. Thus, they use business to solve societal problems. It should be noted that this tendency in women could be the sustaining or stabilizing factor in national and continental development. It promotes quality of life starting with family through communities and the nations.

In another study of entrepreneurship ecosystem and women entrepreneurs' challenges in social capital and network approaches, Newmeyer et al. (2017) used venture typology, race, and ethnicity to examine the entrepreneurship phenomena. They found that minority women (relative to white) do better than men in lifestyle and survival ventures such as fashion, hair care, and restaurant industries. They also found that network connectivity and distribution of social capital are significantly different for men and women. Although this study was done in the USA there are strong relationships between the minority African American women cited and the African businesswomen as well as the industries identified. The lessons are that African women entrepreneurs must seek creative and innovative ways to clear the hurdles or challenges of networking and building social capital. They must find innovative ways to leverage social media. Opportunities abound in technological and telecommunication advancements and growing social media as fiber optic cables are laid across Africa (https://engineering.fb.com/connectivity/2africa/ Facebook Projects).

The point is, recognizing that most of the challenges that have been rightfully identified as inhibiting factors for the entrepreneurial women's success such as limited education and training leading to ineffective business organization and management, lack of access to funding for start-up and growing enterprise, poor planning strategies, networking and mentoring issues, traditional roles and expectations, evolving and dynamic cultural changes, improved opportunities, acquisition of assets, and so forth, are gradually being minimized as women advance in both education and knowledge. They are finding ways to change gendered traditional roles as cultural norms change and opportunities for asset acquisition by women improve.

Summary

Women entrepreneurs have come a long way but still have so much more to achieve. The question is how far could they go if they shed the fear of failure or what societal norms may be violated. Many African girls and married women sometimes underplay potential or delay career opportunities so that they will not be seen as being too forward or trying "to act like a man." Societal norms expect men to make more money than their wives, just as in the saying that "A woman's status is measured by her husband's wealth." Educated, career-oriented, and successful businesswomen are often looked upon as threats instead of being recognized for the socio-economic contributions they make. Many of the young African girls want to be recognized as "marriage material" which is a characteristic or adjective often used both potential groom's and bride's parents. Unfortunately, a man is never scrutinized for potentials of making a good husband.

Johnson (2002) in his book "Who Moved My Cheese?: An A-Mazing Way to Change and Win" deals with the recognition and management of change. What changes do African women entrepreneurs see in the twenty-first-century society and how do these changes affect their roles and status? Most importantly, what would they do if they are not afraid? It is imperative for African women entrepreneurs and women in general, to reevaluate certain terms and their applications in order to strategically influence and manage the socio-economic changes in Africa. They must seize the opportunities offered by technology and global processes. Terms such as empowerment and equality have been used globally to argue the need for inclusion of women in national policymaking. However, empowerment could be defined as "ability to do something about your needs, wants, opinions, beliefs, feelings…" and could be broken up into the following areas—economic, political, cultural, societal, and national empowerment can be achieved with equal opportunities, not necessarily equality (https://quizlet.com/50377873/ss7-5-types-of-empowerment).

African women in general and entrepreneurs specifically must put on their strategic thinking hat and search for areas where they have both comparative, cooperative, and competitive advantages. Think of the key elements of empowerment (which by the way frightens African men who by tradition believe that women should be submissive) which includes authority, resources, information, accountability, etc. These elements connote that when someone is given responsibility or empowered for a task they must also have the tools, which includes the authority to make the decisions, the necessary resources, and information for him or her to be accountable. African women can find ways to empower themselves by using their entrepreneurial tendencies to affect society and culture.

Culture and traditions which have engendered roles are dynamic and have changed tremendously. Technology advancement and globalization have created new and popular culture even in Africa—the way women (girls and women) dress, education, communication, economy, society, information resources and processes, transportation, etc. Changes are in the air and those who will successfully benefit from it are those African women who apply some of their entrepreneurial attitudes and attributes such as resourcefulness, perseverance, future-oriented, industriousness, visionary, etc., to change their life.

- They must explore new opportunities—women can empower themselves if equal opportunities in all sectors exist
- They must create a brand or niche—identify their comparative, cooperative, and competitive advantages
- Be an entrepreneurial leader—seek equal opportunities not equality
- Think strategically—learn to negotiate with diverse groups and individuals (firms, venture capitalist, government, business alliances, partners, etc.)—learn to push the right button with each one by enhancing your communication and knowledge skills
- Be a change agent—"disrupt" the status quo.

Seek Equal Opportunities in Several Sectors for Self-Empowerment

Education	Free, government-sponsored, competitive admissions, primary through university education
Technology	Seek information through the internet, email, smartphones, social media, applications, etc., and become tech literate
Economics	Engage in "Disruptive" innovations, create new value-added products or services, network, and a healthy economic system
Politics/National	Run for political offices, aim to become entrepreneurial leaders, change agent, engage with organizations and alliances
Cultural/Society	Enhance and promote roles in societal development—leverage skills in social entrepreneurship, create and engage in local, national, and international networks, differentiate and find niches

Inequality and disequilibrium or lack of equilibrium breed collaboration. For example, nature created inequality in human hands with the fingers. They are not all equal but must work together to be functional and perform effectively. If you cut or eliminate one finger, the rest will have difficulty in performing their duties. The same could be said of the human body as a system of organs featuring the heart, liver, kidney, lungs, stomach, etc. A healthy body is one where all the organs are in sync and are working together. If one organ malfunctions and therefore out of sync, the individual becomes sick and cannot fulfill his or her duties until the organ is repaired.

> In a similar situation, a socio-economic system that does not recognize and put all its potential resources together and in sync is incomplete and would not function effectively. African nations and the continent must infuse or integrate the female population into the system for sustainable socio-economic development.

Women have come a long way and are still making differences in families and communities. It is apparent and encouraging to note that many are being recognized for the potential impact they could make in motivating and mentoring the youth. For example, Tony Elumelu Foundation joined the United Nations and other global organizations in celebrating International Youth Day on August 12, 2020. The African entrepreneur, known for his promotion and push for "Africapitalism" invited a group of pan-African speakers to discuss the theme, "Investing in Africa's Future: Youth Empowerment through Entrepreneurship" (https://lifandtimesnews.com/tony-elumelu-international-youth-day/).

The interesting take away from this forum is that seven of the eight invited speakers were women. They spoke of the need to recognize entrepreneurship as an essential part of Africa's employment challenge; for governments to start looking at entrepreneurship as a fundamental core topic that needs to be integrated into the educational system; and for the need to make youths co-owners of policymaking process and to give them co-ownership at the table not just to be invited as guests. The fact that this well-known African entrepreneur invited an almost all female panel to speak on entrepreneurship is a sign the compass needle is changing and is pointing toward a greater and better future for women entrepreneurs.

A comparison of African women entrepreneurial growth to Maslow's Hierarchy of Needs (Exhibit 10.2) indicates that women entrepreneurs

Exhibit 10.2 Comparing Maslow's hierarchy of needs to stages in African women entrepreneurs' growth

*Safety and Survival Needs: These two lower levels of the Pyramid represent the Micro-Entrepreneurs/First generation
***Self-Actualization, Esteem, Social/Belonging: Top three levels represent the Second-generation women entrepreneurs

have grown from micro, tradition-induced entrepreneurial ventures (survival and safety-oriented focus) to more established classic and competitive entrepreneurs ready and able to engage in industries formally dominated by men. They are now seeking and seizing opportunities for networking (belonging), self-esteem, and self-actualization through their ventures. As portrayed in the pyramid, many first-generation women still dominate this bottom of the pyramid known as the informal sector. The top three levels of the apex relate to the growth and successful transitions of some second-generation women entrepreneurs who have been able to penetrate the sectors formally dominated by men. These women have found credibility in networking and gained grounds in social capital, thus building and achieving some self-esteem and even reaching self-actualization.

Although most of the African women entrepreneurs still dominate the bottom of the pyramid or what is known as the informal sector, these women contribute immensely to the economy. They are able to apply their intrinsic traits as mothers, daughters, sisters, homemakers, spouses, etc., in their multiple roles. They are great at making good judgment, being resourceful, creative, innovative, courageous, and great problem-solvers as they manage and raise families. They have developed tremendous skills and have become experts in multitasking.

Speaking of multitasking, many years ago I asked one of my sons to stop playing his portable electronic game which was slowing down his effort to clean his room. He responded as follows—"we young ones can multitask, I can do both and more at the same time." My response went as follows—what do you think you know about multitasking? I started multitasking before you were born—as a mother and a graduate student, I kept the apartment clean, cooked (sometimes two different meals at a time) and fed you, did my school work, graded papers as a graduate assistant, and was also an "Avon lady" all in the effort to make ends meet. This conversation reminded me to thank my youngest one who according to the teacher, described my job in his kindergarten "Show and Tell" presentation as follows, "I am not sure what she does because she is always doing many things at a time. Most of the time she is writing or grading papers while she is also cooking, and sometimes checking on our homework as well."

Go figure, my youngest was right I sometimes forget I had something in the oven or on the range while I am working on some research or cleaning the house. Women are naturals when it comes to multitasking. This skill gets even better as they engage in their numerous responsibilities. The trait is a competitive advantage which must be explored and used to grow entrepreneurial ventures and manage families.

The need to recognize and market her multitasking ability is the African woman's ticket to starting and accelerating her business ventures. The ability to wear her multiple hats or roles and manage them effectively should be articulated as they attempt to convince venture capitalists and funding agencies to invest in them. Women should not be afraid nor play down their roles as mothers, caregivers, raising children successfully, etc. These achievements require intelligence and skills and they should be proud to have developed these attributes.

Negotiation skills is another competitive advantage that African women have especially the first-generation women entrepreneurs and they should not take them for granted. Negotiation skills do not only provide women competitive but also cooperative advantages. Sibongeli Sambo (see Profile, Chapter 12) claimed that she acquired her negotiation skills from her mother by watching her haggle and negotiate prices in the local market. She also saw her negotiate positions and responsibilities in the community projects until favorable compromise and cooperation were achieved. This advantage which included patience and collaboration are skills that are common among first-generation women entrepreneurs who juggled responsibilities, engaged, and still engage in price negotiation in their daily market activities. It should be noted that most of the African business activities rely on price negotiation and bidding. There are limited areas of fixed price tags on sales items. There is a common saying that everything is negotiable and women are experts of negotiation.

It is necessary for women to learn how to market their skills—skills developed as a result of their gendered roles and learned from mothers and sisters in their teenage days.

Summary and conceptualized specific areas of modern trends among the African women entrepreneurs are presented in the next chapter with some examples of events and factors supporting the conceptualized trends.

> The future of women entrepreneurs in Africa is very promising as they explore and positively "exploit" areas of equal opportunities to empower themselves. The charge is to: become true entrepreneurial and Invent yourself; Be Brave, Courageous, and create your future.

References

Johnson, S. (2002). Who moved my cheese. *G.P. Putman's Sons, a division of Putman's books*. New York. ISBN 13579108642.

Krotz, J. L. (2017). *Americas first social entrepreneurs were female, black, and millionnaires* (honoring madam C J Walker and Annie Turnbo Malone). www.workingmother.com

Newmeyer, et al. (2017). Entrepreneurship ecosystems and women entrepreneurs: A social capital and network approach. *Small Business Economics, 53*, 475–489, published 3/2018/springerlink.

CHAPTER 11

Conclusions and Trends

INTRODUCTION

It is apparent that the rhythm of the drum beat for African women is changing very fast for several reasons and in various ways. Just as the Kossi proverb (African Missionaries Calendar, 2004) indicates, "if the rhythm of the drum changes, the dance steps must adapt." The roles and status of the African woman are changing and they are adapting quickly and steadfastly to the new roles.

Their participation and contributions to the socio-economic development of the nations and the continent are gradually being recognized. From the first generation, tradition-induced entrepreneurs who persevered to nurture and sustain families with very limited resources (material and skills) to the second generation, twenty-first-century entrepreneurs with more access to education and training, but still with limitations to other necessary resources, the African woman entrepreneur remains the bedrock of society and its development. The 51–55% population of women can no longer be ignored as the continent which is being touted as the world's next economic renaissance forges ahead. Research is showing that the female economy is the world's largest emerging market with potentials to add $12 trillion to the global GDP (McKinsey Report, 2019). Also, the Global Entrepreneurship Monitor reports that the Sub-Saharan Africa has the highest rate of female entrepreneurship globally.

© The Editor(s) (if applicable) and The Author(s), under exclusive license to Springer Nature Switzerland AG 2021
C. Anyansi-Archibong, *The Foundation and Growth of African Women Entrepreneurs*, Palgrave Studies of Entrepreneurship in Africa,
https://doi.org/10.1007/978-3-030-66280-6_11

Trends and Challenges

Technology, telecommunications, social media, and globalization are integrating economies, politics, cultures, societies, etc., changing the rhythm of the drum or rather the environment where the dance steps occur for all, especially the African woman. These factors and their interactive processes have opened the doors for African women especially their structured and gendered roles. African women with their resourceful, persistent, courageous, perseverance, etc., traits have more opportunities to engage in higher level or scaled entrepreneurship in any of the diverse sectors. They could engage and have been engaging in entrepreneurial leadership positions in global organizations. As stated in earlier chapters of the book, they hold leadership positions in many united nations agencies such as the World Bank, International Labor Organization, World Health Organizations, and as ambassadors. They have appointed positions in the African Union (AU) and nationally they have seats in the congress and parliaments such as seen in Rwanda where women represent 56% of Senate and 48% in Senegal.

All the same, it should be noted that this growth in national and continental leadership positions does not mean that the challenges of gender-related domestic violence and other gender issues have been eliminated in the two countries. Economically, and most importantly for the focus of this book, the growth of successful women entrepreneurs in sectors and industries formally dominated by men is noteworthy. Examples include Mrs. Alakija of Nigeria, in the oil exploration industry; Joana Gyan of Ghana, in gold mining, television, petroleum, and a host of other businesses under the Global Empire Legacy Holdings; Njeri Rionge of Kenya, in information technology, consulting, and business incubator; Isabel De Santos of Angola in oil, diamonds, banking, industries, etc.; Sibongile Sambo of South Africa in aviation; and the list goes on in addition to the top 10 women in technology enterprises.

The above strides and successes did not mean the elimination of gender-biased challenges (e.g., limited access to education, ownership of property for facilitating financial loans, limited mobility in business travel as culture frowns on married women who travel for business) faced by African women entrepreneurs. On the contrary, these challenges have become more complex and as the saying goes, "the devil is in the details." Take for example women's access to education: When a family is limited in financial resources, the boy child still gets the first right to go to school before any girl sibling. Admissions in universities favor males for sciences, technology, engineering, and mathematics (STEM) programs. In most African countries limited capacities at both universities and other higher education institutions also discriminate against women. Further barriers to female advancement occur in the employment sector. In many cases where women succeed in achieving university degrees in STEM or other programs, both private and public employers hesitate to hire them. Male graduates are given priority over the females for reasons relating to the gendered roles of marriage, motherhood, and family-caretaker. Employers believe that these create major role conflicts which are more likely to negatively affect the job performances of the female employee.

Similar issues arise as we look at the other apparently minimized challenges in areas of funding and grants for female entrepreneurs. As much as many second-generation women entrepreneurs have been able to acquire property and other assets often required as collateral for loans, venture capitalists, and banks still deny many opportunity for the same gender reasons. They are hesitant to invest in women. They believe that women entrepreneurs are high risks compared to men, even when research reports show that women-led businesses are better managed and have higher returns. In an article by Georgina Varley (2019), the reporter argued that gender diversity in the "tech industry is smart economics." The author followed up by indicating that although women receive less than 50% of venture capital funding, the global technology firms led by female entrepreneurs typically achieve 35% higher returns on investment than those run by men (http://www.women-in-tech-africa-summit.com/). Also, data from Mastercard's Index of women's entrepreneurship showed that there is a growing market for women-led enterprise in Ghana and Uganda with 46.4% and 33.8%, respectively, of each country's business owners. The report also reiterates that the number of African women in business is the highest globally.

Panelists on "Achieving a Single African Market- African Continental Free Trade Agreement (ACFTA)," repeatedly called for the need to create a free track for women and youth by putting "capital at risk" for them; restructuring education to narrow information and knowledge gaps; minimizing government bureaucracy, and most importantly, involving experienced businesswomen in developing the architecture for a successful ACFTA. This last statement came from the fact that many women are already involved in intercountry or cross-border trade. These women complain of many bureaucratic and corruption-based challenges including irregularity in border taxes, confusing and conflicting regulations, absence of legal and enforcement policies, delays in processing passport/visa, and other trade logistics. In addition to trade issues, women complain of gender-related safety in crossing national borders (Davos—World Economic Forum, 2019).

Simon Whuster of Visual Politics (2017) wrote that the "Future of Africa is brighter now than it has ever been." He cited some statistics then such as the status of extreme poverty in Africa in 1999 was 38% but had been reduced to 35% in 2017; the same for child mortality of 18% in 1999 which fell to 8% in 2017 (Bloomberg Philanthropies). The same program also cited some nations it referred to as "African Lions." These countries which are growing at approximately 9% (GDP) annually and what they were doing to effect and sustain the growth, which included Rwanda which is cited for her focus on pragmatic and value-added planning, Ethiopia for her expanded infrastructure development where she has committed no less than 10% of her GDP growth per annum, Botswana for her focus on restructuring of national institutions including education, and Nigeria for the film industry (Nollywood) and its growing impact on the national economy, etc.

As much as the above discussions were fair and show the continent and national progressions toward development, it failed to credit the impact women are making. For example, the 10% drop in child mortality between 1999 and 2017 could be the domino effect of women's access to education (especially health) empowering them to take care of their health during pregnancies (UN MDGs). Africa's future may be brighter now than before, but it cannot afford to overlook the dynamic changes in the global environment. For the countries and the continent to forge ahead successfully, they must think of ways to promote unity with inclusive planning approach that provides opportunities for better quality of life and standard of living for all citizens. The phrase "Sticks in a bundle are unbreakable" (Bondei Proverb, 2004) says it all.

Conceptualized Trends for the Twenty-First-Century Women Entrepreneurs

African women entrepreneurs are actively adapting to the new rhythms of global and technological environmental changes. Based on the past and present accomplishments it is possible to conceptualize and conclude with some certainty the trends for African women entrepreneurs.

Exhibit 11.1 summarizes the conceptualized trends for the twenty-first century. The table predicts not only the status and identifiable characteristics but also, the potential growth, new types of entrepreneurial activities, knowledge and technology literacy, life style, organization and management approaches, etc. These items and others are explained further in the paragraphs below the exhibit and are based on both the African women's deep-rooted culture of entrepreneurial spirit and the anticipated impact of technological and global environment changes. It has also been argued that entrepreneurship is an environmentally driven phenomenon and just as the ecological environmental factors influenced the first-generation micro and sole entrepreneurs, it is expected that current dynamic technology and global environmental factors will have significant influence on the future of African women entrepreneurs.

Exhibit 11.1 Trends in the twenty-first-century African women entrepreneurship

- A. Significant increase in the number of female entrepreneurs with presence in all sectors of the society
- B. New types of female entrepreneurs will emerge, including young female entrepreneurs in tech start-ups, entrepreneurial leaderships in politics, institutions, etc.
- C. More ethically and environmentally conscious female entrepreneurs with significant concerns for the environment, nature, health, and other related enterprises
- D. More tech competent and knowledge-orientation; competition-driven, process innovation orientation, and user-friendly technology
- E. More team player and partnerships oriented
- F. Engage in multiple venture entrepreneurship—serial, seasonal, entrepreneurial teams, opportunistic in contrast to necessity-driven and other related forms
- G. More global reach—engage in more global alliances, network, diaspora relations, etc.
- H. More financially and investment savvy—more opportunistic in seeking and obtaining financial supports and grants
- I. More quality of life and standard of living consciousness—flexible time and holistic work environment that address both family and work responsibilities
- J. Lean more toward entrepreneurial philanthropy with foundations and charitable giving
- K. Slow but growing trend is engagement of university-educated daughters in the mothers' enterprise as will be seen in the profiles

- A. Significant increase in the number of women entrepreneurs is predicted with the expectations that a more pragmatic and inclusive development planning will open doors for more women engagement in all sectors of development, especially the formal economic sector where participation has been very limited. Many are already in Mining, Aviation, Brewery, Banking, Telecommunication, etc. Access to education and relevant training across the nations will boost entrepreneurial activities by women as they learn to manage resources and organize better (http://www.senivpetro.com). Micro-entrepreneurs will pursue opportunities in financing and support for scaling up their enterprises. Studies also show that more educated women than men opt to start their own business rather than seek employment in either public or private sectors (http:// www.FAT Efoundation.org). Evidence also exists to show that more professional women such as dentists, optometrists, and pharmacists in Africa tend to open and operate their own clinics and stores rather than seek employment.
- B. New and younger female entrepreneurs will emerge with start-ups in the tech industry. With potential increase in women's access to higher education and especially training in STEM, young female entrepreneurs will engage in innovative and creative enterprises. The top ten female-led African tech companies (https://www.women-in-tech-africa-summit.com/blog/top-10-female-led-african-tech-companies) list a few of these young and professional entrepreneurs as shown in table.

Company	Service	Founder/Creator
mDoc (Nigeria)	Provides Africans suffering from chronic diseases with a virtual ecosystem where all of their healthcare data is located. mDoc connects its users with medical practitioners such as nutritionists and fitness coaches on a 24/7 basis, and is changing lives across the continent, especially for those suffering from diabetes and hypertension	Dr. Nneka Mobisson, a 2017 Cattier Awards Finalist and a 2014 World Forum Young Global Leader. Dr. Mobisson will speak at Women in Tech Africa Summit (2019) on topic "Troubleshooting with Venture Capitalists: What not to do when Getting their Money"

(continued)

11 CONCLUSIONS AND TRENDS 175

(continued)

Company	Service	Founder/Creator
GirlHype (south Africa)	Provides business opportunities for women in South Africa. It is a not-for-profit which provides programming and app development training for girls and young women. Focus is on after school club programs for 6th—12th graders	Barantang Miya, is a self-taught coder with the goal of getting more women in STEM programs
AppsTech (Cameroon)	Provides enterprise application solutions. With clients in over 40 countries and 3 continents. In addition to a number of software products the company offers services on implementation, training, and application management	Rebecca Ononchong, credits her success to hard work, ability to think big, and never giving up
Tress (Ghana)	A social hair care app that allows black women to discover new hairstyles, products, stylists, and associated costs	The three co-founders, Priscilla Hazel, Esther Olatunde, and Cassandra Sarfo launched their start up in 2016
Empty Tripes (South Africa)	The business matches cargo space demand to supply for transportation of goods. The services reduce carbon emission by optimizing the use of trucks and trains—it has been described as "uber for cargo"	Benji Coetzee, A Singularity Award winner for her AI-enabled transport marketplace
Tiphub (Nigeria)	A tech support and social enterprise which offers clients with funding, mentors, business training, consulting services, and accelerator program. Its goal is to increase the number of socially driven investments in Africa	Amanda Spann, a Business Insider under 30 listings and a future leader in technology by Black Enterprise magazine. She believes that future of start-ups is not in the city

(continued)

(continued)

Company	Service	Founder/Creator
JuaKali (Kenya)	A directory for blue workers allowing them to create an online profile that show their expertise and connects with individual clients and institutions. With the belief that the informal sector is the largest employer in Africa (80%), the founder's goal is to increase female social capital	Judith Owigar—A Change Agent ABIE Award Winner and serves on the board of Swedish Program for ICT in Developing Regions (SPIDER) and the Lumen Labs board
Ghana Code Club (Ghana)	With the belief that a combination of diversity, innovation, creativity, and passion is the key to business success, the company which hosts an after-school program for children with the intent of exposing them early to computer literacy and skills. She envisions a future in which the next generation of Ghanaians has the knowledge to harness the power of technology to achieve economic and personal success	Ernestina Appiah, is named by the BBC in its 100 Women Series for her contributions to Education and Inspiration for the youth
Intelipro (Kenya)	Making headlines in African cloud computing. Company clients which include financial institutions and telecommunication businesses receive insights that allow them to make faster decisions by leveraging big data and machine learning. The platform integrates with high-volume transaction systems like CRM and ERP to present a holistic view of customers progress	Leonida Mutuku, named one of Forbes Africa's top 30 under 30 in 2018. She also leads projects for Africa Open Data Network

(continued)

(continued)

Company	Service	Founder/Creator
iMED Tech Group (South Africa)	The company provides innovative medical solutions to impact healthcare delivery across the continent. With the founder's expertise in 3D Printing applications and has used this technology in developing her custom-made products in the medical area	Nneile Nkholise, a SAB Foundation Innovation Award winner

These tech-led female companies were started by young women under 30 and spans from healthcare to retail to social and media entrepreneurship. Younger women will explore and exploit opportunities in STEM education and business training and develop what could be called "sole-preneurs" with founder as the owner–employee and two or fewer employees. A possible issue with this type of tech-oriented enterprises is its limitation in job creation.

- C. Most modern women entrepreneurs with their natural nurturing and caregiving tendencies will create more environmentally friendly enterprises. They will be more ethically conscious in managing operations with value-added passions for quality of goods and services. Many are likely to engage impact-related activities such as healthcare, social issues, and education industries. Examples could be seen above as well as in GLAM Power's list of the 10 most influential entrepreneurs in Africa, (seven females and 3 males) three of the seven females are identified with businesses in social issues and entertainment, Saran K. Jones of WASH Liberia and Arese Ugwu— Financial Literacy and in entertainment Mo Abudu, founder of Ebony Life TV with interests in showing "the best of Africa to Africans while projecting a positive image of the continent to the world" (http://www.GLAMAFRICA.COM/2017).
- D. There will be evidence of women entrepreneurs becoming more team and partnership oriented. With access to higher education and purposeful training, women are recognizing the benefits of available networking and are therefore more prone to creating alliances for start-ups or scaling up existing ventures. They will be shifting

toward "entrepreneurial teams" and limiting emphasis on "sole-entrepreneurship" or micro-ventures. Management skills are on the rise and will continue to improve with opportunities in business administration education and training. Engagement in international trade through partnerships and alliances with local and international ventures.
- E. The trend is moving toward more opportunity-driven compared to necessity-driven entrepreneurs of the past. As much as necessity women entrepreneurs still exist in many rural communities of Africa; this drive to explore opportunities in the continent and outside the continent will result in engagement in multiple ventures and across diverse sectors. Serial, seasonal, social, team, and entrepreneurial philanthropy are some of the terms that will define the twenty-first-century African women entrepreneurs. They are more likely to engage in better-calculated risk than before and will create conglomerates in both horizontal and vertical-integrated ventures. Ndidi O. Nwuneli, founder of Investment firm with a focus on social innovation, agriculture, and nutrition in Africa and a former Mckinsey Consultant, invests in "numerous ventures across the food value chain." She is also credited with mentoring youth and women across Africa through her association with Leap Africa. Another rising African star is Marcia Ashong, founder of The Board Room Africa, which champions women in executive leadership positions across Africa. She also founded and manages an oil and gas company, among other ventures (https://www.newafricanmagazine.com/december-january-2020).
- F. More global reach through networking, connections with the diaspora, participation in international women's forums, diaspora organizations, and other international invitations related to women issues. Connections with diaspora and other international networks will become a goal as these entrepreneurs seek opportunities for innovative ventures. As late as 2012 I had the pleasure and privilege of being invited to meet with five African women entrepreneurs as they arrived in Greensboro, North Carolina, where I was teaching. Host institution, Bennet College, had an entrepreneurship program and had volunteered to host this program sponsored by the US Department of State. Specific objectives of this three-week program include highlighting the contributions of women to the global

economy and technology development; exploring the gender dimensions of international economics, trade liberalization and international finance; exploring the role of women as agents of social and political change in the USA; and providing network opportunities with influential business and community leaders among others.

Profiles of these women from Cape Verde, Gabon, Kenya, Nigeria, and Zimbabwe included, entrepreneurs and public officers or both such as Ms. Nwanji of Kenya, founder and CEO of professional marketing group with over 230 employees and concurrently serving as the national Vice Chair of Kenya Chamber of Commerce and Industry. I was particularly happy to meet with Ms. Alhassan of Nigeria who credited Students in Free Enterprise (SIFE) which I founded as the key program that spiked her interest in entrepreneurship.

It is international programs such as this that will enhance the African women entrepreneurs' growth and connections to the international and global partners.

- G. With education and special business or professional training, new female entrepreneurs will be more financial savvy. They have the capability to seek, find, and negotiate more effectively for funds. They are able to plan and manage investments for high returns. They are taking on the challenges, breaking barriers to affect the socio-economic environment in a positive and impactful ways. Foreign and indigenous organizations as well as government investment in infrastructures such as the Facebook project. A transformational subsea cables designed to better connect Africa, Middle East, and Europe (https://engineering.fb.com/connectivity/2africa/); this project will help reduce challenges faced by women in tech, especially online trading where slow internet connection and lack of stable power and electricity delay and sometimes discourage business transactions (http:www.dressmeoutlet.com). In the same manner, co-creation hubs across the continent engage young women by training them to accelerate application of social capital and technology including financial acquisitions and services techniques (https://www.cchubnigeria.com/). Another contributing program designed to empower African women to unlock their potentials is the Savings Group for Africa (http://sg4africa.org/consortumteam/) and Empowering African Women (https://www.empoweringafricanwomen.com

- H. Changes in life style—the traditional roles of family caregiver and parenting will be enhanced professionally. The twenty-first-century female entrepreneur is better prepared to balance family and work/business responsibilities. She is able to organize and manage her diverse roles including helping children with school work, organizing and including children in family vacations, maintaining flexible work environment for staff, and creating opportunities for training and mentoring younger staff. They find it easy to travel for both business and pleasure locally and internationally. Examples would be seen in Nike's Art and Museums and other business profiles in Appendix A.
- I. Civic and nonprofit engagements: The trend is toward more active engagement in civic and charitable activities, especially on issues relating to girls and young women. Most will create foundations and will be more philanthropic. However, they will be more oriented toward entrepreneurial philanthropy in contrast to the traditional giving style. Focus for the philanthropy and foundation will most likely be based on their respective personal experiences and challenges as young girls and mothers.
- J. Trend toward active involvement of daughters in mothers' business is on the rise. This movement is becoming a new form of team play. In some cases, such as Keroche Brewery (Appendix A) one of the daughters diversified and created her own company with a different product in the same industry, a form of horizontal diversification but with her mother's blessings.

Conclusions

For the above conceptualizations and discussions of the traits for the twenty-first-century African female entrepreneurs to materialize and impact the development of the nations and the continent at large, the governments and other elements of an entrepreneurial ecosystems must be in place. Recommendations for this enabling environment include but not limited to the following:

1. Both national governments and AU leaders must become more entrepreneurial, innovative, and visionary thinkers

2. Create enabling environments for entrepreneurship by creating motivating ecosystems connections where all the elements are in sync and consistent with the goals and objectives national development. Leaders must recognize entrepreneurship as a comparative advantage of nations including micro-entrepreneurships such as household and market women ventures which fill niches in contrast to high-growth entrepreneurships. The two must interact for sustainable development.
3. Partnerships and alliances with tech and other foreign investors are must especially for infrastructural development in internet and telecommunication infrastructure.
4. Leaders must accelerate efforts to attract, connect, and develop purposeful and sustainable relationships with the diaspora. It is not enough to acknowledge and recognize "the Africa diaspora as the sixth region of the continent." The government must develop appropriate programs and policies to attract and sustain mutual relationship with the diaspora.
5. Develop enforceable policies for equal opportunities across the board irrespective of culture, religious background, socio-economic status, gender, age, etc. This situation must be supported by transparent and moral conscience in governance. In this call, government must pay attention to all the necessary infrastructure development, especially those that impact sustainable development.

The economic distress of Africa's rural communities is the most pressing issues facing the nations and the continent. The absence of businesses and jobs in the rural areas fuels not only poverty but also increases crime and youth migration to cities. A well thought out government collaboration with women entrepreneurs who dominate the rural community could go a long way to create successful micro-businesses with the rural communities' comparative and cooperative advantages of low-cost labor and reasonably lower cost real estate. This collaboration, if well designed and implemented could create a sustainable economic base in the rural communities thus minimizing crimes and poverty. Integration of large businesses and small and medium firms (mostly women-run) will not only enhance economic development but will also provide women entrepreneurs with the training and motivations they need.

With the trend toward entrepreneurial and knowledge economy, there is also the need to restructure educational institutions, especially colleges and universities to develop, grow, and support students' interest in entrepreneurial thinking and entrepreneurship. Governments must focus on developing a purposeful university ecosystem with entrepreneurship-oriented capacity featuring innovation capacity, marketing capacity, relationship capacity (production, R&D, Finance), incubators, governance, etc.

It is the government's responsibility to encourage and promote Research and Development (R&D) institutes, autonomous innovation centers, incubators for start-ups, tech transfer offices, and facilitate a patent acquisition process. A purposeful and goal-targeted university program such as the African Rural University (ARU) for women in Uganda presents future opportunities for women inclusion in national and continental development.

Africa's diversity in culture, traditions, religion, languages, geographic ecosystems, etc., is a gold or platinum mine for sustainable socio-economic development and growth. The role of women is a critical success factor that needs to be carefully and systematically harnessed by the nations' and continent's leaderships. Their knowledge and experiences in organizing and managing both family and business scarce resources are factors to be considered in development planning. They are great disciplinarians in and outside the homes. They are naturally entrepreneurial thinkers and innovators, where innovation is about finding new ways and ideas; ideas that depend on having different perspectives, and different perspectives that come with experience and maturity.

African women have traveled this innovation road in their multiple roles or positions by finding new ways, developing different perspectives, and gaining experiences in both their business ventures and family roles. They are resourceful in finding innovative ways to develop financial independence, self-sufficiency, persistence in achieving goals (protests against colonial policies intended to exploit their livelihood), and they are selfless in their search for creating social goods as they become more ecologically bounded thinkers than men. They are necessity-driven risk-takers when pushed by society and when the welfare of their families is on the line. Nigerian women crossed enemy lines during the civil war (1967–1970) to feed family, earning them the title of "Affia-Attack" Women, and the Umoja village of Samburu County in Kenya, created by women for women, is another evidence of women's resilience and determination to achieve their objectives.

It should not be forgotten, as mentioned earlier that in contrast to men who measure business success by financial yardstick, women in business define and measure success holistically (Malone-Krotz 2017). Trending is not only women entrepreneurs' gravitation toward social entrepreneurship but increasing engagement in non-social entrepreneurial ventures. They seek and find purpose in revenues and profit; using revenue to solve family and societal problems. In other words, "they are doing good by doing well." African women are trending toward entrepreneurial philanthropy. They are becoming more creative in finding ways to empower other women, especially the younger generation. They are motivating them to be more financially independent while balancing family and business roles.

The African Woman is a Phenomenon that is worth exploring; She is naturally entrepreneurial; She is resilient, brave, courageous, and many more.

Is she marginalized? Yes, but she does not see herself as a victim because She faces the challenges, rises to the occasion and upholds her family, business, and the society. The future of the African women entrepreneurs is brighter now than ever before. However, to succeed and excel, Women should see their traditional foundation of entrepreneurial tendencies (especially the nurturing abilities as mothers, home-makers, problem solvers resourcefulness, etc.) as comparative, cooperative, and competitive advantages that could be strategically applied in any appropriate situation for continuing success.

African Women should not be apologetic for doing well and doing good in the society. Bonding together and supporting each other through opportunities for networking, mentoring and training will make them successful, stronger, and "unbreakable" like the sticks in a bundle.

References

Gonzalez, L. (Host, 2019). *Achieving a single African market: Davos world economic forum.* www.youtube.com. Retrieved July 14, 2020.

Malone-Krotz, J. L. (2017). *America's first social entrepreneurs were women, black, and millionaires: Honoring Madam C.J. Walker and Annie Turnbo.* www.workingmother.com.

Varley, G. (2019). *Empowering women in tech for economic development.* http://www.women-in-tech-africa-summit.com/.

Whuster, S. (2017). *Which African countries are taking off?* www.Visualpolitics.en/CCTV@SimonWhuster. Accessed July 9, 2020.

CHAPTER 12

Profiles of Select African Women Entrepreneurs: Their Stories, Successes, Inspirations, and Challenges

INTRODUCTION

This chapter presents the profiles of select women entrepreneurs. The selection is random and designed to showcase African women's engagement in different sectors of the economy as well as their respective personal attributes. The selection is not based on financial success and financial net-worth but on the diverse entrepreneurial attributes and the characteristics they represent.

These profiles focus on the personal background, the business venture, inspirations, aspirations, challenges in starting and managing the ventures, growth strategies, balancing business and family where applicable, and other motivations for becoming an entrepreneur. Passions and specific entrepreneurial attributes of each entrepreneur were considered for selection in an attempt to capture as many diverse characteristics as possible.

Representation of entrepreneurs from each African region was also a consideration. The chapter also includes a profile story a young African woman, Martha Agwang, and her determination to live her dreams despite challenges of school fees and family responsibilities as a girl and the oldest of 10 children. Her story also presents struggles for trending young African women entrepreneurs. Exhibit below presents the summary of select profiles and the business sectors.

© The Editor(s) (if applicable) and The Author(s), under exclusive license to Springer Nature Switzerland AG 2021
C. Anyansi-Archibong, *The Foundation and Growth of African Women Entrepreneurs*, Palgrave Studies of Entrepreneurship in Africa, https://doi.org/10.1007/978-3-030-66280-6_12

List of Profiled Entrepreneurs: Name, Business name, Industry/Sector, and Generation

Entrepreneur	Business name	Industry/sector	.... Generation
Chief/Mrs. Nike M. Okundayo	Nike Art Galleries and Weaving Centers	Art, Painting, and Museums and Retail	First and Second [Started Early and grew into current generation]
Mrs. Marcelina A. Anyansi	Mrs. M.A. Super Market: [On and Off Beer license]	Retail	First ......
Sibongile Sambo	SRS Aviation Limited	Aviation [Flight and Maintenance]	Second....
Salwa Idrissi Akhannouch	AKSAL—Morocco Mall group of Companies	Real Estate/Retail/Manufacturing	Second....
Thabita Karanji	Keroche Breweries Limited	Brewing—Beer/Wine/Spirit	Second....
Isabel Dos Santos	Group of Companies	Conglomerates—Oil, Energy, Finance/Banking, Telecommunications, etc.	Second....
Martha Catherine Agwang	Uganda Youth Development and Training (UYDT)/Global Women Bakery Initiative	Service and Manufacturing	First-generation experience/with second-generation education

In Summary, the following stories are about the African women entrepreneurs' cultural attributes and attitudes: bravery, resilience, perseverance, energetic, determination, assertiveness, Persuasive, resourceful, tolerance for ambiguity, optimistic, self-confident, ability to implement and manage, multitasking, adaptive, Industrious, dynamic, visionary, problem-solvers, inspired, and intrinsic abilities to name a few. They all share similar challenges and struggles but found ways to survive and actually thrive. They are all advocates of equal opportunity for all.

Chief (Mrs.) Nike Okundayo

Owner/Founder and Managing Director Nike Art Galleries and Group of Center for Art and Culture

Inspiration: *__Having the ability to take young girls off the streets and give them skills to live a meaningful and respectful life__*.

Mama Nike, as she is popularly known, had a childhood and teenage life that is as eclectic as her paintings and artwork. Born in 1957, she lost her mother at the age of six, she lived with her father and brother for a couple of years before she was sent to live with her grandmother who was an Adire designer, tie-dye expert, and embroiderer and a great-grandmother who was head of the community as well as a weaver.

As a young teenager in the village, Nike was a stage dancer, an actress in the popular local Yoruba film "Ayaba." Later in life, Nike featured in several documentaries including "Kindred Spirits" sponsored and produced by the Smithsonian Museum in Washington, DC, USA; CNN documentary film, "African Voices"; and as recent as 2016, she was again featured in another CNN documentary, "Inside Africa." Nike has become an internationally accomplished icon in Art. She was a dancer, an actress, and later in life a known artist, painter, textile artist, weaver, and embroiderer, areas where she has won awards nationally and internationally. She has participated and featured in both national and international art shows. She is a member of several professional organizations, a social entrepreneur, and a philanthropist.

Wow! One will wonder how this woman who grew up in a small village population of 200 accomplished above and beyond much more. In a rare interview with Mama Nike (January 2020) she opened up to me with some details of her personal life especially her childhood experiences. After losing her mother at the age when she was supposed to start her primary education, her father, a bead embroiderer for the royal palace ornaments and hats, told her she could not go to school because he could only afford to pay fees for one person, and that means her brother got the priority. She had no option than to stay home, help her father with the bead embroidery, and kept home to cook, clean, and do laundry. "It was during the two years before I went to live with my grandmother and great grandmother that I learned bed embroidery" she interjected.

Nike was a few months away from her eighth birthday when her grandmother (Adire designer and maker) invited her to live with her and her great-grandmother (a weaver). She described her years with both of them as one of her best childhood and teenage years—she was able to start school. The school taught craft and regular embroidery but she got her practical learning in the arts, crafts, weaving, embroidering, and Adire making from her family, specifically her grandparents and father.

Mama Nike worked very hard at school, was very disciplined, and diligent that at the time when her grandparents could no longer afford to pay for school, she received a partial scholarship from the catholic missionary which supervised the school. She needed to come up with 15 shillings (per term) to make up the difference and stay in school. Determined to stay in school, Nike resorted to fetching water and firewood, etc., for sale. She made three to four shillings per month. At this point, Mama Nike pulled up her beautiful Adire long gown to show scars on her legs and knees which she said came from searching for firewood in the farms and wooded parts of the village.

She completed primary six and was at the point where she was wondering what comes next. The scholarship ended and her firewood and water venture could not raise enough money to pay for the 7th grade. Luck struck again as she got a phone call from the missionaries who recommended her for a housekeeping/baby sitter job in the next city. Although the reverend sister told her that the couple will be interviewing her first and that she is not guaranteed the job, the young Nike set out on a two-day journey, and on foot to the city. She was optimistic and just hoped for the opportunity to get an interview.

She got the job and was excited to learn she would be paid one British pound per month (that is 20 shillings). When the couple asked her to go and get her luggage so she could start work immediately, Nike who had arrived in her school uniform, the only decent clothing she possessed, told her new employers, that she had no luggage and she is ready to start. Nike said she looked so dirty and barefoot after two days on the rod that her new employer decided that she could not sleep in the house that first night. She was given an old mat and asked to sleep in the corridor. The next morning, she cleaned up in the back of the house before she received instructions on housekeeping responsibilities.

The issue of communicating became both challenging as well as an opportunity—to Nike. The couple, expatriates from India spoke only English and Nike quickly learned to communicate by hand, headshakes, eye movement, etc. "I learned what I now know as the concept of non-verbal communication. The couple tolerated me and I had the opportunity to improve on my English language" she said smiling.

When she returned at the age of 15, her father decided to marry her off to a local government officer for a dowry of about five British pounds. She arrived at her new husband's home to discover she would become the fifth wife. Nike said she looked so young and skinny that her husband handed her over to the first wife with instructions to feed and "fatten" her up within a year before he could consummate the marriage. She attempted three failed escapes before she succeeded in the fourth.

She hitch-hiked to Oshogbo from Kabba to join a cousin's family. She could not run home because her father would not harbor or protect her and she was not sure if her cousin's family would accept her but they did. Nike remembers, credits her courage to go to Oshogbo as a major break in her life. She remembered getting to work immediately to become financially independent as soon as possible. With a few blank pages and pencils, she went to work, painting black and white Adire and selling them by the roadside.

She made progress as she improved on her paintings and beading art. In the process, she got married and found herself in a polygamous relationship with 14 co-wives. She described her 15 years in the polygamous marriage as challenging in every aspect. Still, in her teenage years, she continued to produce her art and patchwork for sale just kike her other 14 co-wives who were engaged in various retail activities. Being a full-time housewife was not an option since they were all responsible for making enough money to feed, cloth, and in most cases pay school fees for their respective children. It was not just taking care of your children, you have to render your daily account revenue to the husband who will provide for the need for children's school fees will pay out of your account. If, however, your account is not enough your children may have to drop out of school.

We (the co-wives) learned to collaborate for the sake of our children since the money surrendered to the husband at the end of the business day was never returned for feeding or clothing, that was the wives' responsibility. A few of us made more money than others, so we agreed to help each other—My patchwork and beadings business were going well. I was getting orders for specific designs and paintings and made more money than expected, Nike explained. She agreed to teach co-wives who are willing to learn the patchwork business with the agreement that only a percentage of income went to the husband. They should all learn to save possibly for a rainy day. In her case, when she could escape starting her painting and patchwork business.

Her several attempts to leave with her two children failed. When she got permission from her husband to leave it came with the condition that her children stayed back, although some of her co-wives promised to take care of her daughters, she could not leave them behind. "I felt like I was abandoning them in an orphanage" explained Nike.

Mama Nike's big break came in 1972 when she got a call from a government official who she had provided one of her designs and paintings. In her own words—"I was contacted to maybe travel to America to signature my work, wearing and embroidering." She was recommended but was not selected until 1974 and even when she got the call a new obstacle came in the name of her husband who confronted the team from the US National Museum of Art with the fact that he was Nike's husband and that she could not travel without his permission. He even claimed that she was pregnant with his child and as such will not allow her to put his child's life is at risk. After a pregnancy test, according to Nike, it was found that she was not pregnant but her husband's determination to stop her progress continued. He then claims that the only way he could allow her to travel was to be included in the trip so he could protect his "property" the wife. After further negotiations, he was allowed to travel with her. However, the delay in his efforts to stop her delayed trip and she arrived two days later than the other West African artists invited for the show. Of course, Nike was the only female from Sub-Saharan, West Africa in the show.

The trip which took Nike to most of the 50 US states was an eye-opener. Exposure to what women could do to develop society. Nike narrated how she was feted and praised by both US men and women who followed some private invitation to present at universities and organizations. The museum promised grants to establish art studios if the participant could impact their community by training and networking others' local and cultural artwork. Determined to get this grant, Nike came back and organized her 14 co-wives and started teaching them how to make a living from their "natural and traditional skills" and become more self-sufficient.

Nike said she thought she would be appropriate for finding a way to enhance family and community standards and quality of life, but the opportunity was the case. Typical of a male-dominated society, most men saw her actions as activism which was encouraging liberties to women rural communities and allowing them to challenge men's decisions. Some called her out for "desecrating" her culture. Her husband called the community leaders (all male) and the police to arrest her on the accusation that she is encouraging women to become independent and not return their earnings to their husbands. A second arrest came when all the other 14 co-wives decided to leave the marriage following her exit. Several of her arrests followed with accusations around the fact that her efforts to change the status of women in her rural community amounted to "activism" that is encouraging women to disobey husbands and, in some cases, leave their husbands. Nike had to use her sings to get herself out of police custody.

Mama Nike is one of the few African women who were able to survive as a first-generation female entrepreneur. She faced the challenges of limited formal education (taught herself the English language), escaped from child marriage and polygamous enslavement, and applied skills learned from grand and great-grandmothers to build a micro-business.

She transitioned into the second-generation female entrepreneurship with lessons from national and international exposures and is now a worldwide acknowledged artist and philanthropist. However, this transition did not come easy. The challenge of raising the start-up fund was there. She wanted to not only establish a studio for her artwork but to build a center for weaving and "Adire" production. With determination, perseverance, and hard work, Nike was able to raise and save about 10,000 Naira from her short transportation bus business (Kabu Kabu) and continued sales of her patchwork, etc., by 1982.

In 1983 she established the Nike Center for Arts and Culture at Oshogbo with her savings. The center offered free training in various artwork to all Nigerians but it started with 20 young girls who were roaming the streets of Oshogbo and had no hopes for the future. Her entrepreneurial philanthropy was born as she provided these 20 young girls with free accommodation, food, and training materials at her home in Oshogbo and taught them how to use their hands to earn a decent living and become financially independent through art. She has been able to date (2018), to touch the lives of over 3000 young women, most of whom have been violated and abused, by training them in diverse art and embroidery, and thus giving them the skills to earn some decent living.

Nike continued to work hard and grow her business. She built upon the skills she learned from her grand and great-grandmothers to develop her unique styles and techniques of textile design and painting. With experience, she found innovative ways to exhibit her work more effectively. She has developed a national and international reputation in "Adire" textile making, dyeing, weaving, painting, and embroidery (beading and threading) while bagging numerous awards and honorary doctoral degrees and certifications including:

> 2019—Doctor of Fine Arts (Honoris Causa) by Rhodes University, South Africa (2019)
> 2015—Plaque of Excellence by the "Yoruba Arts and Festival Promotion Organization of Nigeria for her outstanding vision, dedication, and commitment to excellence in Art, Culture, and Fashion design.
> 2014—She received the "Women Inspirational Award from" Kogi State (her home) Women Association in recognition of her efforts in motivating and economically empowering the rural women in the state.
> 2015—She received another Women Inspirational Award from the Committee of Wives of Lagos State Official in recognition of her valuable contributions to the empowerment of women in Nigeria.
> 2006—She was awarded "Ordine Della Stella Solidarity Italiana" one of the highest Italian national awards of merit by the Italian government in the appropriation of her efforts in using art to address and solve the problems of Nigerian prostitutes (sex workers) in Italy. Between 2005 and 2019 she had bagged 32 awards for developing the spirit of entrepreneurship, empowering women, promoting Nigeria's culture and heritage through art, and inspiring women activists.

Her hard work, dedication, resilience, internal (intrinsic) motivation, vision, pragmatic and optimistic attitude have brought her to the current status. She is currently the owner and managing director of the center she established at Oshogbo in 1983. Since then she has established the Nike Art Galleries in Lekki, Lagos, Osogbo, Ogidi-Ijumu, and Abuja, the federal capital of Nigeria, where she is the owner/curator. Specifically, in 1994 she founded the "Nike Art Production Limited."

> 1996—She established a textile (Aso-oke) weaving center at Ogidi-Ijummu which employs 200 rural women.
> 2002—She established an Art and Cultural Research Center in Abuja (FCT) with an art gallery and textile museum—the first of its kind in Nigeria to provide a functional platform for research into the Nigerian traditional textile industry.
> 2007—She incorporated the "Nike Art Gallery Limited" and the "Nike Research Center for Art and Culture Limited."

In addition to the galleries, museums, research centers, Nike has diversified into art education, tourism, and publication. The company provides a group of tourists with accommodation and meals at the center's guided tour of art facilities are provided by trained staff.

Nike credits the above accomplishments to hard work and determination, and her vision for promoting Nigeria's culture and traditions through art as well as promoting and empowering women who are naturally artistic and embodies the true cultures of Nigeria and Africa. She also acknowledges the support of her national and international allies (including her ex-British husband) with whom she still regards as a friend. This marriage ended in divorce in 1992 but they had two beautiful girls together.

Nike speaks of her four daughters (two from her polygamous husband and two with her British ex) with pride. She displays pictures of her and her daughters on postcards and business vehicles and she is proud to have them in her establishments.

Nike believes that although she still experiences organizational, management, and other business challenges, she confident that the worst is behind her and is very hopeful of the future as the nation and the continent moves toward an entrepreneurial economy with equal opportunities for women in all sectors!

Sources:
In addition to the personal interview, January 22, 2020.
Other sources—www.nikeartfoundation.com—www.nikeartfoundation.org.
Stitches of Partnership (V); Paintings by Nike & Tola Wewe.

Mrs. M.A. Anyansi SUPER MARKET: [On and Off Beer License]

Inspiration: *"The need to be Financially independent and be able to provide for my personal needs and those of my children without (always) having to wait on my husband's schedule"*

Three weeks after we moved to our new house located strategically on a busy major road, my siblings and I walked home from school to find our mother directing a carpenter on where and how to position the above sign [*Mrs. M.A. Anyansi Super Market: On and Off Beer License*] above the double door entrance to her new and latest enterprise facility.

She was very excited when this two-story building was completed and her husband (our father) agreed to let her continue her expanding business venture in one of the large store spaces on the ground floor. This was our father's way of discouraging or stopping her from making the daily round trip to Ogbete Main Market where she bought a double-spaced stall for her onions, smoked fish, and Irish potatoes business.

Personal Background:

Mama, as she was called by her children and other extended relatives was born in 1914, in the eastern region of a small town in Anambra State, Nigeria. She was the youngest of four children and the only girl. Unfortunately, she lost her mother at the tender age of three and was raised by her father and brothers. More sad news followed as the family's oldest son was kidnapped following a period of robbery and kidnapping around the community. Her father moved the family to her maternal home where she was guarded in a way she referred to as "being in prison." She was only allowed to move within the fenced compound walls. As a result of this restricted movement, she could not attend a school which was far away from the grandmother's house. However, when the family returned to their home in 1924, Mama was able to start school. She completed primary four education and had to stop because of limited family financial resources. Her two older brothers had the priority.

According to Mama, she was at the ripe age of 14 or 15 for possible marriage. She narrated her initial encounter with her would-be husband, Anthony Nwankwo Anyansi. "We met these two men while I was on an errand in the company of three other girls. They stopped us to ask for directions, and although I was still very skeptical about boys and men who I still see s robbers and kidnappers I picked up the courage and responded to their request." A few weeks later, she saw these same two men at her house. She was surprised when her father, in the traditional process, told her that they were there to for her hand in marriage. She avoided the suitor and his family, several times until her aunt convinced her that she will be alright following the aunt's conversations with her "would-be mother and father-in-law." They wedded officially in January 1933 at a catholic church.

Before the traditional betrothal (wedding) of Mama, in 1930, she was first sent to an older married female marriage counselor for marital and home keeping courses and training. She later was sent to Adazi Catholic Women's Economic Center for one year. Upon graduation, Ama returned to her betrothal husband's home who was then based in Ogoja. The marriage was blessed with 13 live births (five boys and eight girls). By the time Mama passed on to be with her maker in January 2017 and at the ripe age of 103 years, she was a proud grandmother of 33, great-grandmother of 57, and great, great-grandmother of four. She was survived by seven of her children.

Entrepreneurial ventures/business life:
Several weeks after arriving in Ogoja, Mama's entrepreneurial "batteries" were charged up. According to our father, he came home one evening to find a small retail table (Affia Table) set up in front of the house. She told him, she was bored and could not just sit at home after cooking and cleaning until he returns. She had paid a nearby carpenter to make her a cheap table. Her start-up capital was a few shillings she received from her family as a wedding gift. There was only one item on the table—"Kola nut." Kola nut is a popular snack for adults in the northern Nigerian town. She said that even though this was her first time of coming into a city of this size, she observed that people chew kola nut all the time, including her husband. A neighbor helped her find a place where she could buy them wholesale. She also learned how to preserve them and keep them fresh until they were all sold. She lost some money early at the start of the business because some kola nuts dried up before she could sell them.

Six months later, the items on the table expanded from one to eight. There was a homemade kola nut complement (ose-oji made from roasted peanuts, peppers, and local spices), dry crayfish, onions, assorted vegetables, etc. In addition to the growing "Affia" table, Ama had started making and selling a popular breakfast drink—"Burukutu" which takes her most of the night to grind, sift, and mix the millet which was the main ingredient for "burukutu" (similar to coco but preferred by residents of the plateau area). In the middle of the business venture was the daily routine trip to the market to deliver lunch to her husband. Mama thrived in her "Affia" table while raising their first four children. However, tragedy struck, she lost two of these children, and therefore after eight years in Ogoja, the family moved southeast to Enugu, a bigger city and the then capital of the eastern region.

Upon arrival in Enugu (where the rest of the children were born) Mama wasted no time in resuming her entrepreneurial activities. She attached herself to a family friend's wife to learn and find a spot for her

"Akara" (fried black bean balls), "Akara local custard, and Okpa (a local bean cake)." She wasted no time in drawing customers in their new neighborhood known as "Hausa" quarters. In her dealings with customers and residents at Ogoja she learned to speak Hausa, Ishibori, and Munchi (Ogoja). She has also picked up two other local languages—Efik and the popular Pigeon English (adulterated/para lingual). She gained the trust of most Hausa residents especially the wives who came to her often for advice. She added, "burukutu" and "tuwo shimkafe" (ground rice and beef stew) which were two popular Hausa meals to her business. She had the opportunity to put her new **Singer brand** sewing machine at work when she started mending clothes for the children and neighbors. She was sewing simple dresses for neighbors as a business.

When asked why she had to work so hard, she indicated that she was in a better position to make money for the family which has just relocated to a new city. "My husband left his clothing materials business and contract with 'John Holt Nig. Ltd.' in Ogoja, and he is currently almost an apprentice in the building materials and construction business" she explained. In an answer to the question of how profitable her business was, she said she was doing very well since she was able to feed her family, help pay rent, and clothe her children as well as their school fees.

In about 12 years her husband (papa) was well established in his building materials and construction business that he built a new house about seven blocks outside the Hausa quarters. The family moved and so did Mama's business enterprise. Her husband could not convince her to stop trading. She told him that business (entrepreneurship) is in her "system." "I discovered that at the catholic domestic center, where we were often challenged to come up with some activity that will help enhance and sustain our married life. I won nine out of ten times – I always came up with moneymaking ideas, be it gardening, cooking, or baking."

Mama reopened her "Affia" table with mostly dry goods. In a few months, she constructed a movable and lockable kiosk with pieces of wood she collected from her husband's construction site. Her creative nature told her that it was easy to find cover for the kiosk, roles it into the hallway at night rather than continue to individually pack all the items, and the rest the next morning. Sooner than later, there were other products in the Kiosk. There were bundles of firewood, small coal bags (Enugu is popularly known as a coal city) and when Mama discovered that many residents cooked with coal instead of firewood, she found a way to purchase extra bags from coal mines and retailed them. When we (the children) needed "brown paper" to cover our textbooks, she cut through the layers of empty cement bags (from her husband's building sites) cleaned and straightened them for us. Before we knew it, book covers from brown cement bags became part of the products sold. We (the children) could never forget the following seasonal products in Mama's entrepreneurial ventures.

1. The "Ogazi" eggs (guinea fowl) which we had to hawk around the Ogbete industrial center, known as "Tinker" with instructions to keep our eyes wide open when and if we get surrounded by more than three individuals to avoid stealing which occurs when friends engage in "egg-gambling games." Sometimes the intent is to distract the seller and steal from them.
2. The fresh corn—boiled roasted, was another business unit set up in the evening under the street light and manned by one or two of the children. The same went for the fresh orange season, roasted and boiled peanuts. The roasted corn was sold hot under the electric pole while the peanuts (roasted and boiled) were cooked at home. Oranges were peeled in an artistic design. Roasted peanuts were shelled and unshelled. The salted and shelled was sold with a complimentary item of popcorn that Mama made at home. The unshelled was systematically soaked in reddish soil dried and then roasted with white dry sand for a special flavored taste. We learned to compete with each other, figured out our marketing strategies, and found ways to build and retain loyal customers who would only buy from us. The goal was to finish selling before others.

We (the children) all took a breath of relief when Mama decided to scale up, leave the home-based businesses, and open a "shop" stall shed at the Ogbete min market (second-largest market in Nigeria, after Onitsha market which is the largest in West Africa). One of my older siblings remembers the exact location and line#—"E, Shed #9." This was an all-women line with retail items such as onions, Irish potatoes, smoked fish, crayfish, etc., Mama ordered goods from the north, taking advantage of traders who were renters in one house but dealt mostly in wholesale items from the north. She had a direct supply of onions, Irish potatoes, and smoked fish from their traders. Although we no longer hawked boiled Ogazi eggs and corn, we had to spend Saturday mornings at the market opening and sorting onions and fish into different sizes. She also continued to sell Ogazi eggs, not cooked but raw. She ordered large quantities to other women who focused on retailing. The business was going very well according to Mama's standard and the yardstick for measuring success-

- "I make enough so as not to ask your father for an unnecessary allowance."
- "Enough to give you, children, pocket money to make up what you get from your father."
- "Enough to buy new clothes for you all without waiting until feasts such as Christmas, ester, or when you are heading back to school when men believe is the on-time children need clothes."
- "I make enough to buy my organizations' uniforms without waiting for your father for money!"
- "It allows me to share my blessings with others who are in need."
- "Most importantly, it gives me financial independence and pride! – she concluded with a gesture that signaled she was done."

In 1962 when her husband completed what he called the family house, a block away from the current location, Mama got another opportunity to scale up. This two-story building was strategically located on a major roadway. With intersecting streets, a bus stop, a small private maternity clinic, a culinary pickup and drop stop, and small shops at adjacent houses. The family occupied the entire top floor while the ground floor had two large spaces built for business rentals. Mama got to open her supermarket store—"Mrs. M.A. Anyansi Supermarket with On and Off Beer License." The Ogbete market operation was shut down as the large store space was fitted with a giant refrigerator, freezer, and the four levels of shelves stocked with all types of imported products from canned to packaged food items, snacks, cigarettes, matchboxes, candies, etc. She created a section for local items including condiments and fresh vegetables which she was able to buy very early in the morning from women who were heading to the market from the nearby rural village (Agbani). She would buy vegetables like spinach, bitter leaf, okra, and other greens in large bundles, and retail them in smaller quantities, the location of the new house made it possible for such purchases as the women must pass in front of the house (Agbani Road) to get to the market.

Within a few weeks, the store space was expanding with locally made awnings to accommodate evening customers who had their beer on the spot (the on license). Visitors to the next-door photography studio and bus stop provided most of the customers in her innovative and creative thinking style she soon added roasted chicken and meat, for beer drinkers. In the afternoon she sold meat roll, puff-puff, and chin-chin, all local snacks, to school children, especially those from Immaculate Heart Girls School, 90% of who must pass in front of her store to get home.

Management and Book Keeping:
Mama, as many of her customers, as well as neighbors, called her, continued to grow, manage, and add seasonal items, to her business. In addition to managing her business, she later went into the poultry business by constructing cages in the backyard. She kept the family on their toes. As a disciplinarian, she made sure every child including relatives who shared her home went to school, worked, and house chores. She made sure she prepared most of the family meals especially those that her husband (Papa) ate. When she did not make them (as she tried to teach us, including the boys, how to cook), she supervised. She belonged to many women's organizations and served as treasurer for two (Sacred Heart Catholic Women's Association and Abagana Women's Organization) for many years.

I had the privilege of recording daily revenues for her business and also recorded dues and fines for her organizations. She kept the cash and books, she always cross-checked the catch with my recordings. Although Mama, like most of her peers and even more than her peers who were semi-illiterate, could count numbers, recite alphabets in vernacular (Igbo), and recognize some English words, I was amazed at her level of intelligence and understand when my bookkeeping misrepresented her record. Sometimes, when I am not immediately able to record, she will leave cash in the register overnight. On this particular occasion, there was a discrepancy or shortage of £1 in my record. We argued for a while before she invited me to her bedroom to confirm the accuracy of her recording.

She opened a cloth blind at one corner of the room revealing chalk marks on the wall. These were color-coded and in symbols. She pointed to the section that belonged to the store revenue and pointed to the total which was £1 more than my entry in the register. She asked me to go back and check the drawer in my room, where she put the register and the money. Of course, I shared this room with one of my sisters and thus my first reaction was to ask her if she removed any money from the register? She answered in negative and as I went back to my room to do a second check, I found one pound (£1) under one of my exercise books. I was doing my homework when I pulled the register to record sales. The one-pound must have slipped from the bundle.

I had to ask Mama about her codes when I went back to correct my mistake. She gave me a lesson on what I later on in life (when I was in college) learned to be a statistical recording. She had strokes in bundles representing different amounts—there were symbols for five, 10s, 20s, 40s, 80s, and 100 pounds. The shillings and pence (coins) were wrapped in papers and in specific amounts. I saw symbols such as ////, 0000, ZZZZ, YY, etc. She told me she knew exactly what each meant. Mama, with her limited formal education, created her own accounting or bookkeeping system. Sacred Heart Catholic Women Association accounts were in the red, while Abagana Women's Organization was recorded in the green color and her business was in black. In between these were other colors used to differentiate specific amounts for each group.

Mama was proud and eager to let me know that both associations have always found their money complete at the annual balancing with the financial secretary who was usually young and more educated.

Mama's multiple and diverse business ventures were doing well until the Nigeria Civil War of 1967–1970 disrupted everything and the family was forced to evacuate from Enugu to home town of Abagana and in less than six months was again forced to move and ended up as refugees in another town for over two years. You may not believe it but Mama was always looking for opportunities to trade even in the refugee camp. She sold some of her jewelry and wrappers during the war to buy food or exchange for food to feed her family.

Personal and Entrepreneurial Characteristics:
Mama as everyone who came in contact with her called her except her husband (Papa) who called her "Mrs." Her peers called her "Gold" as a tribute to her beauty. Her kindness, goodness, and humanitarian gestures toward others were noteworthy. As much as she never established a formal foundation or social enterprise, she indicated that part of her motivation to make her own money was to help the needy. In many of our annual

vacations from the city to the village, we spent the first three to four days delivering packages to families especially widows with children. Each package included rice, onions, salt, beans, garri, cooking oil, etc. Some families also receive clothing for children and wrappers for adults. She inculcated the habit of charity (be it is kind or cash) among her children. She was very outspoken, she stood for the truth and justice for all and was very inspiring. Her intelligence and ability to retain and remember historical details and narrate them systematically earned her titles such as "great orator, oral historian, action-oriented, supercomputer, authoritative but fair, and disciplinarian."

Mama embodied most of the entrepreneurial characteristics that has been described as evidenced by her enterprising ventures. She was very creative, resourceful, innovative, brave, opportunistic, and in some situations, necessity-driven. She was very goal-oriented, intrinsically motivated, high aspirations, pragmatic, etc.

Some of the above characteristics were aptly depicted in the tributes shared over time from family, friends, and community. Some of these phases are presented below:

- "*You were a caring and giving mother. We never lacked. You thought us to be entrepreneurs at a young age and you said it is more blessing to give than to receive. You preached respect, love, and discipline.*" Son Tony
- "*The pride and most beautiful of the family, who loves truth and generosity. You taught us to be always truthful in all our dealings with others.*" Daughter Esther
- "*Mama, you were a school of thought to many young women who had close observation of you, you were a model mother of faith, truth, advisor, hater of idleness, and enforcer of discipline.*" Admirer
- "*Your memory marveled us as you can remember to ask about many grand and great-grandchildren by name.*" Grand Children
- "*Mama your life is worth emulating as you were always honest and forthright in your praise and criticism.*" Victor/Son-in-law
- "*Mama, during your golden years your brain was still active and all your sensors were receptive.*" Chuma/Grand Child
- "*One of the ever-important lessons you gave me was be good to people because nobody will ever spit out something that is sweet.*" Ime/Grandchild

- "*Mama was the type of person who is always willing to help however she could, extremely humble and resourceful, never afraid of new environment and always willing to teach those around her valuable lesson.*" Tony/Grandchild
- "*Mama was a wife, mother, and contractor. Making sure nobody miscalculated the bags of cement, blocks, and bags of nails that the husband used in building houses. How did Mama do that with limited education? By making lines on the wall and crossing them in tens, fives, etc.*" Chinweoke/Daughter
- "*Mama, we call you supercomputer because of your sharp memories, very comprehensive in historical events, Outspoken, disciplinarian with compassionate soul, hardworking, and committed.*" Rev. Sister Josephine/Daughter
- "*The ultimate measure of a successful life is not valued by its duration but by the inspirations and contributions to other lives. Mama embodied strength, exuded love, joy, hard work, and grace.*" Emma/Granddaughter

Finally, in a few words, Mama was a genius, naturally intelligent, perceptive, energetic, outspoken and maybe bold especially when injustice is around the corner, determined, disciplinarian, leader, organizer, etc., but first and foremost she was an entrepreneur—a seasonal entrepreneur.

Source:
 Conversations with the Entrepreneur, her children, grandchildren, friends, and admirers

Salwa Idrissi Akhannouch [Princess of Business and Queen of Fashion]

Founder and CEO AKSAL—Morocco Mall Group of Companies

Inspiration: *Desire to promote equal opportunity for all people through Advocacy*

Salwa Akhannouch is the daughter of Boulagoul Idrissi, a Berber family from the small village of Agnerd-Oudad, Tafraout, and the wife of Aziz Akhannouch, a wealthy business man, and well-known politician. Salwa was born in Casablanca in 1985.

Salwa started her business and built on the fortune she inherited from her grandfather, Haj Ahmed Benlafkih who was a businessman. He dominated the Moroccan tea trade in the 1960s. With this background, she is often being referred to as being born with "golden spoon" in her mouth. However, she has managed to succeed on her own building on the inheritance and capitalizing on her connections and contacts in a country where being a businesswoman is a struggle and full of challenges which in most cases are not of legal or regulatory nature. The struggle is that of stereotyping where the woman has to override the "cultural breaks" if she wants to engage in entrepreneurial venture. In many cases, the woman will have to self-sensor and self-limit and fail to convince herself of the value of her own projects relative to family well-being. She is said to have an impeccable "baksahbi" which is the Moroccan term for having connections and money. She and her husband have three children and mostly are in agreement about having privacy when it comes to family.

All the same, Salwa who had always advocated for women advancement as well as equal opportunity for all, did not waste the opportunities to start business and built an empire of her own. Her entrepreneurial adventures began in 2003 when she created a distribution company for floor-laying materials and immediately followed up with specialization in franchises with Zara in 2004 followed by Massimo Dutti brand in 2006.

In 2011, Salwa opened the Morocco Mall, the largest second shopping center in Africa built at the cost of $240 million in 2007. Guinness World Records (2012) called it the "largest in-store shop façade." Aksal, the parent company owns 50% of the mall. The Moroccan leader in luxury goods, department stores, and retail shopping centers and generates turnover of over 5 billion Moroccan Dirhams ($514 million). The Conglomerate also owns exclusive and sole franchise in Gucci, Fendi, Banana Republic, Massimo Dutti, and Gap. Her love and admiration for luxury which is the background of her Morocco mall includes her pride brands of Prada, Miu Miu, or Louis Viutton which she claimed were not "canvassed" but just emerged.

Salwa's ambition is to make her brand the biggest shopping mall of Africa, second only to South Africa, and possibly dethrone the Algerian Complex of Bab Ezzouar……… Mrs. Akhannouch's latest business is the launching of her newly created cosmetics brand Yan&One. This creation which started in 2017 was launched in the Morocco Mall on October 28, 2020. Yan&One takes a new approach to beauty with multiple products and services including makeup, beauty-care, fragrances, hygiene, accessories, and with tea served to customers while they receive services. It claims to have taken some significant investment in job creation and training with over 200 young recruits hired and trained for six months in various positions. Perfumes were created by "greatmasters of perfumers" from Grasse—World capital of perfume.

Salwa says that the brand drew inspirations from nature in Morocco with new range of "Moroccan Rituals" using such ingredients like argon oil and prickly pear oil. The word Yan in cosmetic name, Yan&One, is a Berber word for one and Salwa selected that word in honor of her roots.

It is noteworthy that Kenza Akhannouch helped in developing Yan&One. She worked on the brand strategy and helped in the implementation of this "world's first beauty smart store" and helped put Zara franchise in the spotlight www.linkedin>uk>kenza-akhannouchwww.linkedin>uk>kenza-akhannouch.

Salwa is a very ambitious, hardworking, and courageous woman. She has been dubbed Moroccan leading lady of luxury goods. She is one of the most influential entrepreneurs in Morocco and wields enormous social and political power. She is a fashion icon who attempts to maintain private personal life as a cultural respect. Forbes 2019 listed her as one of the most powerful Arab businesswomen, Business of Fashion (BOP) listed her as one of the people shaping the fashion world, and in 2012 she won the MIPIM award in Cannes for the category

Salwa represents most of the twenty-first-century African women entrepreneurs in terms of seeking business opportunities and capitalizing on them, working hard, persevering, visionary, energetic, and committed to her goals among others.

Sources:

Nsehe, M. (2013, April 24). Ten African multimillionaires You've not heard of...., Forbes. http://www.forbes.org.

Morrison, A. (2019, March 23). People in news.... Ozy. http://www.ozy.com.

Africa Top Success. (2014, February 14). Business/Salwa Idrissi Akhannouch: Princess of Business and Queen of Fashion. http://www.africatopsuccess.com/tag/Salwa-idrissi-Akhannouch-en/.

Morocco World News. (2017, October 3). Yan&One launched in Morocco Mall. http://www.moroccoworldnews.com.

Wikipedia. (2020, August 2). Salwa Idrissi Akhannouch.... http://www.en.wikipedia.org>wiki>public>salwa_idrissi_akhannouch/.

Business of fashion. (2019, September 2). Salwa Idrissi Akhannouch: Princess of Business and Queen of Fashion. http://www.thebusinessoffashion.com.

SIBONGILE SAMBO FOUNDER AND CEO OF SRS AVIATION LIMITED

Inspiration: *"Being able to invest in people because I am where I am today because someone believed and invested in me."*

Background:
Sibongile Sambo was born in 1974 in a small town in South Africa. She studied at the University of Zululand. She remembers sitting outside her watching airplanes fly by and wondering how she could get the opportunity to work in one. When she traveled to her school, according to her interview with Wisdom Exchange TV, she used to beg her mother to make her reservations with air shuttle where she might get some opportunity to sit in the cockpit with the pilot.

She described herself as a risk-taker who fears nothing. She continued to say that when she puts her mind on doing something, she went for it believing that the worst that could happen was getting the answer "No." but she was convinced that No, will never kill her, and thus "I wake up the following day and do something different." She believed that it was her positive attitude in life that has carried her to the current period.

Ms. Sambo's childhood interest in airplanes led her to apply for flight attendant position with the South African Airways. A position she did get because she did not meet the height requirement. With her university degree in accounting (having rejected recommendations to study nursing or teaching), she took a job with Telecom in Human Resources department.

SRS Aviation Ltd.
SRS Aviation Limited was launched in 2004. However, the groundwork and rekindling of this childhood obsession with airplanes began in 1994 when the government of South Africa announced a new program and policy that encouraged entrepreneurship among the citizens including women. She spent all free time reading every relevant material about establishing and managing an aviation enterprise. She attended workshops and completed forms including all regulatory agencies since this is an industry that is regulated nationally, internationally, and global. Compliance is a critical factor that cannot be compromised according to Ms. Sambo. Many friends, colleagues, and even family tried to dissuade her from continued to chase what many called a baseless dream reminding her that aviation belonged to men not women. She was also touted for not having a degree in aviation which was true.

Her determination to get approval and the license from the Ministry of Aviation motivated her to find and read every publication on aviation and types of airplanes. In one of her interview she described how she went as far as quitting her job so she could have enough time to study and learn the language of the industry. "I was so excited and danced around the day I got a letter from the ministry telling me that all the needed paper work submitted have been approved and I only need to bring in my initial schedule and itinerary as well as the qualifying aircraft or aircrafts to receive my license" Sibongile shared in the interview.

She continued by indicating how she was humbled when she realized that she could not raise the funds she needed to open her dream company. Banks had many reasons to turn down her loan application including the fact that she is a woman, had no experience in the industry, and did not have a diploma or degree in aviation. The same issue hunted her as she approached other potential financial agencies and friends. She needed $800,000.00. Funding salvation came from her mother and her aunt (who raised her) when they both cashed their pensions and invested in her dream. On the question of how she felt using her mother's and aunt's life savings without guarantee of success? Sibongile answered that she never thought of failure and that she was so "fired up with passion" and optimistic that she never even thought of that type of question. For her failure was not an option.

The rest is history, SRS was launched as a VIP charter and Helicopter services. Since then it has expanded to aircraft maintenance, sales, and fleet management services for private jet owners. Her company offers clients professional and personalized, as well as effective and affordable flight options to destinations around the world. SRS Ltd. has since expanded into Ghana and Nigerian markets and is planning to enter India. She described her challenges especially on entering international markets as that of managing the environment which is different from the home base. Policies, internal regulations, and culture of doing business, etc., may be different and it is important that as a business person that you understand and comply with these especially in the aviation industry. Safety and its sustainability were and still is a major challenge. "One safety miscalculation and failure could ruin your entire operation, and you don't want that." She reintegrated.

Ms. Sambo described her leadership and management style as that of learning to build relationship with all stakeholders including her employees as well as partnership with competitors in the industry. For example, she said that SRS "partnership agreement with MCC Aviation allows her company to share office, staff, etc. which keeps the overhead low. We are in a niche market and quality and timely services guarantee us the word of mouth advertisement. Leadership style is based on flexible but determined negotiation with stakeholders. 'I learned negotiations skills by watching my mother negotiate prices at the market,' Sibongile said in the interview. She offered an example of the negotiated salary cuts in her company during the recession and never lost an employee. She credited this success to team effort which she had built in her company. She explained by adding that many people may not look at their mothers" as leaders but they (mothers) truly have all the skills that demonstrate leadership. They are resourceful and diligent as they manage the family budget, raise the children, manage their education and aspirations, etc.

Ms. Sambo credits her positive attitude, open-minded attitude to opportunities, perseverance, ability to think outside the box, visionary attitude, building effective network, communication by learning to speak the language of your enterprise, etc., for her successes. Her successes have earned her many recognitions and awards including:

- 2006—BWA's Regional Business Women of the Year for Start-up Category
- 2006—BIBA [Black women In Business Award]
- 2006—Impumelelo Top Female Entrepreneur of the Year
- 2008—BMF [Black Management Forum Presidential Award in Youth Leadership]
- 2008—Featured in World Bank's Report; Doing Business in Africa…Women
- 2009—Nominated for Queen Victoria Memorial Award (International Socrates Award) by European Business Assembly in London
- 2010—International Women's Entrepreneurial Challenge [IWEC] Award.

In addition to the above accolades, Ms. Sambo is also affiliated with several professional and business organizations including, South Africa's Women Entrepreneurs Network [SAWEN], Southern Africa Women in Aviation [a nonprofit organization that encourages women to seek career in aviation], Women of Color in Aviation and Aerospace in the USA, and Women in Aviation International [WAI].

Ms. Sambo believes that her philosophy of always checking or questioning her intentions and why she is living in this world is what keeps her grounded. She joked on the fact that she still receives mails addressing her as "Mr. Sambo" and she attributes that to the reality that society is yet to accept the fact that a woman would engage in and succeed in aviation industry—a sector reserved for men.

Ms. Sambo, a mother of two young boys, said that she has refused to be changed by the industry. She travels a lot, nationally and internationally. She tries to be assertive without being rude. She dresses professionally for board meetings, does her homework, speak the industry language, and maintain visibility and these have earned her recognition and respect in her company and the industry.

Her advice to the African woman entrepreneur is "As women in Africa, we have so many opportunities to enter any industry, embrace them, however, we must not forget our responsibilities at home."

Sources:

Wikipedia. (2013, April 20). Twenty Young Power Women in Africa. http://www.en.wikipedia.org>Sabongile_Sambo.

eNCA. (2014, August 29). Profiles of remarkable women. Lioness of Africa August Women. http://www.lionessofafrica.com>blog>tag>Sibongile+Sambo.

Stevens, S.F. (2014, June 24). Wisdom Exchange TV. http://www.wisdomexchangetv.com/video/Sibongile….

YouTube. (2014). Sibongile Sambo. http://www.youtube.com/watch?v=5efONmkhic.

Lioness of Africa. (2018, March 13). Entrepreneur Advice from Sibongile… http://www.lionessofafrica.com.

SRS Aviation Ltd. website: www.srsaviation.co.za.

Thabita Karanja Founder and CEO of Keroche Breweries

Inspiration: "*The Support of Kenyans have kept me going. If we support one another, we Kenyans, we Africans, we'll be able to do even bigger than what the multinationals can do*"

Thabita Karanja who has been described by the Lioness of Africa program founder Melanie Hawken as "Africa's Gender-and-Monopoly-busting Brewer" was born into what is described as a normal Kenyan family. Her mother was a farmer and her father were a government office driver. In her 26th year as an entrepreneur, she wears the multiple hats of a spouse/wife, mother of four, and a homemaker in addition to managing her Keroche Breweries.

Thabita Karanga started Keroche Breweries in 1997 as a small wine maker but soon diversified into beer and spirits in 2008. She has been referred to as being an epitome of against-all-odds' entrepreneur. She chose a part that led to confrontations from all sectors of the society including the government, banks, and of course the 87-year-old entrenched foreign multinational monopoly who saw her as a competitor. Kenyan government was equally uncooperative and at one time shut down her offices. She dared into an all-male business monopoly and succeeded in breaking the mold to become Kenya's first homegrown beer and alcohol manufacturer.

Her niche market produces quality and affordable beer products for Kenyans as well as Tanzania and Zambia where Keroche Breweries has expanded. In a video interview Ms. Karanja spoke of her planned $55 million investment for state-of-the-art facility expansion which is expected to provide for the expected 20% market share her company controls.

As one of Kenya's leading entrepreneurs she has been admired as a remarkable trailblazer, inspirational entrepreneur, motivator, and a leader. Official recognitions and awards include:

- 2010, The Moran of the Order of Burning Spear (MBS) award by President Mwai Kabila for liberalizing the liquor market in Kenya
- 2014, Business Woman of the Year, at the East African Round of the CNBC Africa Business leaders Award (AABLA)
- 2015, The Transformational Business Award from Africa Awards for Entrepreneurs (AAE)
- 2016, Entrepreneurial Excellence in Africa, in the Lifetime African Achievement Prize.

The Keroche Foundation exemplifies Thabita's vision on the empowerment of new generation of entrepreneurs. This entrepreneurial Foundation, the Young Entrepreneurs Mentorship Programs is designed to train, sponsor, and mentor the new generation. The founder has plans to extend program to other African countries and has earmarked the some of 50 million Kenyan shillings for the 2021 program.

This encouragement and support for your generation could be credited for wholesome participation of Ms. Karanja's two daughters in the

Management of the Breweries. Her oldest daughter Anerlise Mungai decided in 2013 to prove herself separately by creating and starting her own but related business. Her mother initially wanted to keep her in her company but after reviewing her ideas and plan of action gave her support.

Ms. Mungai started Nero Company Ltd. A company that produces high end bottled water—Executive. She later introduced a more affordable product, Life, which targets families and noncorporate market. Anerlise said that she named her company Nero because the word stands for black in Italian language and water in Greek. Differentiation and quality are her key to success. She prides herself on the fact that her water is not as salt tasty as other existing bottled water.

Anerlise, plans to open an entrepreneur school for the youth in the future. Her motivation for this philanthropic action is the finding that most of her business knowledge and experiences came from her mother and many aspiring young people do not have this opportunity.

Ms. Karanja's second daughter, Tecra Wangari Mungai, who before her accidental and sudden death on May 2, 2020, was credited with and recognized as the brain behind most of the marketing strategies and innovation, including branding, for Keroche Breweries.

Source:
SABC News. (2015, March 4). Video Interview: Thabita Karanja. www.sabc.com.
Hawken, M. (2015, March 5). Lioness of Africa, Thabita Karanja. http://www.lionessofafrica.com.
YouTube. (2020, May 3). Tecra Mungai's death. http://www.youtube.com/nabiswa.
Keroche Breweries Ltd. (2020). http://www.kerochebreweries.com.

Isabel Dos Santos Isabel Dos Santos Group of companies

Inspiration: *Likes being close to the Youth especially students because their energy inspires her.*

Isabel Dos Santos responded to the question of who she is as follows, "I am Angolan, woman, mother, business woman, and an entrepreneur." This Africa's richest woman and first African female billionaire, according to Forbe's magazine (2013 and 2019) was born in 1973 in Baku, Azerbaijan. She is the eldest daughter of former Angolan president, Jose Eduardo Dos Santos (1979–2017), and mother, Tartiana Kukanova, a

Russian born and first wife of the Angolan president. She has dual nationality of Russia and Angola.

Ms. Dos Santos and her husband Sindika Dokolo have three children. The couple met in college and he is the son of a millionaire from Kinshasa, Democratic Republic of Congo and a Danish mother.

Ms. Dos Santos attended an all-girls boarding school in Kent, England. She studied electrical engineering at Kings College, London, England, where she met her husband.

Entrepreneurial Ventures:
Ms. Dos Santos returned to Angola in the early 1990s and joined the father in Luanda where she worked as a project manager engineer for a company who won a contract to disinfect and clean the city, Urbana 2000, a Subsidiary of Jember's Group.

Her first business venture was a trucking company, but the widespread use of walkie-talkie technology paved her way into telecom industry. In 1997 she started what might be deemed her first fully owned business—The Miami Beach Club, one of the first night clubs and beach restaurants on Luanda Island. In the next 20 years, Dos Santos built her wealth by investing and taking stakes in companies doing business in Angola.

Some of the holdings built in over twenty years include:

- Trans Africa Investment Services: A Gibralter-based vehicle founded together with her mother for the diamond business operations
- Unitel International Holdings B.V.: Name change from Kento and Jadeuim based in Amsterdam, vehicle for investment in telecommunication
- Santoro Finance: Vehicle for investment in Banco BPI based in Lisbon
- Esperaza Holding B.V.: based in Amsterdam for oil, energy, etc.
- Condis: A retail chain based in Luanda, Angola.

Ms. Dos Santos has diversified internationally with investment operations in Portugal, Netherlands, Spain, Cape Verde, etc. Some investments in Portugal, starting in 2008, include her interests in telecommunications, media, retail, finance, and energy industry in Angola and Portugal. In addition to commercial interests in oil and diamonds, she owns shares in the Angolan Cement company, Nova Cimangola; Jadeium which is owned by Santos acquired 4.9% of ZON Multimedia shares from Spain's

Telefonica. However, through her Unitel International Holding B.V. (Netherlands), she became the main shareholder of ZON multimedia with over 29% interest in 2012. Other major stakes include partnerships and relationships in Angolan State oil company, Sonangol, Founding member of Banco BIC Portugues, which acquired the nationalized Banco Portugues de Negocios. In 2013 the merger of ZON and Sonaecom created the new company, ZOPT.

In Angola specifically, Dos Santos in 2017, used her ownership in Unitel to acquire 2% interest in Banco Fomento De Angola (BFA) from BPI and thus owns a controlling share of 51% of the bank. Most of her telecommunications focus includes the Unitel created in partnership with Portugal telecom; acquisition of the mobile operator T+ in Cape Verde and also received the license to open a second telecom company in Sao Tome and Principe. Dos Santos promised that Unitel will invest in education in Sao Tome and Principe to train engineers, managers, and other technicians with a focus on creating jobs in the community where her diverse family background has roots. Her grandparents from her father's side were from Sao Tome and Principe. In 2015 Dos Santos invested in the Satellite TV operation, ZAP with the rights to distribute Forbes magazine in a number of Portuguese-speaking countries including Portugal, Angola, and Mozambique.

Isabel Dos Santos life and entrepreneurial ventures could be described as nothing but success after success. She seeks opportunities and strategically employ her negotiation skills and connections to make business deals. In her storyline on her website, she reintegrates the need for countries and businesses to include women in leadership positions. She indicated that women's intrinsic qualities which is a great competitive advantage could be seen in their performance of responsibilities as mothers, daughters, spouse, homemaker, etc., and entrepreneurs. She believed that these women possess and share social and communication skills, they have good judgment, they are innovative and creative, have great problem-solving abilities, and team leadership capabilities. She called all of these "essential ingredients for leading and managing a business or a country."

She credits African women with flexible, versatile, and multitasking abilities. Ability to implement and monitor projects which she believed are critical factors for success. She sees the future as promising for women as awareness of their impactful contributions in society—from family to business world, in politics, entertainment, sciences, technology, etc., reach unparalleled level.

Ms. Dos Santos' energy, determination, perseverance, goal orientation, and other entrepreneurial attributes speak for themselves as you observe her entrepreneurial ventures and contributions to her country and the world. She is an advocate of equal opportunity for all irrespective of gender, religion, or ethnic origin. She calls on African women to make themselves heard and make a difference. She is convinced that youth and entrepreneurship are the future of Africa and the following statement sums it up… "I believe in talent, and every day I invest in empowering the next generation of leaders because the development of Africa and my country is my priority as an Angolan business woman."

Sources:
Website: www.isabeldossantos.com.
Google Search. (2020, August 28). Isabel Dos Santos. http://www.en.wikipedia.org>wiki>Isabel_dos_santos.

Martha Catherine Agwang

Serial Micro-preneur and Founder, Uganda Youth Development and Training (UYDT)

Inspiration: *Intrinsically driven by need to do the right thing; do what she loves especially when challenged; and to inspire all African women to thrive and change the current status quo*

Martha Agwang was born on February 9, 1983 to family of 10 children, seven girls, and three boys. She is the oldest and as such had to bear most of the family expectations from the oldest child especially a female. In a traditional Ugandan family, she is expected to help take care of the other nine siblings including cleaning, cooking, gardening, or farming for food, etc. The family was within the poverty bracket and parents were peasant farmers that only worked for food for survival of the family.

As the family grew so did expenditures for basic needs like food, medical bills, school fees, etc. Her mother became more hard-working and resourceful as she led the children into farming for cash crops which was much needed to help pay for school fees, clothing especially school uniforms, and other necessities.

Martha's childhood (0–18 years) was full of challenges not just because she was the oldest but also, she was a female. She described her role in the family, especially when her mother got very sick and was hospitalized as automatically taking over her role as head of the family. "I will always stand as a head of the family in raising my own siblings (finding food for them, Cooking, getting school materials ……and making sure they attend school, including visiting school as their older sister and family representative, getting clothing, and many other needs. In addition, I did the farm work at home and coordinated all work at other gardens. And I also had to go to school and do my school work as well." Martha explained that sometimes she was amazed as to how she was able to take care of her siblings starting from the age of nine and in primary three. Between the ages of 10 and 17 she coordinated various activities at home and community where she would engage the rural community children in farming including planting, weeding, spraying, harvesting, cleaning, and packaging agricultural produce for sale. She needed to sell these produces so she could help pay her mother's hospital bills.

Martha was very enthusiastic about learning and getting education despite the challenges of poverty and family responsibility. Hard work, and self-confidence earned her opportunities for higher education. She completed her university education with bachelor of science in Business Computing and Master's degree in Accounting and Finance through persistence and with scholarships from the university programs. She also completed a short course and training in leadership and governance from the Leadership Academy in Kampala and got an opportunity for a five-weeks course in entrepreneurship, leadership, and social innovation organized by the African Change Makers fellowship Program in 2018. She defied odds since by tradition and culture she was supposed to be a source of funds for her family who expected her to get married and produce generate money through her dowry payment.

Martha skipped pre-primary education because her parents could not afford the fees. She starts public primary school when she turned seven. She remembered walking, bare foot, seven miles each way to attend school. Without breakfast and no lunch at school, she was able to endure the 7 am to 4 pm school program. She was encouraging and inspired with the thought that education could be the one thing that will help change her current situation of poverty. She and her siblings woke up at 3 am and worked in the farm until about 6 am when they would clean up and get ready for school. She was very active in school and participated in many co-curriculum activities including debate team, sports, and leadership positions such as class captain and school timekeeper.

Martha's entrepreneurial spirit and ventures intensified in her secondary school years when, although her father has now started work as a gateman, his earnings did not help much with the family needs.

Although family continued to farm for revenue, she knew she needed to make extra money to support herself in secondary school. She put some of her arts and crafts skills into action. She made and sold table cloths, liquid soap, etc., to pay for school fees and uniforms. She sent home extra money to help the family. However, in her fourth year and at the age of 16, her parents especially her mother was convinced that she has had enough education as a girl child. She (her mother) believed that further education was a waste of money and it was time for her to get married. Luck smiled on her when the school headmaster offered her a scholarship to complete her O level education.

Her parents were still not happy as they went ahead to arrange for a suitor in marriage whom she practically told that she was not ready to get married. It took my grandfather who was a retired school teacher to convince my parents to allow her to continue with the next level (Advanced or A level) since she has been making good to excellent grades. She performed so well she got admitted into the top Makerere University which is well known around Africa. Once again, Martha faced the financial challenges as well as pressure from parents and community for marriage but succeeded in completing her University education by using partial scholarships, baking and selling cakes and other goodies on campus to complement her scholarship.

Entrepreneurial Ventures
Martha described her entrepreneurial adventures in economic and social welfare by outlining the challenges she faced and the drive that helped her turn the challenges into opportunities. She started with the economic entrepreneurial activities designed to earn her money for survival, with some of her business ventures happening between the ages of 14–18. She remembers a particular period when a new breed of groundnuts (peanuts) seeds, promoted in the community for yielding higher and better yield crop than the current seed. According to Martha, the new variety was very expensive and her parents were out of town because of her mother's illness. Family had no money but there was maize in the home so she took the initiative and sold the maize. She then bought the new variety of groundnuts. She planted the groundnuts and the yield was more than she expected. Her profit from the sales of this new breed was more than enough to cover the family's expenditure including her mother's hospital bill.

She and her siblings at various times sold soya nuts, small baked bread, deep fried and roasted cassava on the streets during the holidays. In addition to holiday business activities were college entrepreneurial ventures of making and selling table cloths, birthday cakes, etc., to students and faculty so she can meet her school needs especially books and other personal needs.

Post university education found Martha working in several organizations such as the Cavendish University, African Rural University, Uganda Rural Development and Training Program including Non-government organizations like the Red Cross and Action Aid Uganda. Experiences from these positions inspired and helped Ms. Agwang start over five businesses which failed. However, she never gave up. Her optimistic attitude, experiences, and values such as doing the right thing and "helping people around me always made it possible for me to bounce back" she concluded.

Ms. Agwang is currently the founder and Chief Executive Officer of Uganda Youth Development and Training Program (UYDT). UYDT is, according to Martha, both an economic and social enterprise which delivers programs designed to train microenterprises and support growth. It also creates jobs and builds communities. Martha recently started a bakery business in collaboration with three other women.

Her motivations for founding UYDT were based on her experiences as a young girl in rural Uganda and the struggles she had to go through to get meaningful education. She still saw young girls struggling and many, even in the twenty-first century, still believe that the culture that defined them without adequate education, good for household responsibilities, and later a source of revenue for the family when the dowry comes from marriage, etc., are their ultimate destiny. Most importantly, she wrote that the thought of seeing fellow African women who were (and still are in some Ugandan clans) being regarded as "donkeys, properties, and many more" drove her toward this training and motivational program which focuses more on girls and women.

According to Ms. Agwang, this is a transformational center where different groups of people in the community will meet, be trained, mentored, nurtured, economically empowered, and supported so as to change the lives in their homes and communities. Her goal is to develop a critical mass of value-driven citizens especially among women, who will take responsibilities for their own situations without necessarily waiting on someone else to do it for them.

Sources:
http://www.uydt.org.

Email Communications with Ms. Agwang, followed by documentation titled "African Women Entrepreneurs and their challenges/Agwang Catherine Martha/August, 2020."

References

Academy of Management (AFAM) 5th Biennial Conference. (2020). *Globalization, pan Africanism, and the African business climate*. Hosted by Lagos Business School, January 8–11, Lagos, Nigeria. https://www.africaacademyofmanagement.org.

Adusei, M. (2016). Does entrepreneurship promote economic growth in Africa. *African Development Review, 28,* 201–214.

Africa Continent. www.Britannica.com/Place/Africa.

Africa's Secret Weapon: The Diaspora. www.CNN.com, 1 November 2013.

African Union (AU) meeting in Kigali, Uganda. (2018). *Establishing the Africa continental free trade agreement*. www.youtube.com. Retrieved August, 2020.

Ahmed, F., & Charrad, M. M. (2002). States and women rights: The making of post-colonial Tunisia, Algeria, and Morocco. *Contemporary Sociology, 3*(1).

Ahmed, N., & Salvadori, K. (2020). *Building 2Africa: A transformational subsea cable for better connectivity*. https://engineering.fb.com/connectivity/2africa.

Allam, A., & Nwankwo, S. (2013). Entrepreneurship development in Africa: An overview. *World Journal of Entrepreneurship Management and Sustainable Development, 9,* 82–86.

Alvord, S. H., et al. (2004). Social entrepreneurship and societal transformation: An exploratory study. *The Journal of Applied Behaviioral Science*. www.Sagepub.com; https://doi.org/10.1177/002188634266847.

Ammar, N. H., & Lababidy, L. S. (2002). Women's grassroot movements and democratization in Egypt. In J. M. Bystydzienski & J. Sekhon (Eds.), *Democratization and women's grassroot movements* (pp. 150–179). Bloomington, IN and New Delhi, India: Indiana University Press and Kali for Women.

Ankoma, B. (2020, January). *Some progress on SDGs, but still a long way to go—ACBF Report*, New African, an IC Publication.

Anyansi-Archibong, C. B. (1987). *Strategy and structure of enterprise in a developing country*. Avebury: Gower Publishing Company Limited, England. ISBN056605471X

Anyansi-Archibong, C. (1995). *Planning in developing countries*. Chicago, IL: The Planning Forum.

Anyansi-Archibong, C. (2005). *Role of women in the socio-economic development of the continent*. African Forum—Global Leadership Institute, University of the Virgin Island, St. Thomas, USVI.

Anyansi-Archibong, C. (2014). African entrepreneurs and their philanthropies: Motivations, challenges, and impact. In M. Taylor, et al. (Eds.), *Handbook of research on entrepreneurs' engagement in philanthropy: Perspectives*. Northampton, MA: Edward Edgar Publishing Inc.

Anyansi-Archibong, C. B. (1996). African women in economic development. In P. J. Dubeck & K. Borman (Eds.), *Women and work: A handbook* (pp. 487–489). New York: Garland Publishing, Inc.

Anyansi-Archibong, C. B. (2006). Entrepreneurship as the missing factor in the economic development of developing nations. *Global Entrepreneurship Monitor*.

Apraku, K. (1991). *African émigré in the United states: A missing link in Africa's social and economic development*. Westport: Praeger Publishers.

Ayitte, G. B. N. (1998). *Africa in chaos*. New York: St Martins Press.

Babooza, S. (2013). *Why African philanthropists seek "Africapitalism"*. Retrieved at http://www.thisdaylive.com.

Baharul-Islam, K. (2012). Rural entrepreneurship for women: A case of wealth creation by African rural poor amidst global financial crisis.

Baradi, E. M., & Tahir, R. (2019). Behind the veil: The challenges and impediments encountered by women entrepreneurs in United Arab Emirates. *Journal of Entrepreneurial Venturing, 11*(3), 258–282.

Baranik, L., Gorman, B., & Wales, W. J. (2019). *What makes Muslim women entrepreneurs successful: A field study examining religiosity and social capital in Tunisia*. Available at https://doi.org/10.31235/0sf.i0/gkg6u. Accessed April 2020.

Baumol, W. J. (1990). Entrepreneurship: Productive, unproductive, and destructive. *Journal of Political Economy, 98*(5), 893–919.

Bello, D., et al. (2009). Exposure to nanoscale particles and fibers during machining of hybrid advanced composites containing carbon nanotubes. *Journal of Nanoparticle Research, 11*, 231–249. https://doi.org/10.1007/s11051-008-9499-4.

Berner, E., Gomez, G., & Knorringa, P. (2012). Helping a large number of people become a little less poor: The logic of survival entrepreneurship. *The European Journal of Development Research, 24*(3), 382–396.
Biggest Obstacles for Start-Ups in Africa. (2016). http://venturebuirn.com/2016/03/6/biggest-obstacle-startups-face-africa.
Boston Consulting Group Study, in I. Ichikowitz. (2019). Africa can stand toe-to-toe with the big guys. *New African Magazine* (An IC Publication), December 2019/January 2020, No. 599.
Braukman, U. (2006, February 8–10). *Entrepreneurship career development: An innovative impulse from Wuppertal entrepreneurship education.* Presented at the Third AGSE International Entrepreneurship Research Exchange, Auckland, NZ.
Broel, W. G., Jr. (1978). *The village entrepreneur.* Cambridge, MA: Harvard University Press.
Brooks, G. (1976). *Women traders in pre-colonial Senegal.* https://www.wikipedia/history-women-in-Africa.
Bruin, A., & Flint-Haitie, S. (2006, February 8–10). *The search for equity capital: Implications for women entrepreneurs.* Presented at Third AGSE International Entrepreneurship Research Exchange, Auckland, NZ.
Bruno, A. V., & Tyebjee, T. T. (1982). The environment for entrepreneurship. In C. A. Kent, D. L. Sexton, & K. H. Vesper (Eds.), *Encyclopedia of entrepreneurship.* Englewood Cliffs, NJ: Prentice-Hall, Inc.
Bruton, A., Ahlstrom, D., & Obloj, K. (2008). Entrepreneurship in emerging economies: Where are we today and where should research go in the future. *Entrepreneurship Theory and Practice, 32*(1), 1–14.
Building a More Inclusive Entrepreneurial Ecosystem. https://www.ToigoFoundations.org.
Burkina Faso/YouTube. (2019). *Burkina Faso: Religion and family life.* www.youtube/burkina Faso. Retrieved April 10, 2020.
Challenges: African Entrepreneurs. (2017). http://www.africanpreneurs.com/some-challenges-faced-by-entrepreneurs-in-africa.
Chandler, A. D. (1977). *The visible hand: The managerial revolution in American business.* Cambridge: Harvard University.
Chepchirchir, T. (2018). *Women Enterprise Fund (WEF).* www.Techmoran.com. Accessed March 15, 2020.
Chocomilo, A. S. (2020). *Igbo laws: Igbos disagree as supreme court upholds the right of a female child to inherit her father's property.* https://www.lifeandtimesnews.com/08/27/2020.
Cobb, C. Jr. (2005, September). Africa in fact: A continent's numbers tell its story. In *National Geographic,* Africa special issue. http://www.nationalgeogrphic.com/magazine.

Cooper, S. Y., Ward, T., Lucas, W. A., & Cave, F. (2006, February 8–10). *Developing self-efficacy and entrepreneurial intent for technology entrepreneurship: The role of work experience*. Presented at the Third AGSE International Entrepreneurship Research Exchange, Auckland, NZ.

Co-Creation HUB Nigeria. (2017). https://cchubnigeria.com; http://faceboo knigeria.fb.com.

Cypher, J. M., & Dietz, J. L. (2004). *The process of economic development* (2nd ed.). London: Routledge.

Davos. (2019). Africa Union (AU) on discussion of the potential benefits of proposed Africa continental free trade agreement. *World Economic Forum*. www.youtube.com.

Dangote, A. (2017). *Discussions on powering Africa*. World Economic Forum. www.weforum.org; www.youtube.com.

Davos World Economic Forum. (2017). *On powering Africa*. www.youtube.com. Accessed April 14, 2020.

De Bruin, A. C., & Brush, C. (2006). Introduction to the special issue: Towards building cumulative knowledge on women's entrepreneurship. *Entrepreneurship Theory and Practice, 30*, 285–593.

Dekker, E. (2018). Two types of rationality: Or how to best combine psychology and economics. *Journal of Economic Methodology, 26*(4), 291–306. https://doi.org/10.1080/1350178x.2018.1560486. Accessed June 13, 2020.

Diaspora African Women's Network (DAWN). www.dawners.org.

Dolan, K. A. (2013, April 18). African charitable giving gets a boost with new launched African philanthropy forum. *Forbes.com*, p. 1.

Edoho, F. M. (1997). International technology transfer in the emerging global order. In F. M. Edoho (Ed.). *Globalization and the new world order, promises, problems, and prospects for Africa in the 21st century* (pp. 99–126). Westport, CT: Preaeger Publishers.

Ehigiamusoe, A. (2006). Impact of illiteracy on women. In D. Fick (Ed.), Africa: Continent of opportunity (pp. 73–75). Johannesburg, South Africa: STE Publishers.

El Baradi, M., & Tahir, R. (2019). Behind the veil: The challenges and impediments encountered by women entrepreneurs in United Arab Emirates. *International Journal of Entrepreneurial Venturing, 11*(3), 258–282.

Elkan, W. (1988). *Entrepreneurs and entrepreneurship in Africa* (pp. 171–188). World Bank Research Observer.

Empowering Africa's Women-Led Entrepreneurial Business Ecosystem. (2018). https://m.buscommunity.Africa/.

Entrepreneurial Ecosystem: Why They Matter and How to Build Them. http://www.fasttrack.org/blog/entrepreneurial-ecosystems.

Entrepreneurial Ecosystem Momentum and Maturity—Ewing. http://www.kau ffman.org/entrepreneurial-ecosystem-momentum.

Entrepreneurial Ecosystem as a Model for Economic Development. http://www.kauffman.org.
Fick, D. (2002). *Entrepreneurship in Africa: A study of success.* www.amazon.com/books/dp/1567205364.
Fick, D. (2006). *Africa: A continent of economic opportunity.* www.realafricanpublishers.com/most-popular/business/africa-continent-of-economic-opportunity-detail.html; www.amazon.com/books/dp/1919855599.
Fick, D. (2014). *African entrepreneurs in the 21st century and their stories of success.* Ghana: Excellent Publishing and Printing. ISBN 978-9988-0-7807-2.
Fick, D. (2016). *Africa entrepreneurs: Success studies.* www.eppbookservices.com.
Folade, K. (2011). *Fashion icon-Foloronshe Alakija at 60.* http://www.thenationonline.net/2011/indes/php.
Francee, E. (2016). *Senegal: Gender and colonial legacy.* New Magazine of American Association of Historians.
Fredrick, H. H., & Chittock, G. (Eds.). (2005). *Global Entrepreneurship Monitor (GEM)* (Executive Report. Unittec New Zealand's Center for Innovation & Entrepreneurship Research Report Series), Vol. 4(1), Auckland. ISBN 0-473-10827-5.
Gigerenzer, G. (2000). *Adaptive thinking: Rationality in the real world.* Oxford: Oxford University Press.
Gigerenzer, G. (2007). *Gut feelings: The intelligence of the unconscious.* New York, Vikings, Cross Reference/Google Scholar.
Gigerenzer, G. (2015). *Simple rationality: Decision making in the real world.* Oxford Press, Cross Reference/Google Scholar.
Gigerenzer, G., & Todd, P. M. (2012). Ecological rationality: The normative study of heuristics. In P. M. Todd & G. Gigerenzer (Eds.), *Ecological rationality: Intelligence in the world* (pp. 487–497). New York: Oxford University Press, Cross Reference/Google Scholar.
GLAM Africa Magazine. (2017, December). *The digital innovator in GLAM Africa: The GLAM powerlist of Africa's most influential entrepreneurs.* London: Quarterly Publication by GLAM Africa Ltd.
Gnyawali, D. S. (1994). Environment for entrepreneurship development: Key dimensions and research implications. *Journal of Entrepreneurship, Theory and Practice.* https://doi.org/10.1177/104225879401800403.
Gonzalez, L. (Host, 2019). *Achieving a single African market: Davos world economic forum.* www.youtube.com. Retrieved July 14, 2020.
Gray, K. R. (2001). Small business management in Africa: Prospects for future development. In F. M. Edoho (Ed.), *Management challenges in the twenty-first century: Theoretical and applied perspectives* (pp. 259–275). West Port, CN: Praeger Publishing.
Guye, F. B. (2017). Colonial and post-colonial changes and impact on pastoral women's role and status in Northern Kenya. *Pastoralism, 7*(13), 1–9.

Harvey, C. M., et al. (2011). Andrew Carnegie and the foundations of contemporary entrepreneurial philanthropy. *Business History, 53*(3), 425.

Hayes, M. J. (1976). *How economic changes in pre-colonial Kenya affected Luo women.* https://www.wikipedia/history-women-in-africa.

Hayes, R. N., & Robinson, J. A. (2012). An economic sociology of African entrepreneurial activity. *International Journal of Entrepreneurship, 16*(Special Issue), 51–67.

Henley, A. (2016). Does religion influence entrepreneurial behavior. *International Journal of Small Business: Researching Entrepreneurship.* https://doi.org/10.1177/026624261656748. Sage Publishers Journals.

Hirsch, R. D., & Bush, C. (1985). *The woman entrepreneur: Starting, financing, and managing a successful new business.* Lexington, MA: Lexington Books.

Howorth, et al. (2005). Rethinking entrepreneurship methodology and definitions of the entrewpreneur. *Journal of Small Business and Enterprise Development, 12*(1), 24–40.

Human Development Report. (2006). *Beyond scarcity: Power, poverty, and global water crisis.* New York: United Nations Development Programme.

Ibid. Nigerian Women Entrepreneurs, pp. 500–502.

Ibrahim, M. (2019a). African youths: Jobs or migration, governance weekend. Mo Ibrahim Forum, Abijan, Cote d'Voire.

Ibrahim, M. (2019b). *African youths: Jobs or migration?* Speaking at the governance weekend forum, Abijan, Cote d'Voire, West Africa. www.youtube.com. Retrieved May, 2020.

Ichikowitz, I. (2020). *Africa can stand toe-to-toe with the big guys, New African.* An IC Publication, January 2019–December 2020.

Igbokwe, E. M., & Ozor, N. (2007). Roles of biotechnology in ensuring adequate food security in developing societies. *African Journal of Biotechnology, 6*(14), 1597–1602. In N. Ekekwe (2010, ed.) *Nanaotechnology and microelectronics: Global diffusion, economics, and policy.*

Imaralu, D. (2012). *Ugandan billionaire Ashish Thakkar launches venture capital fund for young entrepreneurs.* Available at www.maragroup.com/2010; http://www.ventures-africa.com/2012/07/ugandanbillionnaire.

Irogbe, K. (2003). Transformation in South Africa: A study of education and land. *International Third World Studies and Review, XIV*, 11–28.

Isenberg, D. (2011, May). Nature or nurture; Born or made?—Do ecosystem evolve naturally or can they be intelligently designed? *Forbes.com.*

Isenberg, D. (2014a, May 12). What an entrepreneurship ecosystem actually is. *Harvard Business Review, 5*, 1–7.

Isenberg, D. (2014b). *Entrepreneurial ecosystem and growth-oriented entrepreneurship* (p. 6). In Mason and Brown (Eds.).

Jackson, D. J. (2011). *What is an innovation ecosystem.* Washington, DC. Retrieved http://erc-assoc-org/siters/default/files/download-files/DJackson_what-is-an-innovation-ecosystem.pdf.

Jackson, T. (2020). *There are not enough women-led tech startups and it is costing us all.* http://www.disruptafrica.com.

Johnson, S. (2002). Who moved my cheese. G.P. Putman's Sons, a division of Putman's books. New York. ISBN 13579108642.

Kadiri, I. (2020a). Moroccan saying, girls have two exits in their lives: One to their husband's home and one to the grave. New African-Pan-African Magazine, December 2019–January 2020, #599, p. 23.

Kadri, I. (2020b). The Alchemist. 100 most influential Africans. *New African Magazine* (An IC publication), December 2019/January 2020, No. 599.

Kent, C. A., Sexton, D. R., & Vesper, K. H. (Eds.). (1982). *Encyclopedia of entrepreneurship.* Englewood Cliffs, NJ: Prentice Hall, Inc.

Kent, C. A. (1974, April). *Education for entrepreneurship.* AACSB Bulletin.

Kierulf, H. E. (1973, June–July). Can entrepreneurship be taught. *MBA Magazine.*

Kieruff, H. E. (1974, October–December). Developing a curriculum for effective teaching of entrepreneurship. *MBA Magazine.*

Kiggundi, M. N. (2002). Entrepreneurs and entrepreneurship in Africa: What is known and what needs to be done. *Journal of Developmental Entrepreneurship,* 7(3), 239–258.

Kirzner, I. M. (1973). *Competition and entrepreneurship.* Chicago: University of Chicago.

Kisubi, A., Anyansi-Archibong, C., Kamalu, N. C., Kamalu, J. A., & Adikwu, M. U. (2010). Emerging technology transfer, economic development, and policy in Africa. In N. Ekekwe (Ed.), *Nano technology and microelectronics: Global diffusion, economics, and policy.* Hershey, PA: Information Science Reference (IGI Global).

Kramer, H. E. (1971). New entrepreneurial dimensions of business education. *Collegiate News and Views, XXV* (1, Fall).

Krotz, J. L. (2017). *Americas first social entrepreneurs were female, black, and millionnaires* (honoring madam C J Walker and Annie Turnbo Malone). www.workingmother.com

Lambini, C. (2006, February 8–10). *Rural women entrepreneurs and access to socio-economic development in Northern Ghana: A case study of Chereponi sub-district.* Presented at the Third AGSE International Entrepreneurship Research Exchange, Auckland, NZ.

Leisure, S. (2002). Exchanging participation for promise: Mobilization of women in Eritrea. In J. M. Bystydzienski & J. Sekhon (Eds.), *Democratization and women grassroot movements* (pp. 95–110). Bloomington, Indiana and New Delhi, India: Indiana University Press and Kali for Women.

Lejarranga, J., & Pindard-Lejarrana, M. (2020, June 26). *Bounded rationality: Cognitive limitations or adaptation to the environment? The implications of ecological rationality for management learning*. Academy of Management Learning and Education.

Lucas, W. A., & Cooper, S. (2006, February 8–10). *Enhancing self-efficacy for entrepreneurship and innovation: An educational approach*. Presented at the Third AGSE International Entrepreneurship Research Exchange, Auckland, NZ.

Lulat, Y. G. (2005). *A history of African higher education from antiquity to the present: A critical synthesis* (pp. 154–157). Greenwood Publishing Group, ISBN 978-0-313-32061-3.

Luoto, S., & Ristimaky, K. (2006, February 8–10). *Gendered entrepreneurship in Finnish students' narratives: A social semiotics approach*. Presented at the Third AGSE International Entrepreneurship Research Exchange, Auckland, NZ.

Madichie, N. O., & Gallant, J. (2012). Studies on Islam, muslim women, and entrepreneurship in context of restrictive culture. *Journal of Business Ethics, 129*(4).

Mafela, L. (1979). *Botswana women and law: Society, education, and migration [1840–1980]*. https://doi.org/10.4000/etudesafricaine.7962.

Malone-Krotz, J. L. (2017). *America's first social entrepreneurs were women, black, and millionaires: Honoring Madam C.J. Walker and Annie Turnbo*. www.workingmother.com.

Mason, C. (2018). *Domains of entrepreneurial ecosystem*. www.researchgate.net/profile.colin_mason2/publication. Accessed June 12, 2020.

Maswana, J.-C. (1998). Africa's future needs to include the informal sector. In Spring & B. E. McDade (Eds.), *Entrepreneurship in Africa: Theory and reality*. Gainesville: University Press of Florida.

Maya, W. (2020). *Show case Africa*. www.youtube/ghana/liberia. Retrieved July 8, 2020

McKinsey Inc. (2019, August 10). *The female economy is the world's largest emerging market with potentials to add $12T to global GDP*. https://mckensey.com; www.pleasuremagazine.com.ng.

Meier, F., & Selhan, Z. (2014). *Missionaries and colonial disempowerment in colonial Uganda: New evidence from protestant marriage register, 1880–1915* (pp. 74–112). http://doi.org/10.1080/20780389.2014.927110. Retrieved March 26, 2020.

Millennium Development Goals and Sustainable Development Goals. www.unitednations.org.

Moeti, M. (2018, November–January 14–20). Health is a good investment for development. *New African Woman Magazine* (An IC Publication), Issue 44.

Mohammed, A. J. (2018, November–January). You cannot put a band-aid on the world's problems. *New African Woman Magazine* (An IC publication) Issue 44, Interview by Regina Jane Jere, pp. 6–11.

Moremong-Nganunu, T., Hindle, K., & Cunningham, E. (2006, February 8–10). *A preliminary evaluation of the world's largest skills enhancement program for entrepreneurs*. Presented at the Third AGSE International Entrepreneurship Research Exchange, Auckland, NZ.

Moreno-Gavara, C., & Jimenez-Zarco, A. I. (Eds.). (2019). *Sustainable fashion: Empowering African women entrepreneurs in the fashion industry*. Macmillan-Palgrave Publishing company. ISBN 978-3-319-91265-3.

Morino, M. (2007, September 28). *Business entrepreneurs and philanthropy: Potentials and pitfalls, keynote Speech-Legacy*. National Philanthropic Trust Forum.

Morris, N. H. (1998). *Entrepreneurial intensity: Sustainable advantages for individuals, organizations, and societies*. Westport, CT: Quorum Books. ISBN 0-89930-975-5.

Nabi, G., Liñán, F., Mitra, J., Abubakar, Y. A., & Sagagi, M. (2013). Knowledge creation and human capital for development: The role of graduate entrepreneurship. *African Journal of Economics*. www.Emerald.com.

Nana-Fabu, S. (2011). An analysis of economic status of women in Cameroon. *Journal of International Women Studies, 8*(1), 148–162. http://vc.bridgew.edu/jiws/vol8/issi/11. Retrieved March 27, 2020.

Nasr, S. (2018, November–January). Women need equal opportunities not equality. *New African Woman Magazine* (An IC Publication) Issue 44, pp. 23–40.

Nayantra, J. (2018). *This 26-year-old from Kenya is churning out bricks from plastic waste*. http://www.weetracker.com.

Nenes, M. F. (2009). *International cuisine* (pp. 501–542). Hoboken, NJ, Africa: Wiley.

Newmeyer, X., Santos, S. C., & Kalbfleisch, P. (2018). Entrepreneurship ecosystem and women entrepreneurs: A social capital and network approach. *Small Business Economics, 53*, 475–489 [Springer link].

Newmeyer, et al. (2017). Entrepreneurship ecosystems and women entrepreneurs: A social capital and network approach. *Small business economics, 53*, 475–489, published 3/2018/springerlink.

Nickels, G. M., Mchugh, J. M., & McHugh, S. M. (2019). *Understanding business* (10th ed.). New York: McGraw-Hill Education Publishers. ISBN 978-1-259-92943-4.

Nnadozie, E. (2020, January). Capacity imperatives for the SDGS: In line with the African Union Agenda 2063. In B. Ankoma (Ed.), *Some progress on SDGs, but still a long way to go—ACBF Report*, New African, An IC Publication.

Nzekwe, H. (2018, October 23). *From fighting depression to amassing USD2Mn fortune: The Zed farmer's extraordinary journey*. http://www.weetracker.com (free reads).

Oliveira Jr., M. M., Cahen, F. R., & Borini, F. M. (Eds.). (2019). *Startups innovation ecosystems in emerging markets: A Brazilian perspectives*. Palgrave Macmillan. ISBN 978-3-030-10864-9.

Olusoluon, S. (2012). *Aba women riot: Women's war*. http://www.en.m.wikipedia.org%3Ewomen%5Fwar; www.blackpast.org%3Ea-women-riot.

Oyewunmi, N. (1997). *Application of women cases in pre-colonial context*. https://www.wikipedia/history-women-in-africa.

Osabuohien, E. S. C. (2010). Technological innovations and Africa's quest for development in the 21st century. In N. Ekekwe (Ed.), *Nanotechnology and microelectronics: Global diffusion, economics, and policy*. Hershey, PA: Information Science Reference (IGI Global).

Osirim, J. (2013). *African women in the new diaspora: Transnationalism and the (re) creation of home*. https://repositorybrynmawr.edu/cgi/viewcontent.cgi/article=1005andcontent=soc.pubs; www.researchgate.net/publication.

Pennell, C. (1987). Women resistance to colonialism in Morocco: The RIF-1916-1926. *Journal of African History*, 28, 107–118.

Pio, E. (2006, February 8–10). *Inspirational parables: Ethnic minority Indian women entrepreneurs in New Zealand*. Presented at the Third International Entrepreneurship Research Exchange, Auckland, NZ.

Pocket Planner. (2004). *Missionaries of Africa*, 1622 21st Street, NW. Washington, DC 20009-1089.

Rajuili, K., & Burke, I. (2002). Democratization through adult popular education: A reflection on the resilience of women from Kwa-Ndebele, South Africa. In J. M. Bystydzienske & J. Sekhon (Eds.), *Democratization and women's grassroot movement* (pp. 111–128). Bloomington, Indiana and New Delhi, India: Indian University Press and Kali for Women.

Rasod, H. (2017). Impact of colonial rules on women's rights: Case study specific to Egypt under the rule of British consul-general, Lord E. Cromer. *Journal of Religious Studies*, 2(2), 1.

Roscoe, J. (1971, June–July). Can entrepreneurship be taught? *MBA Magazine*.

Saee, J. (2006, February 8–10). *Entrepreneurship education and training: A Panacea for the European Economic Malaise in the third millennium*. Presented at the Third AGSE Entrepreneurship Research Exchange, Auckland, NZ.

Salami, M. (2013). *Change makers: Women of the African diaspora*. www.newint.org>blog>2013/o8/01>women-of-the-africa.

Sanyang, S. E., et al. (2010). The impact of agricultural technology transfer to women vegetable production and marketing groups in the Gambia. *World Journal of Agricultural Sciences*, 5(2), 169–179.

Schoch, S. (1979, September). How business schools handle entrepreneurship. *Venture Magazine, 1*(8).
Schrein, J. W. (Ed.). (1975). *Training and education for entrepreneurship*. Proceedings of Project ISEED. Milwaukee Center for Venture Management.
Schumpeter, J. A. (1936 first published 1911). *Theory of economic development*. Cambridge: Harvard University, Rpt. Oxford 1961.
Schumpeter, J. A. (1939). *Business cycles: A theoretical, historical, and statistical analysis of the capitalist process*. New York: McGraw-Hill Inc.
Senor, D., & Singer, S. (2009). Start-up nation: The story of Israel's economic miracle. Twelve: Hachette Book Group, New York. www.HachetteBookGroup.com.
Sheriff, M., & Muffatto, M. (2015). The present state of entrepreneurship ecosystem in selected countries in Africa. *African Journal of Economic and Management Studies, 6*(1).
Shilcola, A., & Prester, C. (1998 [1992]). *Role and status of women in pre-colonial versus colonial society*. www.wikipedia.com/history-women-in-africa.
Singh, G., & Belwai, R. (2008). Entrepreneurship and SMEs in Ethiopia. Evaluating the role, prospects, and problems faced by women in this emerging Sector, Gender in Management—An International Journal.... Emeraldinsight.com.
Smith, A. (1937). *The wealth of nations, editor, Edwin Cannon*. New York: Modern Library.
Smith, V. L. (2003). Constructivist and ecological rationality in economics. *The American Economic Review, 93*, 465–508. https://doi.org/10.1257/000282 9803322156954.
Smith, V. L. (2015). Conduct, rules, and origins of institutions. *Journal of Institutional Economics, 11*(3), 481–483. https://doi.org/10.1017/517441374 14000605.
Soetan, F. (2012, August 2). *Finance, Fashion, Philanthropy: Folorunsho Alakija, FAMFA Oil*. http://www.ventures-africa.com/2012/08/finance-fashion-philanthropy-folorunsho-alakija.
Spring, A., & McDade, B. E. (1998). *African entrepreneurship: Theory and reality*. Gainesville: University Press of Florida.
Sub-Saharan Africa Has the Highest Rate of Female Entrepreneurship Globally. www.Global-entrepreneurship-monitor.org. Accessed May 12, 2020.
Swoyer, C. (2003). The linquistic relativity hypothesis. In E. N. Zalta (Ed.), *The stanford encyclopedia of philosophy*. http://plato.stanford.edu/archives/win2003/entries/relativism.
Tanas, J. K., & Yamin, S. (2006). *Entrepreneurial education for the new millennium*. Presented at the Third AGSE International Entrepreneurship Research Exchange, Auckland, NZ.

Taylor, M. L., Strom, R. J., & Renz, D. O. (2014). *Handbook of research on entrepreneurs' engagement in philanthropy: Perspectives*. Northampton, MA: Edward Elger Publishing Limited. ISBN 978-1-78347-100-3.

Terborg, R., & Rushing, A. B. (2018). *Women in Africa and the Africa diaspora: A reader*. www.amazon.com/women-africa-adfrica-diaspora-terborg.

The Entrepreneurial Ecosystem of South Africa: A Strategy for Global Leadership. (2017). http://sabcms.blog.core.windows.net.

The Importance of an Entrepreneurial Ecosystem for Creating a Systemic Entrepreneurship: Lessons from Amazon Rainforest and Silicon Valley. http://eenetwork.org…/the-importance-of-an-entrepreneurial-ecosystem-for-creating.

Tlaiss, H. A. (2014 [2015a]). How Islamic business ethics impact women entrepreneurs: Insights from four Arab Middle Eastern countries. *Journal of Business Ethics, 129*(4). Also Available https://doi.org/10.1007/s10551-014-2138-3.

Top 50 Black African Women Entrepreneurs to Watch Out for on a Global Stage. https://www.experthub.info.

Top 10 Female-Led African Tech Companies. https://www.women-in-tech-africa-summit.com/blog/top-10-female-led-african-tech-companies.

Ufuk, G., & Ozgen, A. (2001). Role conflict for married women entrepreneurs in Turkey.

Umoja Uaso Village in Samburu County, Kenya. www.nbcnews.com; www.Youtube.com; www.shewillsurvive.com.

UNDP. (2007). Human Development Report. *Fighting climate change: Human solidarity in a divided world*. United Nations Development Programme. New York: Palgrave Macmillan.

UNESCO Literacy Definition. (2018). https://www.litworld.com/unesco/definition.

Varley, G. (2019). *Empowering women in tech for economic development*. http://www.women-in-tech-africa-summit.com/.

Vesper, K. H. (1976 [1979]). *Entrepreneurship education: A bicentennial compendium*. Milwaukee Center for Venture Management.

Vesper, K. H. (1980). *Research on entrepreneurship education*. Presented at the Conference on Research and Education on Entrepreneurship, Baylor University, Texas.

West Africa's Growing Startup Ecosystem Is Built for Small Growing and HIGH-Impact Companies. www.impactAlpha/west-Africa-growing.

What an Entrepreneurial Ecosystem Actually Is. http://hbr.org/2014/05/what-an-entrepreneurial-ecosystem/.

Whuster, S. (2017). *Which African countries are taking off?* www.Visualpolitics.en/CCTV@SimonWhuster. Accessed July 9, 2020.

Why Is It Important to Build a Startup Ecosystem? Ye! http://yecommunity.org/en/blog/why-is-it-important-to-build-a-startup-ecosystem.

Wikipedia. (2018). *Senegal women: Changes in roles during the colonial era*. www.wikipedia.org/Women-in-africa. Retrieved February 11, 2020.

Wilson, J. (2012, December 5). Richest black woman in the world, Folaronshe Alakija was a major fashion designer in Africa. *Huffington Post*. http://www.huffingtonpost.com/2012/12/05/folaronsho-alakija-richest-blac-woman-fashion-designer-n-2245703.html.

Wintz, M., & Volkmann, C. (2019). *Social entrepreneurial ecosystems as a means for creating sustainable urban development*. www.isscbookofblogs.pressbooks.com [in dialogues of sustainable urbanization: social science research and transitions to urban contexts] Accessed July 1, 2020.

World Bank Economic Report. (2016). https://www.worldbank.org/Africa.

World Bank Economic Report. (2018). https://www.worldbank.org/Africa.

World Economic Forum. (2015). Entrepreneurial ecosystem around the globe and company growth dynamics.

World's Oldest University. http://www.guinnessworldrecords.com/world-record/oldest-university; http://www.pewforum.org/2015.

World's Oldest University. http://www.en.m.wikipedia.org.

Yesufu, A. (2020). *Igbo apprenticeship system makes people hate Igbos*. www.ne.np.facebook.com>posts>igbo-.

Zakaria, F. (2019). Nigeria-Americans' contributions to the US economy. www.cnn/GPS/nigeria-american-economic-contributions

Zakaria, F. (2020). *Analysis of Trump's controversial travel ban list*. https://www.cnn-africa/GPS/february/17/2020.

www.dangote.com.
www.dangotefoundation.org.
www.Kauffman.org.
www.lulu.com/hfredrick.
www.nationsonline.org.
www.tonyelumelufoundation.org.
www.songaga.inflibnet.ac.in.
www.UNICEF.org.
http://www.usabe.org/page/2020conference.
www.data.worldbank.org.
http://www.wikipedia.org.
www.wikipedia.com/africa-facts.

Index

A

Aba, 34
Abagana women organization, 50
Abandonment, 136
Aba women, 34
Abeokuta, 34, 35
Abeokuta ladies club, 35
Abudu, Mo, 177
Abuja Art Gallery, 91
Abundance resources, 26
Acada, 51
Academic discipline, 3, 10
Accredited, 9, 10, 91
Action-oriented, 7, 136, 201
Adazi Catholic Women's Economic Center, 194
Adesina, Akinwumi, 117, 120, 123
Adire, 75–77, 187–189, 191
Affia, 119, 195, 196
Affia-Attack, 69, 182
Africa, 3, 6, 8, 12–14, 19–23, 25, 26, 28–36, 53, 57, 58, 65, 66, 80, 90, 95–97, 104, 106, 107, 109, 114–120, 123, 125, 126, 128, 130–132, 134, 137, 141–143, 160, 177, 178, 193, 203
Africa Continental Free Trade Agreement (ACFTA), 22, 120, 121, 123, 124, 171
Africa Development Bank (ADB), 120, 123
Africa Diaspora in Asia (ADIA), 141
Africa Diaspora Initiative Web Portal, 141
Africa-female entrepreneurs, 89, 92, 103, 106
Africa in chaos, 31
Africa Leadership and Progressive Network (ALPN), 141
African Academy of Management (AFAM), 91
African American, 162
African economies, 8, 26
African ecosystem, 86, 109
African Lions, 172
African Queen, 21

INDEX

African Rural University (ARU), 80, 182
African Union (AU), 92, 106, 107, 112, 114, 116, 123, 125, 146, 170, 180
African women entrepreneurs, 13–15, 23, 52–54, 64, 86, 92–95, 102, 103, 106, 119, 120, 160, 162, 163, 166, 168, 170, 172, 173, 178, 179, 185, 186
Africapitalists, 29
Africa Rural University (ARU), 157, 158, 160
Africa's Secret Weapon, 146
Africa Technology Business Network (ATBN), 105
Africa-USA International Conference, 144
Agbani road, 199
Aggregates, 6
Agnerd-Oudad, 202
AGOA, 100
Agricultural technology, 114
Agriculture, 25, 44, 72, 73, 92, 100, 113–115, 117, 178
Agro-products, 115
Agwang, Martha Catherine, 186
Ahmed, F., 85
Akasai Group, 97
Akhannouch, Aziz, 202
Akhannouch, Kenza, 204
Akhannouch, Salwa idrissi, 94, 97, 186, 202
Aksal, 203
Akwa Group, 97
Akwa-Ibom state, 144
Alakija, Folorunsho, 29, 30, 37, 94, 96, 149
Alemu, Bethlehem T., 94, 96
Al-Fihri, Fatima, 23
Algeria, 57, 62, 85
Aligator pepper, 49

Aljazeera, 117
Allah, 64
Alliance for Arab Women (AAW), 99
Almsgiving, 64
Alphabets, 59, 62, 199
Alvord, Sarah H., 85
Amal salih, 60
Ambitious, 105, 130, 204
Amsterdam, 211
Anambra State, 194
Anglophone nations, 33
Angola, 27, 58, 94, 95, 170, 211, 212
Ankara textiles, 56
Anthony Nwankwo Anyansi, 194
Anyansi-Archibong, C., 112, 125, 126
Anyansi, Marcelina A., 186
Anyansi, Peter, 144
Appiah, Ernestina, 176
Apprenticeship, 81, 150–152
Apraku, K., 100
Arab explorers, 62
Araia, Semhar, 146
Architectural Culture, 59
Architecture, 133, 171
Argentina, 11
Argon oil, 204
Artisans, 35, 56
Asante kingdom, 66
Ashanti, 107
Ashoka Fellow, 158
Asia, 23, 63, 106, 115, 116, 143
Asian-Indian, 63
Aso-oke, 91, 192
Assignment, 20, 47
Association for the Study of Worldwide African Diaspora (ASWAD), 141
Athens of Africa, 23
Attitudes, 59, 61, 133, 157, 160, 164, 186

Attributes, 137, 164, 167, 185, 186, 208, 213
Auckland, 8
Austria, 10, 96
Aviation, 94, 96, 170, 174, 205, 206
Ayaba, 187
Ayittey, George, 31
Azerbaijan, 210

B

Babson College Entrepreneurship Center, 10
Badran, Hoda, 99
Baking, 48, 49, 62, 150, 196, 215
Baksahbi, 203
Baku, 210
Banana, 62
Banana Republic, 203
Bantus, 63
Baradi, E.M., 77
Baranik, L., 85
Barboza, S., 28
Bareness, 80
Batik, 56
Bazar markets, 43, 57
Beijing, 20
Beliefs, 57, 60, 61, 64, 73, 125, 163
Bello, D., 117
Belonging, 166
Belwal, R., 36
Bend-down-boutique, 140
Benin, 27, 30, 57, 66, 76
Benin and Ijebu kingdoms, 66
Benlafkih, Haj Ahmed, 202
Bennet College, 178
Berber, 202, 204
Biafra war, 69
Bicycle, 42
Billionaire, 29, 210
Biodiversity, 32, 127
Biological resources, 23

Birth control, 25
Bitter-leaf source, 63
Blood, 63
Bloomberg Philanthropies, 172
Blue Bunny, 144
BMF award, 207
Bobotie, 63
Boko Haram, 61
Bolmus Group International, 97
Borehole, 140
Boserup, Ester, 43
Botswana, 12, 27, 58, 67, 71, 172
Boubou, 76
Bounded rationality, 124, 132, 136
Brain drains, 147
Brain repatriation, 147
Braukman, U., 12
Brazil, 9, 10, 115, 142
Breaking barriers, 54, 97, 179
BRICS (Brazil, Russia, India, China, South Africa), 115
Bridal gifts, 41
British colonies, 65
Brooks, 43
Brother(s), 19, 45, 49, 76, 139, 143, 152, 187, 194
Brown, L.D., 85
Bruin, A., 9
Bruton, A., 32
Buganda, 45
Build, Operate, and Transfer (BOT), 100
Burke, I., 101
Burkina-Faso, 27, 45
Burukutu, 49, 195, 196
Burundi, 24, 28, 57
Bush, C., 6, 8
Business education, 82, 100
Business leadership, 29
Butter, 45, 48, 49

C

Cairo, Egypt, 99
Cameroon, 27, 30, 56, 58, 67, 72
Canada, 11, 106, 144
Capabilities, 127, 133, 212
Cape Maley, 63
Cape Verde, 57, 84, 179, 211, 212
Capital, 21, 25, 26, 31, 36, 48, 49, 64, 80, 94, 98, 101, 105, 111, 118, 119, 121, 127, 151, 160, 161, 171, 204
Capital at risk, 171
Care Clubs, 101
Caregivers, 37, 167
Cargo charter, 96
Casablanca, 105, 202
Cash crop, 45, 72, 93, 213
Cassava, 42, 62–64, 72
Cassava sellers, 81
Cattle, 63, 71
Central Africa Republic, 24, 26, 28
Central Planning Office (CPO), 112
Chad, 27, 58
Challenges, 5, 6, 10, 12, 14, 21–23, 25, 31–33, 36, 37, 62, 65, 69, 73–75, 77–80, 82, 85, 89, 90, 93–96, 103, 104, 106, 107, 114, 115, 119, 121, 134, 141, 150, 156, 160, 162, 165, 170, 171, 179, 180, 185, 186, 190, 191, 193, 203, 206, 213–215
Chandler, A.D., 4
Change makers, 214
Charrad, M., 85
Charter, 206
Cheap labor, 113
Chepchirchir, Tabitha, 85
Chief Executive Officer (CEO), 29, 91, 93, 95, 104–106, 179
Chiefs, 66
Chieftaincies, 66
Chihombori-Quao, Arikana, 107
Child and dependent care, 36
Child bearing, 43, 80
Childcare, 44–46
Child mortality, 83, 84, 117, 172
Children, 9, 30, 34, 43, 45, 46, 49, 50, 52, 53, 60, 64–66, 69, 71, 77–81, 84, 99, 119, 120, 126, 140, 148, 155–157, 176, 185, 189, 194, 207, 211, 213
Chile, 11
China, 11, 20, 22, 84, 112, 113, 115, 116, 121, 147
Chin-Chin, 199
Chisolum, 155, 160
Christian Igbos, 63
Christians, 24, 59, 61
Cigarettes, 49, 198
Civic society, 45, 145
Civil freedom, 114
Civil war, 69, 119, 182
Classic, 29
Classic entrepreneurs, 7, 52, 166
Cleopatra, 68
Climate change, 82
Clinton, Hilary (Senator), 53
Coal city, 49, 196
Coastal, 26, 58
Cobb, C., 25
Coca Cola, 85
Coetzee, Benji, 175
Cognitive limitation, 124
Collectivity and market taxes, 72
Colombia, 142
Colonial culture, 56, 59, 68
Colonial heritage, 33
Colonialism, 43, 65, 68
Colonization, 70, 72
Colorful basins, 45
Commercialization, 10, 71, 72
Communities, 9, 23, 31, 32, 35, 36, 52, 59–61, 64, 86, 90, 94, 107, 108, 115, 125, 130, 140, 143,

INDEX 237

145, 147, 148, 158, 160, 162, 165, 178, 181, 190, 216
Community Alliance for Renewal of Inner-South Manchester Area (CARISMA), 146
Computer, 11, 26, 161, 176
Concepts, 3–6, 10–13, 22, 28, 32, 34, 35, 102, 124, 132, 147, 188
Condis, 211
Conglomerate, 30, 95, 97, 98, 103, 178, 186, 203
Consul general, 66
Consumption, 48, 49, 63, 105, 114
Contextual, 13, 15
Continent, 3, 13–15, 19–23, 25, 26, 28–32, 35, 37, 45, 46, 48, 53–55, 60, 61, 65, 66, 73, 77, 80, 82, 84, 86, 92, 96, 99, 105, 107–109, 111–117, 120, 121, 124–126, 130, 131, 133, 134, 136, 137, 140, 142, 144–147, 152, 157, 160, 161, 169, 172, 174, 177–181, 193
Cooking pots and pans, 41, 42
Cooper, S., 12
Corn husk, 62
Corn porridge, 63
Corruption, 32, 34, 36, 106, 117, 133, 137, 152
Corrupt leaders, 21
Cottage industry, 56
Coupland, C., 11
Courageous, 68, 90, 109, 114, 136, 167, 170, 204
Couscous, 56, 62
Cow, 48, 62, 63
Co-wives, 64, 76, 81, 189, 190
Craft, 43, 53, 56, 76, 77, 136, 187, 215
Crayfish, 42, 49, 195, 197

Creative, 4, 7, 32, 89, 104, 119, 130, 158, 162, 167, 174, 183, 196, 199, 201, 212
Creativity, 7, 128, 130, 137, 144, 146, 176
Criminals, 46
Critical success factors, 103, 112, 182
Crocheting/crochets, 49
Cromer, Lord, 66
Cuisine, 44, 56, 59, 62–64, 140
Cultural centers, 55
Cultural dynamics, 46
Cultural elements, 34, 36, 58, 64, 73, 128
Cultural-induced tendencies, 34
Culture, 5, 8, 9, 14, 34–37, 43–45, 47, 48, 52, 53, 55, 56, 58, 61, 64–66, 73, 77, 79–81, 90, 93, 94, 97, 98, 104, 105, 108, 109, 113, 125–128, 131, 148, 155, 164, 170, 173, 181, 206, 216
Culture and tradition-driven entrepreneurs, 3
Culture-induced, 55, 60, 78, 79
Cunningham, E., 12
Curator, 77, 91, 192
Curriculum, 12, 23, 48, 53, 71, 72, 78, 119
Curry, 63
Cypher, J.M., 114

D

Dangote, Aliko, 29, 30, 111, 117, 118
Dangote Group of Companies, 29
Danish, 211
Danjuma, Theophilus, 29
Deep-fried cassava, 216
Dekker, E., 124
Denmark, 10
Dentistry, 152
Deserts, 26

Determination, 34, 70, 73, 90, 91, 93, 94, 104, 105, 112, 146, 147, 157, 182, 185, 186, 190, 191, 193, 206, 213
Developed economy, 4, 7, 11, 15, 22, 126, 142
Diarrhea, 140
Diaspora, 14, 116, 121, 137, 152, 160, 178, 181
Diaspora African Women Network (DAWN), 141, 146
Diaspora women, 139, 140, 145–147
Dietz, J.L., 114
Dike, Tonto, 109
Diowera, Fatoumata, 146
Disciplinarian, 47, 182, 199, 201, 202
Discontinuation, 136
Diseases, 46, 70, 83, 174
Disrupt, 114, 164, 200
Diverse ecology, 26
Doctoral program, 90
Doctor of philosophy (Ph.D.), 91
Dokolo, Sindika, 211
Dolan, K.A., 149
Dollars, 81, 91, 92, 100, 139, 145
Domesticity, 43
Domestic skills, 43, 48, 52, 53, 55, 75, 78
Domestic violence, 53, 94, 98, 108, 170
Dos Santos, Isabel, 94, 95, 186, 210, 212
Dowry, 41, 43, 45, 48, 60, 64, 73, 76, 79, 81, 98, 156, 188, 216
Dowry payments, 64, 99, 214
D.R. Congo, 28
Dressmeoutlet.com, 106
Driven, 6, 13, 26, 44, 61, 70, 89, 91, 93, 94, 106, 113, 119, 130, 134, 173, 216
Driving forces, 28, 31, 90
Drum beat, 169

Dutch, 65
Dynamic, 14, 34, 35, 44, 90, 98, 104, 108, 113, 131, 134, 162, 164, 172, 173, 186
Dysfunctional, 46

E
Early marriage, 43, 55
East Africa, 30, 36, 43, 63, 67, 79, 81, 95, 99, 156
East African cultures, 43
Eastern Europe, 8
Eastern region of Nigeria, 49
Ecofriendly, 145
Ecological, 3
Ecological elements, 125
Ecological factors, 22, 125, 126
Ecological Rationality (ER), 124–126, 131, 137
Economically-deprived, 21
Economic Community of West African States (ECOWAS), 100
Economic development, 4, 5, 13–15, 21, 23, 25, 26, 84, 111–114, 116, 117, 120, 121, 124, 126, 130
Economic development models, 22
Economic equilibrium, 5, 94, 119
Economic milieu, 125
Economic opportunities, 31
Economic renaissance, 28, 112, 169
Economics, 3, 5, 6, 13, 14, 101, 126, 164, 171, 179
Economic sociological perspectives, 33
Ecosystem(s), 3, 6, 15, 20, 22, 26, 30, 32, 48, 52, 58, 62, 73, 109, 112, 113, 117, 121, 126–128, 130, 131, 134, 136, 137, 147, 148, 158, 161, 162, 180
Edoho, Felix, 117
Educated African man, 44

Education, 5, 8, 10–15, 23, 25, 26, 37, 43, 44, 52, 55, 61, 62, 65, 70, 71, 73, 77–79, 82–84, 86, 89–91, 93, 94, 97, 98, 100–104, 107, 108, 116–120, 127, 128, 133, 136, 137, 142, 151, 155, 157, 160–162, 164, 170, 172, 177, 187, 193, 207, 212, 214, 216
Educational institutions, 10, 72, 127, 181
Education ecosystem, 160
Education-induced, 78
Efik, 196
Egusi, 42, 49
Egusi source, 63
Egypt, 27, 57, 66, 99
Egyptian Baharat, 62
Ehigiamusoe, A., 103
Elumelu, Anthony, 28–32
Embroider, 76, 187, 191
Emerging economies, 8, 9, 32, 55
Empirical research, 21
Empowering African women, 52
Enabling environment, 14, 25, 26, 37, 79, 113, 119, 142, 147, 152, 180
ENACTUS, 142–144, 147, 149
Energetic, 7, 130, 137, 186, 202, 204
Energy infrastructure, 111, 114
England, 105, 142, 144, 211
Enterpriser approach, 12
Entrepreneurial-based economy, 19
Entrepreneurial capitalism, 4
Entrepreneurial characteristics, 7, 14, 200, 201
Entrepreneurial development, 14, 21, 132, 161
Entrepreneurial economy, 13, 22, 23, 25, 26, 37, 116, 121, 193
Entrepreneurial ecosystem, 3, 5, 13, 14, 109, 112, 121, 126–128, 130, 134, 136, 137, 160, 161, 180
Entrepreneurial education, 11, 36, 86, 160
Entrepreneurial government, 113, 160
Entrepreneurial man, 7, 13
Entrepreneurial phenomenon, 28
Entrepreneurial philanthropist, 28, 118
Entrepreneurial philanthropy, 13, 147, 148, 150–152, 178, 180, 183, 191
Entrepreneurial team, 8, 178
Entrepreneurial woman, 13, 160
Entrepreneurs, 3–9, 11, 13–15, 29–31, 34, 36, 37, 51, 52, 55, 62, 64, 73, 78, 82, 84, 92–94, 96, 106, 116, 123, 125, 128, 131, 133, 136, 137, 141, 149, 150, 157, 158, 160, 162, 165, 167, 169, 174, 204, 209, 212
Entrepreneurship, 3–6, 8–15, 23, 26, 28–37, 118, 120, 128, 131, 148, 170, 171, 173, 177, 179, 181, 196, 205, 213, 214
Enugu, 49–51, 144, 195, 196, 200
Enugu Technical College, 143
Environmental protection, 82, 114
Equal opportunities, 90, 101, 107, 108, 115, 119, 127, 133, 137, 157, 161, 163, 181, 186, 193, 203, 213
Equatorial Guinea, 27, 58
Equatorial rainforest, 23
Eritrea, 57, 84, 99
Eritrean People Liberation Forum (EPLF), 99
Esparaza Holdings BV, 211
Essential commodities, 69, 70
Establishment, 26, 72, 113, 114, 119, 193
Ethiopia, 27, 36, 57, 63, 66, 94, 172

Ethnicity, 9, 33, 68, 162
Europe, 106, 143, 179
The European Agenda for entrepreneurship education, 12
European authors, 35
European countries, 36
Euros, 139
Eweniyi, Odunayo, 105
Ewing Marion Kauffman Foundation, 10
Executive water, 210
Extended family, 45, 51, 52, 64, 80, 126
e-zine bellanaija.com, 105

F
Factors of production, 14, 23, 26, 31, 113
Faculty advisor, 143
Falah, 60
Family constellation, 125, 126
Farmers, 55, 63, 84, 94, 114, 208, 213
Farmer, Zed, 94, 95
Farming, 45, 72, 93, 100, 115, 140, 213, 214
Fashion, 42, 44, 52, 59, 62, 64, 92, 96, 105, 106, 109, 150, 161, 162, 204
Fashion designer, 81
Fashion industry, 37, 52
Fasting, 64
Father, 30, 45, 47, 49, 75, 76, 79, 81, 93, 94, 150, 158, 159, 187, 188, 194, 195, 214
Father-in-law, 194
Fathers' day, 46
Feasibility studies, 112, 113
Female population, 24
Femme libres, 72
Fez, 23

Fiber optic, 162
Fick, David, 31, 32, 100
Financial success, 185
Firewood, 50, 76, 188, 196
First-generation entrepreneurs, 98
Fiscal resources, 77
Fish sellers, 81
Five-Year Development Plan (FYDP), 112
Flint-Haitle, S., 9
Folade, K., 149
Forbes corporation, 89
Forced female labor, 34
Foreign, 22, 28, 36, 90, 97, 107, 113, 116, 130, 153, 157, 179, 181, 209
Foreign aids, 31
Foreigners, 32
Foreign languages, 65
Foreign multinational corporation, 107
Forestry resources, 45
Formal business, 14, 95
Formal education, 37, 43–45, 47, 48, 51, 53, 61, 62, 65, 73, 77, 78, 90, 91, 93, 94, 98, 101–103, 151, 155, 191, 200
Formal entrepreneurial activities, 33
Formal network, 81
Formal wage, 35
Foundation, 8, 97, 137, 146, 149, 180, 200, 209
Francee, E., 71
Francophone, 33
French, 65, 67, 68, 70
French colonial legacies, 33
French colonial masters, 70
Fresh milk, 45
Functioning institutions, 114

G
Gabon, 27, 58, 179

Galleries, 186, 192, 193
Gambia, 28, 57
Gems, 22
Gender, 3, 5, 32, 35, 45, 53, 68, 70, 72, 77, 107, 108, 145, 172, 179, 213
Gender-based violence, 45
Gendered, 43, 48, 55, 66, 80, 83, 113, 119, 162, 168, 170, 171
Gender equality, 83, 108
Gendering role, 64
Gender-neutral, 70
General Counsel, 108
Generic Incremental Value-Added (GIV), 130–132, 134, 136
German, 65
Germany, 12, 20, 22, 142, 144
Gestures, 59, 62, 76, 200
Ghana, 9, 27, 35, 36, 45, 57, 66, 107, 140, 144, 170, 171, 175, 206
Ghana Association of Women Entrepreneurs (GAWE), 100
Ghatak, S., 114
Gigerenzer, G., 124
Gikuyis, 63
Gjenge Makers Limited, 104
Global Entrepreneurship Monitor (GEM), 8–11, 169
Globalization, 14, 21, 86, 90, 93, 98, 104, 106, 164, 170
Global organizations, 31, 99, 165, 170
Goal-oriented, 89, 90, 116, 118, 121, 201
Goat, 43, 48, 62, 63, 71
The Gods Must be Crazy, 21
Gold, 58, 98, 200
Golden Stool, 107
Goldman Sachs, 89, 98, 153
Google, 106, 141, 153
Google Scholar, 28

Gorillas in the Mist, 21
Governance, 65, 68, 114, 116, 131, 157, 181, 182, 214
Government, 4, 5, 12, 15, 25, 26, 30, 31, 66, 71, 72, 76, 77, 92, 99, 107, 112, 115, 127, 132, 133, 141, 142, 147, 148, 150, 152, 180, 181, 188, 205
Government bureaucracy, 33, 171
Government ministry, 96
Government policies, 25, 31
Government policies and programs, 29, 89
Grandmother, 75–77, 91, 107, 187, 191, 194, 195
Gray, Alan, 29
Greece, 10, 11
Green Revolution, 115
Grinding stone, 41
Gross Domestic Product (GDP), 24, 46, 84, 92, 120, 126, 127, 169, 172
Gross National Income (GNI), 26–28
Groundnuts, 49, 215
Group decision-making, 124
Guinea, 27, 57
Guinea-Bissau, 28
Guinea fowl, 197
Guinea fowl eggs, 50
Guinness World Record, 23, 203
Guye, F.B., 71
Gyan, Joana, 170

H

Hairdressing, 35
Haiti, 142
Hand-me-down, 140
Haqq and Adl, 60
Hardworking, 52, 89, 95, 118, 130, 137, 204
Haruna, Fatima, 93

Harvesting, 44, 214
Harvey, Charles, 148
Hausa, 196
Hausa-Fulani, 68
Hawken, Melanie, 208
Hayes, Jean, 43
Hayes, R.N., 33
Hazel, Priscilla, 175
Health, 9, 25, 52, 82, 94, 103, 106, 114–117, 119, 120, 125, 145, 172
Heart of Darkness, 21
Helicopter, 206
Hindle, K., 12
Hisrich, R.D., 6, 8
Hitch-hike, 189
HIV, 83, 84, 86, 102
Homecare, 46
Housefly, 140
House-helps, 47
Household servants, 72
Howorth, C., 11
HSBC, 106, 108
Human capital, 25, 26, 101, 116, 127, 128, 131, 137, 160, 161
Human Development Index (HDI), 127, 132, 133
Human Development Report, 116
Humiliated and inadequate, 103
Hungary, 9, 10
Husband, 30, 41–46, 48–52, 57, 61, 64–66, 72, 77–81, 91, 155, 156, 163, 188–191, 193–196, 198–200, 203, 211
Hut-taxation, 72

I

Ibrahim, Mo, 25, 29, 37, 117
Ideologies, 114, 125
Idrissi, Boulagoul, 202
Igbokwe, E.M., 115
Igboland, 68, 70
Ihsaan, 60
IKE's Café and Grill, 140
Illiterate, 21, 103, 127
Imaralu, Douglas, 30
Immaculate Heart Girls School, 199
Impactful contributions, 109, 212
Impactors, 128–130
Imperial taxation, 72
Inadequate access, 25
Incentives, 80, 105, 113
Inclusive development, 28, 174
Inclusive socio-economic development, 107
India, 115, 116, 147, 188, 206
Indian diplomat, 76
Indigenes, 32, 113
Indigenous entrepreneurs, 28
Indonesia, 115
Industrial center, 197
Industrious, 89, 186
Infant mortality rate, 23–25
Informal business, 14
Informal entrepreneurial activities, 33
Information literate, 97, 118
Information Technology (IT), 92, 94, 95, 170
Infrastructure, 4, 22, 32, 37, 105, 111, 115, 119–121, 127, 133, 137, 141, 160, 172, 179, 181
Ingredient, 31, 62, 64, 141, 195, 204, 212
Inhibiting factors, 36, 137, 161, 162
In-laws, 30, 145
Innovation, 5, 6, 8, 10, 85, 91, 104, 106, 111, 113, 114, 116, 117, 119, 128, 130, 142, 148, 176, 178, 182, 210, 214
Innovation ecosystem, 105
Innovative, 7, 31, 32, 85, 90, 104, 119, 136, 137, 141, 144, 158,

162, 167, 174, 178, 180, 182, 191, 199, 201, 212
Inside Africa, 187
Insite, 95
Inspiration, 14, 35, 66, 185, 204
Inspired, 21, 90, 91, 93, 96, 186, 214, 216
Inspiring change, 54
Integration mechanism, 36
Intellectuals, 160, 161
Intelligence, 61, 90, 167, 199, 201
Intelligent, 47, 131, 202
Interdisciplinary and experiential entrepreneurship education, 11
Internal locus of control, 7
International, 187, 191, 193, 206–208
International Labor Organization (ILO), 12, 106, 170
International Monetary Fund (IMF), 25, 31
Intrapreneur(s), 7, 29
Intrinsic traits, 167
Investors, 22, 28, 104–106, 113, 181
Invisible hand, 4, 132
Invisible hand of markets, 131
Irio, 63
Irish potatoes, 194, 197
Irogbe, Kema, 119
Isenberg, D., 127, 128, 130, 131
Ishibori, 196
Islamic, 45, 57, 59, 60, 62, 125
Islamic values, 45
Isoken, 51
Israel, 131, 147
Isusu, 81
Isuzi, 81
Ivory Coast, 27
IWEC award, 207

J
Jalade-Ekeinde, Omotola, 109

Jamaica, 9, 11, 142
Jamme, Mariamme, 106
Japan, 10, 96
Jewelry, 45, 56, 57, 70, 99, 200
Jimenez-Zarco, Ana Isabel, 52
John Holt Nig. Ltd., 196
John, Silvester, 143
Jones, Saran K., 177
Jordan, 11

K
Kaba, 76
Kabila, Mwai, 209
Kabu Kabu, 191
Kadri, Ilham, 91
Kagadi, 158
Kakhu, 140
Kalbfleisch, P., 162
Kano riot, 34
Kansas City, Missouri, 143
Kanuri women, 68
Karanja, Tabitha, 94
Karanji, Thabita, 186
Kent, C.A., 5
Kenya, 27, 29
Kericho county, 85
Keroche Breweries, 97, 180, 209, 210
Khadija, 60
Khoikhoi, 63
Kidney, 165
Kieruff, H., 11
Kigali, 121
Kikuyis, 63
Kindred Spirits, 187
King's College, 211
Kin groups, 68
Kings, 66
Kinshasa, 211
Kirzner, Isreal M., 5, 119
Kitchen, 42, 48
Knitting, 49, 72, 100

Knowledge, 12, 26, 28, 31, 35, 94, 97, 101, 102, 116, 118, 121, 124, 131, 133, 134, 136, 137, 150, 158–162, 173, 176, 181, 182, 210
Knowledge gaps, 171
Knowledge workers, 31
Kogi state, 91
Kola-nuts, 49
Koran, 59
KPMG, 143, 144
Kramer, H.E., 12
Krotz, Joanna L., 162
Kukanova, Tartiana, 210
Kumasi, 140
Kwashiorkor, 70

L

Labor, 9, 26, 31, 44, 107, 119, 128, 181
Lackluster, 114
Lagos, 24, 30, 75, 105, 144, 192
Lagos Art Gallery, 91
Lamb, 62
Lambini, C., 9
Land, 26, 61, 71, 119
Land disputes, 125
Landmass, 21, 24, 66
Land topology, 113
Latvia, 11
Launchpad Fund, 30
Leadership Academy, 214
Lemba, 72
Lentils, 62, 63
Lesotho, 27, 58
Letts, C.W., 85
Liberal, 44, 47, 59
Liberia, 28, 57
Libya, 27, 45
Life, 186, 187, 189, 190, 196, 200, 204–206, 210, 212

Life expectancy, 23–25
Lifestyle, 7, 29, 44, 52, 59, 61, 64, 71, 73, 105, 162
Lioness of Africa, 208
Liquid soap, 215
Liquor market, 209
Literacy, 25, 26, 100–103
Literacy education, 102
Literacy rate, 23–25
Literature, 22, 23, 32, 34, 36
Liver, 165
Live-stock, 34, 43, 45, 48
Local broom, 41, 42
Local markets, 45
Local Native Courts, 34
Logic, 133
Logic road map, 160
Lolosoli, Rebecca, 156
Lolosolu, Rebecca, 53
London, 144
Louis Viutton, 203
Luanda Island, 211
Lucas, W.A., 12
Lugard, Lord, 68
Luo women, 43
Lynn University, 104

M

Maathai, Wangari, 147
Madagascar, 28
Madichie, N.O., 60
Mafimisebi, Taiwo, 114
Maghrib, 85
Maize, 215
Makerere University, 215
Malaria, 83, 84, 86
Malawi, 24, 28
Male-dominated society, 190
Male domination, 58, 77
Mali, 27, 45
Malnutrition, 69

INDEX 245

Mama Nike, 61, 64, 75, 77, 78, 81, 91, 186–188, 190, 191
Mangoes, 50
Mara Launchpad Incubator, 30
Marginalized, 43, 44, 53
Marginalized-women, 21
Market women, 3, 34, 35, 37, 43, 78
Marrakesh, 56
Marriage payment, 60
Marriage rites, 64
Masai, 63
Mashed plantain, 63
Master Card, 98
Maswana, Jean-Claude, 34
Matake, 63
Matee, Nzambi, 104
Material culture, 59, 62
Maternal health, 83, 84
Matriarchal society, 45
Matriarch village, 157
Matrilineal, 9
Mauritania, 28, 57
Mauritius, 24, 26, 27
MBA, 90
McDade, B.E., 34
McKinsey, Inc., 92
McKinsey Report, 169
Meat, 62, 63, 69
Meat roll, 199
Media, 89, 105
Media and movie production, 108
Mediocre performers, 46
Meier, F., 71
Mentors, 29, 94, 104, 105, 128, 175, 209
Mentorship, 81, 89
Merchants, 23, 84
Metro women, 70
Mexico, 10, 11, 115
Miami beach club, 211
Miami Beach night club, Angola, 95
Microenterprises, 216

Micro financing, 81
Micro-flush toilet, 139, 140
Micropreneurs, 7
Micro restaurants, 64
Microsoft, 106
Middle East, 106, 179
Midwest, 91
Milano, Benny, 144
Millennium Development Goals (MDGs), 82–84
Millets, 42, 44, 45, 62, 63, 195
Mineral resources, 22
Ministry of National Planning (MNP), 112
Minority ethnic groups, 33
MINT, 115
Misfit, 46
Missionaries, 71, 72
Miya, Barantang, 175
Mmakau Mining, 98
Mobisson, Nneka, 174
Model of ecosystem, 128
Moeti, Matshidiso, 84, 108
Mohammed, Amina J., 89, 97, 108
Monitor, 212
Moral ideology, 72
Moran of the Order of Burning Spear (MBS), 209
Moremong-Nganunu, T., 12
Moreno-Gavara, Carme, 52
Mores, 61
Morino, M., 150, 152
Moroccan Mall, 186
Moroccan rituals, 204
Morocco, 23, 27, 45
Moser, Tom, 143
Moslem, 45, 60
Mosquito, 83
Mother hen, 46
Mother-in-law, 194
Mothers, 34, 37
Mothers' day celebration, 46

Mountain, 26, 58
Mozambique, 28, 212
Mrs. Anyansi, 51, 52, 78
Mrs. M. Anyansi Super Market, 51
Ms. Alhassan (of Nigeria), 179
Ms. Nwanji, 179
Multiple ethnicity, 33
Multiple roles, 45, 46
Multitasking, 167
Munchi, 196
Mungai, Tecra Wangari, 210
Music, 11, 56
Musical instruments, 56
Muslim, 24, 57, 60, 61, 63, 64, 68
Muslim culture, 56, 62
Muslim society, 97
Mutuku, Leonida, 176
Muzaif Farms, 93
Mwangi, James, 29

N
Nachami, 157
Naira, 191
Nairobi, Kenya, 104
Nana-Fabu, S., 73
Nanaya Asantua, 107
Nanotechnology, 117
Nashat, 66
Nasr, Sahar, 46
National governments, 31
National identities, 33
National Reconstruction and Development programs (NRDP), 101
The National Union of Eritrean Women (NUEW), 99
Native revenue ordinance, 34
Natural resources, 21, 26, 31
Nayantra, Jha, 104
Ndhlukula, Devine, 96
Necessity, 8–10, 51, 128, 157, 178

Necessity-driven, 52, 173, 178, 182, 201
Need assessment, 112
Needle work, 43, 48
Nefatari, 68
Nefatiti, 68
Negotiation, 190, 207, 212
NERO Company Limited, 210
Network capital, 160
Net worth, 95, 96, 185
Newly-weds, 42
Newmeyer, X., 162
New Zealand, 8–11
Niche, 164, 181, 207, 209
Nickels, William G., 7, 31
Niger, 28, 45
Nigeria, 19, 24, 27, 29, 30, 34, 35, 112, 113, 115
Nigerian, 90, 91, 106
Nigerian legal tender, 70
Nigerian society, 30
Nigerian soldiers, 69
Nigerian Women Union, 35
Niger Network of Women Business owners and Credit Union for Women Enterprises, 100
Nike center for Art and Culture, 91
Nisa Food and Bakery, 93
Njiri, 43
Nkholise, Nneile, 177
Nnadi, Isaac, 144
Nnaji, Genevieve, 109
Nneka, 41, 48
Nobel Laureate, 147
Nomadic lifestyle, 45
Non-achievers, 47
Non-Governmental Organization (NGO), 99–102
Non-quantitative, 12
Non-verbal communication, 188
Non-visionary, 137
Norms, 34, 41, 44, 45, 57, 59

North Carolina African Services Coalition (NCASC), 141
Nuances, 22, 33, 35, 36
Nuclear family, 126
Nurturers, 37, 105

O

OBGYN, 152
Obloj, O., 32
Ogazi eggs, 198
Ogbete market, 50, 198
Ogidi-Ijamu Gallery, 91
Ogoja, 49, 195, 196
Okoro, Sandie, 108
Okoye, Oge, 109
Okra source, 63
Okrika, 140
Olatunde, Esther, 175
On and Off beer License, 51, 186, 198
Onions, 194, 197, 198, 201
Oniru, Olatorera, 106
Onitsha, 34
Onitsha market, 197
Ononchong, Rebecca, 175
Onwuneli, Ndidi O., 178
Opinionated, 51
Opportunity cost, 46
Opportunity(ies), 5, 8–10, 14, 21, 29–32, 35, 36, 45, 48, 52, 53, 55, 61, 71, 72, 75, 77, 82, 90–92, 94–98, 100–104, 106–109, 114, 117, 120, 121, 127, 128, 133, 134, 140, 142, 143, 147, 150, 158, 160–163, 166, 170–172, 174, 175, 177–180, 182, 188, 190, 196, 198, 200, 203–205, 207, 208, 210, 212, 214, 215
Opportunity-seeker, 29
Optimistic, 186, 188, 192, 206, 216
Optometry, 152

Oral historian, 201
Oranges, 50, 197
Orator, 201
Organs, 165
Ornaments, 187
Orphanage, 189
Osabushien, 116
Oshogbo, 77, 91, 189, 191, 192
Oshogbo Gallery, 91
Osirim, J., 145
Ottoman empire, 68
Owerri, 34
Owigar, Judith, 176
Owner–employee, 177
Oyewunmi, N., 43
Ozgen, A., 36
Ozor, N., 115

P

Palm oil, 63
Pan African Diaspora Women's Association (PADWA), 141
Parents, 19, 20, 41, 43, 47, 48, 51, 53, 60, 62, 64, 66, 69, 75, 104, 139, 147, 150, 158, 159, 163, 213–215
Passionate entrepreneurs, 31, 32
Patriarchal, 9
Peasantry, 213
Pedagogical changes, 13
Pedro, Uche, 105
Pennell, C., 68
Persistence, 91, 96, 104, 109
Persistent, 52
Perspectives, 19, 21, 22, 33, 35
Phenomena, 22, 43, 162
Phenomenon, 3, 10, 13
Phidora, 43, 48
Philanthropic entrepreneurship, 96
Philanthropic organizations, 10
Philimena, 145

Piggybank.ng, 105
Pilgrimage, 64
Pillars of Islam, 64
Pio, E., 9
Pipelines, 111
Planet, 82
Political freedom, 114
Polygamous marriage, 64
Pondu, 63
Poor education system, 25
Poorest nations, 25–28
Poor feeding, 46
Poor health, 46
Population, 23–25
Portuguese, 212
Positive attitude, 152, 205, 207
Pound, 76, 139, 188, 200
Pounded yam, 63
Powering Africa, 111
Prada, 203
Precious metals, 22
Pre-natal care, 83
Pre-primary, 214
Private sector, 25, 29, 31, 35
Process, 3, 6, 8, 12, 13, 15
Productive resources, 22
Profiles, 185
Property inheritance, 55
Prosperity, 82
Psychology, 5, 6
Public nuisance, 46
Puff-puff, 199
Pumpkin, 63
Purchasing power parity (PPP), 24, 27, 127

Q
Queens in Egypt, 68
Quran, 68

R
Radebe, Bridgette, 94, 97, 98
Raffia baskets, 56
Rain forest, 26
Rajuili, K., 101
Ransom kuti, 35
Rasod, H., 66
Rate of growth, 23, 24
Refinery, 111
Refugee camp, 69
Refugees, 200
Regional conflict, 21
Regional economic blocs, 32
Regional perspectives, 14
Religion, 33, 44, 48, 56, 58–60, 66–68, 70, 71, 73, 113, 125, 182, 213
Religious diversity, 23, 33
Republic of Congo, 27
Researchers, 28, 31, 36, 37
Research methodologies, 33
Research models, 22
Resilient, 81
Resource assessment, 112
Resourceful, 78, 81, 82, 89, 109
Retail traders, 43
Revolutionary, 99, 100
Rhodes University, 192
Rhythm, 169, 170, 172
Rice, 42, 44, 45, 62, 63, 201
Richest nation, 24
Rionge, Njeri, 94, 95
Risk-takers, 29, 89
Road-side restaurants, 64
Robinson, J.A., 33
Role conflict, 36
Roles of women, 9, 34, 35, 37, 58, 60, 72, 105, 108, 114, 115, 128, 179, 182
Rooster, 46
Roots, 21, 147, 204, 212
Roscoe, J., 11

Rosie, 145
Rotary International, 149
Rotating credit, 81
Rural transformation, 160
Rusel Hanout, 62
Russia, 115, 211
Rwanda, 27, 45

S

Sacred heart women association, 50
Saee, J., 12
Saka-Saka, 63
Salami, 146
Sambo, Sibongile, 94, 96, 170, 186, 205
Samburu tribe, 53
Sam Walton fellow, 143
San Francisco, 149
Sanitation, 83
Sans, 63
Santoro finance, 211
Santos, 162
Sanyang, Saikou E., 114
Sapir-Whorf hypothesis, 61
Sarfo, Cassandra, 175
Savannah, 26, 58
Schoch, S., 11
Scholars, 28, 29, 35, 43, 112
Scholarship, 30, 76, 119, 149, 187, 188, 214, 215
School materials, 214
Schreier, J.W., 11, 12
Schumpeter, J.A., 4, 5, 8
Sciences, technology, engineering, and mathematics (STEM), 171, 174, 175, 177
Scientific Equipment Development Institute (SEDI), 144
Scotland, 10
Seamstress, 35, 81
Seasonal, 197, 199, 202

Seasonal entrepreneur, 50, 52
Second-generation, 91, 93–96, 98, 103
Second-generation entrepreneurs, 14
Second-hand, 140
Second-hand knowledge, 35
SECURICO, 96
Self-actualization, 102–104
Self-efficacy, 12
Self-employed, 81
Self-employment, 33
Self-esteem, 102–104, 166
Self-generating, 158
Self-motivated, 81
Self-nurturing, 7
Self-reliance, 158
Self-study, 112
Self-sufficiency, 51, 52, 85, 125, 150, 182
Self-sufficient, 36, 41, 52, 53, 145, 150, 161, 190
Semi-deserts, 26
Sen, Amartya, 127
Senegal, 27
Senegalese women, 44
Serial, 29, 52, 173, 178
Serial entrepreneur, 7, 128
Seven and half dates, 51
Sewing center, 81
Sewing machine, 41–43, 48
Sewing skills, 48
Sexton, D.R., 5
Sexual harassment, 108
Sex workers, 192
Seychelles, 24, 26, 27, 45, 58, 84
Shagaya, Hajia Bella, 94
Sharia law, 59
Sheep, 63, 71
Shilcola, A., 43
Shillings, 43, 76, 104, 187, 188, 195, 200, 209
Shuttleworth, Mark, 29

Siblings, 47
Sidik and Amanah, 60
Sierra-Leone, 28
Singh, G., 36
Single Africa Market, 120
Sisterhood, Excellence, Empowerment, Diversity, and Service (S.E.E.D.S.), 146
Sisters, 69, 107, 139, 167, 168, 188, 200, 214
Skilled labor, 26
Slovania, 10
Small-scale traders, 34
Smith, Adam, 4, 124
Smithsonian museum, 187
Smith, Vernon, 124, 126
Smoked fish, 194, 197
Snyder, Christina, 84
Soaked bread, 63
Social, 6, 25, 29, 31, 36, 46, 52, 59, 64, 65, 78, 82, 84, 85, 89, 96, 98, 107, 118, 124–126, 128, 131, 137, 139, 145–150, 160, 162, 175, 177–179, 183, 200, 204, 212, 214–216
Social capital, 85, 162, 166, 176, 179
Social contract, 146
Social entrepreneur, 7, 85, 187
Social environment, 31
Social media, 162, 164
Social milieu, 125
Social needs, 82
Social rights, 45
Social structure, 34, 44, 51, 54–56, 59, 64, 77, 80, 90, 93, 95
Social transparency, 160
Societal burden, 46
Societal roles, 43
Socio-economic, 82, 84, 86
Socio-economic development, 9, 12, 15
Socio-economic status, 20, 99, 181

Sociology, 5, 6
Socio-political, 127
Soetan, F., 30
Sole authority, 35
Sole-preneur, 177
Sole Rebels, 96
Solvay, Belgian Chemical Group, 91
Sonangol, 212
Sosaties, 63
South Africa, 8–10, 27, 29, 30, 115, 119
South Africa Women Entrepreneurs' Network (SAWEN), 207
South America, 8
Southern African Women Aviation, 207
South Korea, 115
Soya nuts, 216
Spain, 11, 96, 142, 211
Spann, Amanda, 175
Special Economic Zones (SEZ), 112, 113
Spot On Global Solution, 106
Spouse, 37, 44, 46, 49, 60, 167, 209, 212
Spring, A., 34
SRS Aviation, 186, 205
Stable political systems, 33
Stakeholder, 130, 133–137, 150, 206, 207
Standardized methodologies, 33
Start and improve Your business (SIYB), 12
Startup enterprises, 29
State University of New York (SUNY), 93
Status quo, 114, 115
Stereotyping, 66, 77, 203
Story(ies), 185, 186
Strategic capital, 160
Strategic patterns, 125
Structural patterns, 125

Structural tension, 158
Students in Free Enterprise (SIFE), 142–145, 149, 152
Subordinate, 44, 68
Sub-Saharan Africa, 35, 92, 98, 190
Subsistence cultivation, 45
Subsistence farming, 72, 100
Successes, 14, 28, 32, 84, 85, 90, 93, 95, 152, 170, 207
Sudan, 27, 29, 57
Suitor, 79, 80, 155, 194, 215
Supalaky, 157
Super computer, 201
Super market, 51, 186
Survival, 52, 60, 120, 161, 162, 166, 213, 215
Sustainable Development Goals (SDGs), 82, 83
Sustainable economic development, 28, 30
Sustainable Urbanization, 147
Sweden, 10
SWOT analysis, 133
Swoyer, 61
Symbolic, 41
Symbols, 62, 199, 200

T
Table cloths, 215, 216
Tafraout, 202
Tahir, R., 77
Tanas, J.K., 12
Tanzania, 27
Tarzan, 21
Taxation, 34, 35
Taxation-in-kind, 71
Taxation ion Gambia, 146
Taxation of wives, 34
Tax breaks, 113
Taylor, M., 29, 65
Technical know-how, 36

Techniques, 22
Technology, 90, 93, 104–106, 108
Telecommunication, 21, 37
Tembo women, 72
Tempest, S., 11
Textile museum, 92
Thakkar, Ashish, 29, 37
Things Fall Apart, 21
Tie-dye, 56, 91, 187
Tinker, 197
Tlaiss, H.A., 60
Todd, P.M., 124
Togo, 28
Tolerance for uncertainty, 7
Tomato patch, 95
Tomato Queen, 95
Trade blocs, 32
Trade logistics, 172
Traditional entrepreneurship, 33
Traditional kebabs, 63
Traditional marriage, 41, 42
Traditional rulers, 33
Traits, 7, 91, 118, 119, 130, 137, 170, 180
Trans Africa Investment Services, 211
Transformational education, 158
Transforming industries, 54
Transgenerational, 44
Tribes, 56, 59–61, 64–66, 125, 151
Tripod stand, 41
Tropical grassland, 26
Tunisia, 27, 57, 62, 85, 144
Turkey, 36, 93, 115
Tuwo shimkafe, 196
Tuzini Farm Limited, 95
Two-story duplex, 156

U
Ubuntu philosophy, 158
Ufuk, G., 36
Ugali, 63

Uganda, 12, 27, 29, 30, 43, 45, 48, 56, 57, 67, 71, 79, 158, 171, 216
The Uganda Project, 160
Uganda Red Cross Society, 216
Uganda Rural Development and Training (URDT), 157, 158, 160
Uganda Youth Development and training Program (UYDT), 186, 216
Umoja, 53, 156, 157, 160, 182
Unaccredited, 10
Uncle, 45, 79, 80
UN Deputy Secretary General, 89, 108
UNDP, 116
Unemployment, 25
UNESCO, 102
United Kingdom, 20, 96, 142
United Nations Agencies, 89, 170
United Nations (UN), 25, 92, 99, 117, 127, 153, 165
United States, 10, 19, 20, 77, 91, 96, 100, 107, 141, 142, 147
Unitel international, 211, 212
University of Karueein, 23
University of Uyo, 144
Unsatisfactory, 12
Unskilled labor, 26, 128
Unsystematic, 12
Unwed mothers, 45
Urban migration, 160
Urban population, 23, 24
US Agency for International Development (USAID), 100
US Department of State Exchanges, African Women Entrepreneurs Program (AWEP), 98

V
Value-added, 28, 29, 31, 46, 172, 177

Values, 44, 57, 59–61, 64, 73, 85, 101, 148, 216
Van Niekerk, Francios, 29
Vegetable farmers, 43, 55
Vegetable gardens, 48
Vegetables, 43, 52, 62, 64, 94, 195, 198
Venezuela, 9, 10, 142
Venture capitalists, 104, 105, 167, 171, 174
Venture-preneur, 29
Vesper, K.H., 5, 6, 11
Viable stay-home mothers, 49
Victorian value, 70
Virgin cow, 48
The visible hand, 4
Visionaries, 29
Visual politics, 172
Vocational Training Team (VTT), 79, 149

W
Wado Maya, 140, 145
Wait-hood, 25
Walkie-talkie, 211
Wangari, Amina Hassane, 100
Wannanchi Online, 95
Warrant chiefs, 34, 70
Washington, DC, 187
Wasta, 85
Watson Institute Incubator, 104
Wealth, 211
Wealth of Nations, 4, 124
Web-based entrepreneurs, 7
Weberian perspective, 33
Wedding gifts, 41, 42, 48
Weeding, 44, 48, 214
Well-being, 14, 60, 102, 120
West Africa, 19, 34, 35, 43, 63, 100, 190, 197

West Africa International Business Linkages Programme (WAIBL), 100
West African Businesswomen Network (WABNET), 100
West Africa Regional Programme (WARP), 100
WhatsApp, 161
Wheat, 62
Whuster, Simon, 172
Widowed, 72
Wifi, 161
Wildlife, 23, 58
Wild life expedition, 21
Wilson, J., 149
Wives on Strike, 53
Wolof Kingdom, 66
Women education, 61, 82, 84, 86
Women Enterprise Fund, 85, 98
Women in Aviation International (WAI), 207
Women inspiration award, 192
Women on Strike, 73
Women rights, 45, 68, 70–72, 85
Women's revolt, 34, 35
Wooden mortar and pestle, 41
Work ethics, 59, 65
Work-overload, 45
World Bank (WB), 26, 31, 54, 92, 98, 106–108, 116, 132, 170
World Economic Forum (WEF), 25, 120, 128
World Health Organization (WHO), 84, 106, 108, 170
World Trade Organization (WTO), 106
Wrapper, 41, 42

Y

Yamin, S., 12
Yamor, 120
Yams, 62, 63
Yan&One, 203, 204
Yen, 139
Yoruba arts and festival, 192
Yorubas, 63
Yoruba women, 68
Youth bulge, 25
Youth migration, 25, 181
Yuan, 139

Z

Zahida Jibril-Usman, 93
Zaloumi, Maria Zileni, 94
Zambia, 27, 30, 36, 94
Zambia National Farmers Union, 95
Zara, 203, 204
Zimbabwe, 12, 27, 58, 96, 144, 179
ZOPT, 212
Zulu community, 56
Zulu kingdom, 66